RICHARD WILLIAMS

RACERS

PENGUIN BOOKS

PENGUIN BOOKS

Published by the Penguin Group
Penguin Books Ltd, 27 Wrights Lane, London W8 5TZ, England
Penguin Putnam Inc., 375 Hudson Street, New York, New York 10014, USA
Penguin Books Australia Ltd, Ringwood, Victoria, Australia
Penguin Books Canada Ltd, 10 Alcorn Avenue, Toronto, Ontario, Canada M4V 3B2
Penguin Books (NZ) Ltd, Private Bag 102902, NSMC, Auckland, New Zealand

Penguin Books Ltd, Registered Offices: Harmondsworth, Middlesex, England

First published by Viking 1997
Published in Penguin Books 1998
5 7 9 10 8 6 4

Printed in England by Clays Ltd, St Ives plc

ACKNOWLEDGEMENTS

Some of the material in this book first appeared in different forms in the *Guardian*, the *Independent on Sunday*, the *Sunday Times Magazine*, *GQ* and *F1 Racing*. Thanks go to my editors at those publications: Ian Jack, Simon O'Hagan, Simon Kelner, Neil Morton, Louis Jebb, Alan Rusbridger, Roger Alton, Sabine Durrant, Ian Mayes, Mike Averis, Nick Mason, Neil Robinson, Ben Clissett, David Robson, Stephen Wood, Angus MacKinnon, Jessamy Calkin and Mike Herd. And also to my fellow writers, principally David Tremayne, Nigel Roebuck, Alan Henry and Andrew Benson.

'Look upon the inmost causes of things, stripped of their husks; note the intentions that underlie actions; study the essences of pain, pleasure, death, glory; observe how man's disquiet is all of his own making, and how troubles never come from another's hand, but like all else are creatures of our own opinion.'

MARCUS AURELIUS

'There is always something to learn. One never stops learning. Particularly when one is losing. When one loses, one knows what has to be done. When one wins, one is never sure.'

ENZO FERRARI

PREFACE

This is a book about the men who drive racing cars and about their place in our lives. That place has grown larger in recent years, thanks to television, but it does not mean the men themselves are much different from their predecessors in their motives, desires or reactions. Sport is still about winning or losing, the refinement of technique and the pleasure of taking part; the difference, in the television age, is that the spectator is allowed a closer view of the player's character. Sometimes transparent, sometimes obscured by layers of deception, that character can be strengthened or distorted by the exaggerated and incessant attention. The simple compensation for being subjected to this unnatural process is the money. The forfeit varies from person to person.

Here, over the course of a season, a three-way rivalry plays itself out with unusual intensity. This is not a detailed reconstruction of a season's races; the relevant statistics may be found elsewhere. But it is the story of three men, their effect on each other, their effect on us, and our effect on them.

RICHARD WILLIAMS
London 1997

I

I'm standing here in the paddock at Monza on a sunny day in September, talking to a girl dressed all in black who came up a couple of minutes ago and started a conversation. We know each other slightly. But now she isn't even looking at me. Behind her sunglasses I can see her eyes flickering from side to side. Sometimes she turns right around, scoping out the scene in a glance. It's obvious that she hasn't got anything much to say, that she doesn't expect me to say anything interesting and that, anyway, the point is not for the two of us to talk. The point is for her to be seen to be talking to someone.

In an inoffensive sort of way, she's using me. She just wants to stand here in the paddock, at a point equidistant between the motor homes of the big three teams, a spot representing the vortex of all the rumours on a weekend in which everyone in the place seems to have a secret to share. She wants to stand here, at the sunlit centre of this land of shadows. And she doesn't want to be seen standing here alone, with no one to talk to, as if her presence were of no consequence or she didn't have access at that very minute to important and confidential information.

The point of all paddock dialogue is the barter of information, since its possession is the key to the extension of influence. If you play this game, you are never just standing around and talking – and you certainly never just stand around on your own, like a spare part. This girl wanted to stand between the temporary headquarters of the biggest racing teams so that she could see if anything was going on, so that she would feel she wasn't missing anything. I was simply a convenient prop.

When television turned motor racing into mass entertainment, information became currency. Nowadays the course of a rumour is pursued as avidly as the story of a race. While television coverage provides the bare bones of the narrative structure the newspaper journalists, led by the representatives of the tabloids, add the flesh of characterization and motive. The screen will show you how one car overtook another, but the tabloids will add layers of dramatic meaning by telling you exactly how much the two drivers concerned hate each other because one of them stole the other's girlfriend or, of even greater emotional impact, stole his seat in the best car in the field. The psychological dimension of the conflict seems to occupy as much time as the technical side. The drivers and other team members have learnt that they can sometimes make profitable use of journalists whose existence depends on not missing a story. A quiet conversation can be used to leak information or plant rumours that are damaging to a rival's commercial or technical interests. A carefully timed aside at a press conference can undermine the morale of a fellow driver who may be sitting only a couple of feet away or may be in another country.

The most important thing is to be seen to be busy, to be occupied, to be engaged in some important aspect of the unfolding tale of the season and therefore integral to the narrative. Sometimes you see people walk the length of the paddock and back again and you know they haven't been doing anything or going anywhere. They've just been hoping for eye contact, for a word, for acknowledgement of their existence as part of this ultra-privileged and highly seductive world.

So when the girl came up and said hello it gave her an excuse to stop and check things out. Now we seem to be conversing, in a disengaged sort of way. What are we talking about? Maybe about how ridiculous an Italian driver called Giovanni Lavaggi looks as he parades himself in the company of two semi-dressed models wearing T-shirts proclaiming them to be members of his fan club. Or perhaps we're comparing views on the fashion for titanium gearbox casings, as found on the latest Ferrari. Or trying to decide whether the disgraced and disinherited son of the Duke of Marlborough has finally found his niche in life as the Benetton team's 'co-ordinator of hospitality and logistics', which means he gets to wear a team uniform and stand around handing out canapés to the people who pay the bills.

Well, probably she and I aren't talking about gearbox casings. But it really doesn't matter what it is. Anything would do. The point is to be standing here, talking. And watching. And not to be alone.

Inside the world of Formula One, things are rarely as they seem. That's partly because, as professional sports go, it is run and contested by a set of people with above-average intellects. True, you don't see many people sitting around in the pits reading experimental fiction. But not all first-rate minds work that way. In Formula One, the combination of a high degree of technical challenge and the vast amounts of sponsorship money make it attractive to some extremely clever people. Also to others who are not so clever, of course, but they rarely stay around for long once their novelty value as canapé-servers has been exhausted.

Since Formula One is, first and foremost, a sport – and therefore based on competition – and since survival within it is based on results, one of the things that happens to the clever people is that every aspect of their professional life is turned into a struggle for supremacy. Their whole existence becomes a game of disguise and deception, of bluff and counter-bluff, played with 100 per cent intensity all the time. Most of them eventually develop such expertise that to wrong-foot someone is an essential part of the day's work, and probably the most pleasurable. They start their careers by designing a better wheel-nut and end up getting their kicks by playing multinational corporations off against each other.

The rewards for this sort of thing are fabulous. Even in the Thirties, Tazio Nuvolari owned his own private plane – an elegant little single-engined Saiman with his tortoise emblem painted on the side of the fuselage – and a grand villa in the countryside outside Mantua, his home town. Sixty years later, Michael Schumacher, who is more or less Nuvolari's contemporary equivalent, flies a £10 million Canadair jet and lives in great luxury on ten acres of land on the shores of Lake Geneva. The men who run the successful teams are even richer. By and large, these are people who started without much in the way of worldly resources and they are keen to hang on to the winning edge that has made them rich.

In such an unremitting, high-stakes game, the intensity of the psychological competition is exhausting. A driver or constructor cannot afford to concentrate simply on whatever is happening this particular weekend. They have to think months, and even years, ahead. The driver needs to know where he will be going next season and who is standing in his way. He must be prepared for disappointment, for the discovery that he has been deceived. The constructor must think about where next season's engines are coming from and about how to fend off the rivals who are trying to get there ahead of him. And this is not the sort of forward planning that invites relaxation when the deals are signed. In Formula One, deals are made to be bent.

This weekend, at the Italian Grand Prix, a record amount of standing around and talking is going on – a reflection of the fact that inside the motor homes a series of double-bluff games is being played. Monza always has an element of that: coming towards the end of the season, it is the time when contracts are being renewed or torn up, when double- and triple-crosses are being finessed. Everybody is twitchy, except those in possession of the secret knowledge of a deal signed or a colleague about to be jettisoned. And even those happy few have their own anxiety, the fear of someone figuring out that they have the knowledge, working out what it might be and finding a way to neutralize it.

But nobody can remember a weekend quite like this one. Damon Hill has just been sacked by Frank Williams, or at least told that his services will no longer be required next season, after six years with the team. The comparatively unknown Heinz-Harald Frentzen will be his replacement. Jacques Villeneuve, Hill's combative team-mate, and Michael

Schumacher, the Englishman's greatest rival, are having trouble concealing their amusement at the whole charade. Hill arrived at Monza for the fourteenth of the season's sixteen races with a thirteen-point lead in the 1996 world drivers' championship. All he needs to do to wrap up the title is win the race, taking the ten points that would give him an unassailable lead. Now he has been given something else to think about, something that might well destabilize the apparently flimsy foundations of his self-confidence at a time when he is most vulnerable.

There seems to have been a press conference every couple of hours during the practice days at Monza, each one an opportunity to indulge in another bout of psychological warfare in front of an avid audience of hundreds of journalists. Competition in Formula One has never been keener, nor more keenly observed and enjoyed by a worldwide television audience whose true size is impossible to estimate, but which is certainly big enough to sustain a billion-dollar branch of the sports-entertainment industry.

The increasingly bitter rivalry between Hill, Schumacher and Villeneuve is exactly what Formula One had been praying for but could scarcely have expected a couple of years earlier, when Nelson Piquet, Alain Prost, Ayrton Senna and Nigel Mansell slipped into the wings. With their departure a whole narrative, a ten-year tangle of plots and sub-plots of ferocious complexity, vaporized overnight. The two Brazilians, the Frenchman and the Briton embodied the era in which Formula One racing grew from the interest of a sizeable minority into a worldwide entertainment phenomenon. Their rivalries, far more explicitly intense than those played out between the drivers of previous eras, had become the stuff of tabloid headlines. Their willingness to stamp on each other's toes on and off the track lent a new and compulsive element of personal animosity to a sport in which the conflict had always been spiced by physical danger.

To the great benefit of sponsors, television broadcasters and other financially interested parties, they had been the first generation to treat motor racing as a contact sport. The danger, you might say, changed its nature from passive to active. Their frequent collisions were endlessly replayed and analysed. When Senna and Prost smashed into each other, the sport became more like a medieval joust than ever. Although hidden inside their visored helmets and their high-sided cockpits, each driver had gradually established a defining image in the public mind: Piquet the carefree hedonist, completely at ease with the glamorous side of his job, with speedboats, jetskis and blondes on Copacabana beach; Prost the bloodless professor, constantly fighting political battles behind the locked doors of the motor homes, arranging the details of his personal life to suit his accountant's tax plan; Senna, the virtuoso whose assumption of complete superiority was reinforced by an adoring family and his own private line to God; and Mansell, the horny-handed *arriviste* whose combination of greed and gaucheness could not quite obscure his admirable willingness to get into a car and fight anyone on equal terms. When they went, one by one, in their various ways, who could replace them? Their collective dramatic range was never more clearly expressed than in the contrast between their final exits, ranging from tragedy to bathos.

Such characters were not created overnight: they needed to be marinated in the brine of conflict and controversy.

The outlines of their distinguishing characteristics – Senna's ruthlessness, Mansell's courage, Prost's rationality, Piquet's volatility – took years to reveal themselves. Without them the traditionalists accepted that Formula One was about to enter a quiet period, such as it had sometimes passed through before. In the absence of authentic box-office stars, for a while at least there would simply be motor races between the best available cars and drivers.

There were those who thought this might be a blessed relief from all the showbiz razzmatazz created by the modern cult of personality. They were wrong. So high was the financial investment in motor racing by television companies and commercial sponsors that it could not be permitted to happen. The sport had to be prevented from following the path of natural evolution, with peaks and troughs of public interest. It needed, above all, to keep up the show, to sustain the high broadcasting ratings to which its sponsors had become accustomed and on the strength of which their huge subsidies had been negotiated. If the stars were not there, they had to be found. Or, if necessary, created. And it would not be good enough for them just to race each other, to see who was the most skilful or whose car was fastest. There had to be another level of competition: a contest between men's minds.

The man most concerned to create that contest was Bernie Ecclestone, the cleverest of Formula One's many clever people. Ecclestone's unprepossessing title is vice-president in charge of promotional affairs for the Fédération Internationale de l'Automobile, the sport's worldwide governing body. What he actually does is run grand prix racing.

Since he is both a senior executive of the FIA and chairman of the Formula One Constructors' Association, the body representing the competitors, and also chairman of something called Formula One Administration – a company which collects, divides and distributes the revenues from the circuit owners, race sponsors, television companies and trackside advertisers to whom, by agreement with the FIA, he is empowered to sell the rights to the world championship events – he is in a unique position: poacher, gamekeeper and lord of the manor too. The arrangement goes unchallenged because it works so well, in the interests of so many parties. As far as the FIA is concerned, Ecclestone has raised Formula One to a position of pre-eminence virtually unimaginable before he became involved. To the constructors, he is the man whose subtle vision and tough deal-making made it possible for the most successful of them to ride around in private jets, and for the least successful to survive. So vital is Ecclestone to the synergy of Formula One that during 1996, the year in which he turned sixty-five, a great deal of backstage debate was devoted to speculation about what would happen when he decided to retire.

Like Fidel Castro, he seems likely to leave many devoted *apparatchiks* but no obvious successor. And, extending the analogy, there appears little likelihood of a voluntary retirement. His drive is prodigious, matched only by his imagination. He is a complicated and subtle man who sometimes takes on quite a different protective coloration. And he makes you think about the nature and exercise of power. Reflecting on his methods of operation one day, I wrote down this slightly opaque thought: 'Someone's temporary standing is expressed not just in how much power they themselves actually wield but in how much influence their existence bestows upon a person with whom they have a relationship.' In other words, if Ecclestone wants to negotiate with, say, Porsche about a series of one-make support races for the grand prix season, his hand is strengthened by an existing deal with, say, Renault – and that, in turn, gives Renault more clout in their dealings with Ecclestone.

He is the most easily identifiable figure in the paddock: no more than five feet four inches tall, invariably wearing a crisp, open-necked white shirt and black trousers or, in moments of extreme relaxation, a pair of freshly laundered and perfectly tailored jeans, with polished black loafers and, in cooler climates, an expensive suede jerkin. His unfashionably long grey hair is neatly barbered and brushed, falling in a fringe above eyes that are normally narrowed in an expression of shrewd appraisal.

At all the European grands prix he can usually be found in his mobile headquarters, the large trailer painted grey and silver with dark grey tinted windows through which, unobserved, he can survey the comings and goings of the paddock. Inside, where the influence is wielded and the deals are made, the furnishings and upholstery are grey, grey and grey again. Bernie's world is a place of logic and order. Nothing is allowed to disrupt this stark, rigorous aesthetic. He stands for neatness, self-control, fresh paint, straight lines and clean surfaces.

Ecclestone's involvement in motor sport goes back to the early Fifties, yet more than four decades later he can still be found at the leading edge of its development, pointing it towards the new millennium on a wave of technological innovation that has nothing to do with the cars themselves.

His trailer is the centrepiece of a ring of similar grey vehicles, drawn up like a wagon train at rest, from which the technicians of Ecclestone's television team control their cameras and their links to national networks around the world. Not far away, nowadays, a massive silver marquee with glass doors and a vase of fresh flowers in the foyer contains the future: a new generation of television equipment representing Ecclestone's personal investment of at least £40 million in the digital future. In 1996 its output was being received by a few thousand subscribers to a German station. In 1997 France was due to join in. Tomorrow, the world.

Ecclestone knows about pistons and camshafts, having sold second-hand cars and motorbikes in his youth and later run his own racing teams, but the mechanical side is not where he made his mark. While others were tinkering with aerodynamics and computerized gearboxes, he was the first to realize the power and potential of the broadcast media and the information technology revolution.

His origins are mysterious, a state of affairs which he has taken a mischievous pleasure in maintaining. He was born in Suffolk in 1931 but moved during childhood to Bexleyheath, in the Kentish suburbs. His father was either a trawler captain or an engineer; perhaps both. During the course of an interview in 1981 he told me that he had taken a B.Sc. in chemical engineering at Woolwich Polytechnic but left a subsequent laboratory job to devote himself to selling motorbikes. He was already buying and selling them, he said, when he was fifteen – in other words, before he was old enough to ride them on the public roads. He worked briefly for a motorcycle dealer before going into partnership in a garage in Bexleyheath. After buying out his partner he built up the business, acquiring premises and dealerships until it became the third largest operation of its type in Britain.

It made him rich enough to indulge his fondness for motor sport, first racing motorbikes then competing in the tiny Formula Three cars of the early Fifties, powered by 500cc motorcycle engines, alongside such rising stars as Stirling Moss and Peter Collins. He also met and became fast friends with a young driver named Stuart Lewis-Evans, against whom he raced and whose father also ran a garage in Bexleyheath. When an accident at Brands Hatch made Ecclestone reconsider his future as a driver he began to follow Lewis-Evans around the circuits, watching him develop into a grand prix driver with the small Connaught team and, later, the championship-winning Vanwall outfit sponsored by Tony Vandervell, the ball-bearings magnate.

Ecclestone enjoyed his new role as travelling fan, but he wanted a greater involvement. He bought a pair of cars from the expiring Connaught concern, intending to rebuild the team around Lewis-Evans, but the driver's death in the 1958 Moroccan Grand Prix put an end to his plan. For a while he retreated back into business, expanding to include property development and a finance company. At some point he disposed completely of his businesses, in a single deal which made him very rich indeed. Curiously, for a man so precise about figures when they come with pound or dollar signs attached, he claimed not to remember whether this took place in the mid-Sixties or mid-Seventies.

But his interest in racing remained keen, and while he was absent from the grand prix scene he used his time to run teams in other kinds of racing, notably motorbikes for the British champion Phil Read and others. In the Seventies, however, he found a replacement for Lewis-Evans in the Austrian driver Jochen Rindt, an aggressive and charismatic character who put the management of his career in Ecclestone's hands. But, towards the end of the 1970 season when Rindt was about to win the world championship, he crashed badly during a practice session at Monza. Ecclestone, who was in the pits, broke through the cordon and ran down the track to the wrecked Lotus. By the time he arrived, Rindt had been taken away in an ambulance. Eventually Ecclestone found his way to the hospital, but Rindt was already dead.

This second tragedy did not deter Ecclestone. A year later he bought the entire assets of the troubled Brabham team, spent a lot of money on new cars and drivers (including Graham Hill and Carlos Reutemann) and waited for their fortunes to turn. In 1974, after Hill had left to start his own team, Reutemann was joined by a young Brazilian, Carlos Pace, who accepted the friendship previously enjoyed by Lewis-Evans and Rindt. The team won three grands prix that season, finishing the year with a one-two in the US Grand Prix at the old Watkins Glen circuit, and Martini offered substantial sponsorship for the following season. Their fortunes continued to improve, although Pace was killed in a light-plane accident in 1977, replaced first by John Watson and eventually by the talented young Nelson Piquet, while Niki Lauda took Reutemann's seat two years later. With backing from Parmalat, the giant Italian dairy-products company, expressed in livery which was clearly the product of many hours in the graphic design studio, Piquet won the world championships of 1981 and 1983 in a Brabham. As well as favouring nice graphics, Ecclestone's team was also tactically inventive: they reintroduced refuelling stops to

Formula One, allowing the cars to run lighter for longer, turning each race from a marathon into a series of sprints.

The Brabham factory shared premises in an industrial estate in Chessington, Surrey, with the Formula One Constructors' Association, also run by Ecclestone. In exchange for a licence fee, FOCA had been given the rights to run and promote the Formula One world championship series and Ecclestone employed a team of people to that end, as well as to administer the business of transporting fifty cars, 600 people and ninety tons of freight around the world in chartered jumbo jets. He was already distributing the income and prize fund according to an arcane and highly secret formula based not just on results but on the length of time a team had been in existence and on its past record of success. This method, in a simplified and less secretive form, is still in use today; its benign effect is to assist the continuity of Formula One by helping teams through lean periods. Thus, in this most high-capitalist of sports, is the immediate impact of market forces gently mitigated.

By the end of the Eighties, after winning a series of bitter battles with the FIA, Ecclestone had grown more interested in running Formula One than in running a team, and the name and effects of the Brabham concern were sold. Now absorbed into the FIA and sitting as a member of its World Council, Ecclestone was in a perfect position to expand the audience and the profile of Formula One, signing deals for live television transmission around the world and thereby making the sport attractive to a growing number of multinational companies with marketing budgets big enough to encompass the sponsorship of a team or two.

His associate, Paddy McNally, concentrated on maximizing the income from trackside advertising through a company called Allsports Management. He developed the Paddock Club concept, enabling companies to buy corporate entertainment packages at each grand prix, giving their clients and favoured employees a treat in gigantic white marquees staffed by uniformed attendants serving champagne and canapés at a cost, in the mid-Nineties, of around £1,000 a head.

Ecclestone's other close collaborator, the lawyer Max Mosley, who had been one of the original partners behind the March racing team in the early Seventies and then became FOCA's lawyer (and, therefore, Ecclestone's *consigliere*), eventually won an election campaign for the presidency of the FIA itself, giving the trio a practically unbreakable grip on the power over Formula One, and control of the proceeds that came from it.

The success of this enterprise can be gauged by the fact that, in the financial year 1993–4, Bernie Ecclestone drew a salary of £29.7 million, the highest ever recorded in Britain. The following year's figure was down to £29.4 million. And the year after that he gave himself the biggest pay cut ever recorded, reducing his income to a mere £600,000: a 98 per cent reduction which reflected his personal investment in the resources necessary to get digital television off the ground.

He loves making deals, he loves the game of manipulation, and most people in the paddock – even those earning salaries comparable to his – are, in some respect, frightened of him. He can seem brusque and abrasive, but there is another side to his exercise of power. You don't have to go far to find someone unknown to the general public, perhaps a mechanic or a motor home driver, who has reason to be grateful for

Ecclestone's practical generosity during a difficult time: an introduction, a pit pass, a helpful word when a team has gone belly-up. Which doesn't make him Mother Theresa, but does help to explain the longevity of his reign.

As the 1996 season reached its climax, no one could claim greater responsibility than he for the way Formula One had recovered from Senna's death and the retirements of Piquet, Mansell and Prost. Not only had Ecclestone created the setting but he had also worked with great energy to ensure that the Formula One field would not lack competitive balance. Having fanned the flames of the dispute between Damon Hill and Michael Schumacher, which had helped maintain box-office interest in the preceding two seasons, he now saw a danger that Schumacher's first season with Ferrari would not be a competitive one for the German, and that Hill would cruise to the title in the vastly superior Williams. So, knowing that the young Canadian driver Jacques Villeneuve, son of the late Ferrari star Gilles Villeneuve, was interested in transferring from US Indycar racing to Formula One, he interceded on Villeneuve's behalf with Frank Williams, in the hope of providing serious opposition for Hill. Or for Schumacher, come to that, if the Ferrari should turn out to be a winner, in which case Ecclestone did not believe that Hill would be good enough to challenge the new combination. Williams could see the logic.

Villeneuve tested for the team at Silverstone in mid-1995 and his immediate speed, in unfamiliar surroundings and using strange equipment, raised eyebrows throughout Formula One. He was in, and suddenly Hill had a new and most significant threat from within his own team, his adopted family, the one place he believed himself to be secure.

Thanks to this astute piece of stage-management, there would be three generations of drivers, practically speaking, and three sets of personal imperatives contesting the 1996 world championship. Hill at thirty-five, searching for his first championship; Schumacher at twenty-seven, looking for a third title to confirm his pre-eminence; Villeneuve at twenty-four, making his entrance. At Monza, many months later, Ecclestone could be happy with his work as Hill headed for the title showdown in a blizzard of psychological warfare that had begun before the cars had so much as turned a wheel.

2

The middle-aged man walked nervously across the airport lounge and held out a pen and a piece of paper, muttering something in a half-embarrassed way. Damon Hill glanced up at him, opened his briefcase and took out a glossy black and white photograph of himself, pre-autographed in black marker pen, from a sheaf. He handed it to the man, acknowledging him with a quick nod. A few minutes later another man came up, holding a small camera, and asked if he could take Hill's picture. 'No,' Hill said, barely glancing up.

At this point, on the eve of the 1996 season, Hill looked as full of tensions as ever. With his quick, jerky movements, his strangely empty smile and the intense, forbidding glare that darkened his face in moments of intense concentration, the public Damon Hill seemed perennially uncomfortable in his own skin, mystifyingly uneasy with the accolades, the rewards, the affection and the admiration of the millions who were getting ready for another season of cheering him on every time he left the starting grid.

That was the perception. And, as with politics, perception is what counts in the modern world of commercial sport. Reality is something else, as Damon Hill has known since he was a small child, when he observed his famous father and gradually became aware of the perilous gap that could open up between the image and the truth. The problem for this sensitive man was to bring the perception close enough to the reality to make it possible to live with himself in the world in which he had chosen to exist, or which had perhaps been chosen for him.

Hill had always tried to make the big decisions himself. Other drivers had used managers: Nigel Mansell had Sheridan Thynne; David Coulthard and Johnny Herbert had the massed suits of Mark McCormack's International Management Group; Michael Schumacher had Willi Weber (plus some assistance from McCormack's people); the newcomer Jacques Villeneuve had Craig Pollock and, to examine the fine print, Julian Jakobi, who had looked after Ayrton Senna's business affairs. But until 1996, Hill, whose big break into Formula One did not come through high-level, top-dollar negotiations, had attempted to supervise his own career, with assistance from his lawyer, Michael Breen, and his sister, Brigitte. 'I do everything myself,' he said as the plane took off for Lisbon, *en route* to a pre-season testing session at Estoril. 'I work with some good advisers, both inside and outside racing, but I'm not comfortable with the idea of having someone do things on my behalf. In some ways that's left me a bit exposed. But I suppose, quite simply, I can't bear to be told what to do. I'd rather work things out for myself. That's how I get my satisfaction. And if I make mistakes ... well, they're my mistakes. I can't go around telling people that it went wrong because I didn't have the right management team.'

Three years earlier, on the day he signed to drive alongside Alain Prost for the Williams-Renault team, Hill had been surrounded by the jumble of his young family in a terraced house in Wandsworth. Now, on the eve of the 1996 season, he had arrived at Heathrow to catch the flight to Portugal from a new home in a mansion overlooking Killiney Bay, just south of Dublin, where he had been spending time with his wife, Georgie, and their three children, trying to absorb and understand the lessons of his motor racing career to date.

Winning the world championship, he said, would mean 'a confirmation of the work I have done', by which he meant the work that had begun, in effect, five years earlier when he signed up as the Williams team's test driver, helping develop the car that gave Nigel Mansell his world championship in 1992. In 1993, the relationship moved into a higher gear. Riccardo Patrese, the experienced Italian who had been the team's number two driver, jumped ship in the expectation that Alain Prost would be taking his seat alongside Mansell. He was right about that, but wrong about the consequences. Mansell, upset at the arrival of a three-time world champion and his new team-mate, failed to agree a new contract with Frank Williams, leaving the team to select their test driver as the new number two, under strict orders not to hinder the Frenchman's progress to a fourth title.

The choice of Hill was widely criticized, not least by those British drivers who considered themselves better qualified than a man who had previously started only two grands prix for a Brabham team that was on its last legs. Nevertheless, Hill did everything that could have been expected of him in that first season, and more, winning three races and finishing third in the championship behind Prost and Ayrton Senna. He kept the seat for 1994, hoping to hone his skills further by sharing the team with Senna, who had come in to replace

Prost. But, when the great Brazilian was killed in the third race of the season, Hill did not shrink from the task of pulling a traumatized team together and fighting Schumacher all the way through the season.

Although doubts were being cast on the legality of Schumacher's Benetton-Ford, which was widely believed to be making use of banned computer-controlled driver aids, Hill managed to win six races and lost the title by a single point when Schumacher's half-crippled car lurched unerringly into his path during the final race in Australia, knocking them both out of the race and giving the title to the German driver.

In 1995 Hill won four races and finished runner-up again, but this time he had been thoroughly undermined by Schumacher's gift for psychological warfare. The worst moment came at Silverstone. After exchanging insults through the media (Schumacher called Hill 'a little man'; Hill branded Schumacher 'a clone'), the two men had put on a show of making up. But on the Sunday afternoon a collision caused by Hill's panicky overtaking manoeuvre put them both out of a race that should have been a walkover for the Englishman. Hill came out of it looking inept and unworthy of the privilege of driving what was easily the best car in the field.

Humiliated again by Schumacher at Aida and Suzuka, the Japanese circuits, towards the end of year, Hill used the fortnight before the last race of the season in Adelaide to reflect on the previous three seasons and to take a good look at himself. What he saw was a beaten man. 'Everything had run straight through from the moment I got the Williams drive,' he said. 'It felt like I just hadn't stopped. By the time I got to Japan I'd run out of puff, to be honest. I knew I wasn't going to win the title and I'd lost the appetite for the competition because, in my own mind, I'd failed. I was taking quite a beating, psychologically, from all quarters. I felt like I was banging my head against a brick wall. Then you realize that if you stop, it won't hurt so much. So you have to stand back, get a fresh perspective and try to junk all the things that you've built up in your head as being important when they really weren't.' Such as? 'You know, the peripheral stuff that comes with the territory. The press speculation, the immense coverage of what was happening. That made it really unpleasant for me. I'd tried my hardest. I'd failed. But in the process I'd still won races and fought for the championship and been the only serious challenger to Michael for the title. It wasn't really such a disaster.'

During the two free weeks between Japan and the last race in Australia, he reached a vital conclusion. 'I didn't have much to do and it was too far to come home, so I had a holiday in Bali with Georgie and then we went to Perth with a couple of friends and spent a few days relaxing. And it suddenly hit me. I'd been working so hard to do everything for the past three years and, before that, the time I'd spent trying to get into Formula One, that I'd become a bit of a workaholic. I decided to come back refreshed for 1996, with renewed enthusiasm for doing what I love doing but which had become a bit of a job of work.' He cleared his mind, came back to win the final race of 1995 at Adelaide and then disappeared again to plan an entirely different approach to a season in which, with Schumacher switching to the troubled Ferrari team, his main threat would almost certainly come from a young and ambitious new team-mate.

The factors were physical, technical and mental. The first and second could be dealt with by extra training in the gym, under the supervision of the team's new physiotherapist, Erwin Gollner, and a rational programme of pre-season testing with the new Williams-Renault FW18. 'I took the view that I didn't want to test too much until I could get my hands on the new car. We tested a hell of a lot in 1995. I think we did twice as many testing miles as Benetton, and we'd already done as many miles by June as we'd done in the entire previous season. I often said at the time that I couldn't see what progress we were making. We were just doing miles. I suppose I brought it upon myself because I was adamant that I wanted to develop and improve the car and win the championship. I just can't let myself rest sometimes, because I'll always curse myself for having let up if I don't achieve my goal. But, after a while, it was difficult to distinguish genuine progress from just another change. You have to stand back every now and then. That's what I've been doing this winter – doing other things, but at the same time preparing myself.'

The third factor, his mental preparation, was where his weaknesses had been spotted by his opponents. It required special attention. 'There's a great deal more to sport than just playing the game,' he said. 'It's something that I've become particularly aware of in the past two seasons, and it's a product of my rapid exposure to the sharp end of Formula One. When I moved from Brabham to Williams I leapt straight from the back of the grid to the front row and I had to sink or swim. I think I swam quite well. There's no problem with what I do when I drive, as far as I can see. But there's the whole political and public relations aspect to Formula One which I've resisted trying to conform to, to a degree, because I want to be myself. I don't want to be a product. I don't want to be packaged. I don't want people putting words into my mouth. You can find yourself paying a price for that.'

But the price of relying on his own resources had proved too high and, in an attempt to reduce it, Hill was going into the 1996 season with a team of reinforcements. 'One of the things that has changed for me this year is that I no longer feel the need to do everything myself,' he said. 'I've learnt to trust other people. I use the people around me to make my life easier, so I can focus on driving.' I asked him whom he went to for advice, whom he trusted. 'I wouldn't be prepared to discuss that here. I take my counsel from many sources. I have one or two people close to me who I talk to all the time, from outside racing and within it.'

The outlines of an informal 'Team Hill' became clearer as the season progressed. Headed by Breen, a partner in the London firm of Edward Lewis, and Georgie, it also included Hill's aide-de-camp, Jamie McCallum, formerly Frank Williams' nurse; his friend, the photographer Jon Nicholson; Erwin Gollner; the *Daily Telegraph* journalist Michael Calvin, who provided advice on handling the media from time to time; and, most controversially, an American image consultant, Mary Spillane.

Their job was to rebuild the public image of a man who, in the eyes of Fleet Street's tabloids, had committed the cardinal sin of not being Nigel Mansell. The newspapers gave him three chances to follow in Mansell's footsteps by winning the championship, and he blew them all. Third in 1993, behind Prost and Senna in his first full season, then second in 1994 and again in 1995, both times trailing Michael Schumacher, his nemesis: it wasn't good enough for editors needing stories of British heroes, and the pack turned on him. From the BBC's Sports Personality of the Year at the end of 1994 to 'The Formula One Whinger' (the London *Evening Standard*'s headline) in less than a year represented quite a fall from grace. 'I wasn't so much shocked as amazed at the severity of it,' Hill said. 'But I suppose it's just part of being in the arena and taking on the challenge. You've got to be up for that. Michael gets the same thing in Germany. Prost got it in France. Nigel certainly got it. I don't know about Senna. It doesn't take much in this sport for there to be some controversial material and I guess there was plenty to go on last year. But I've learnt from first-hand experience.'

The greatest pressure, he claimed, was exerted by himself. 'You do your damndest, but then sometimes you feel you get nothing but criticism for it. That can be a bit upsetting. But in any business you can't expect too much in the way of praise at the top level. Sport, in a way, is one of the few places where you can expect some praise when you get the opportunity to do well. I'm certainly one of the first people to pick up the paper and read about how wonderful I was.'

It was worth asking why, at this point in his career, we were so ready to expose him – apparently a modest young Englishman of impeccable public behaviour – to such scorching public criticism. Partly it was to do with the expectations aroused by the kind of money he was making, which by 1996 had risen to around £5 million for the season from Williams, plus whatever he made in personal sponsorship and endorsements. It was also, more to the point, a product of the relentless newspaper circulation war with its vocabulary of violent confrontation and recrimination.

Until the Seventies, grand prix racing was reported as if it were no different from rowing or polo, more of a gentlemen's recreation than a sport. The battles between Niki Lauda and James Hunt began to change that, impelled by the increasing coverage on television. Gradually a *modus operandi* emerged: television provided the pictures while the newspapers supplied the characters. The techniques were honed in the Eighties when Piquet, Mansell, Prost and Senna were in a state of permanent conflict. Even in Hill's first season, while he was still learning the trade and was confined by the terms of his agreement to play second fiddle to Prost, the tabloids were pushing the hype. When Frank Williams refused to give Prost instructions let Hill win the British Grand Prix, the *Sun* splashed the alleged scandal under the headline, 'Don't be a Blank, Frank!'

By 1996, after two years of non-stop war between Hill and Schumacher, it seemed that motor racing now existed only in these terms. A week or two before the start of the season, the *Mirror* ran a four-paragraph story based on a couple of harmless quotes from Jacques Villeneuve under the headline: 'Hill on His Jacques!' It began: 'Jacques Villeneuve put the boot into Damon Hill . . .' This took its place among a spread of sports stories with headlines such as 'Tel Hits Out', 'My World of Hate – Tyson', 'Fans Spit on Mac', 'Athers Faces New Torment' and 'Fans Stand There and Call me a Fat B******, says Paul Gascoigne'. To command space in such pages it had become necessary to speak the language.

In Hill's case it was also a question of being his father's son. Damon walked on to the stage of Formula One and received a big hand just for being Graham's boy. Yet that was the last thing he wanted to be known for, and it set up tensions that were a long way from being unwound. On the one hand, in his own life – the life that he had made with his wife, children and his network of family, friends and assistants – he seemed centred and secure. Yet from the world outside came this constant scratching away at the business of living up to his father's achievements, which would have been easier to cope with had the preoccupation of outsiders not happened to coincide with something genuinely unresolved and largely unacknowledged in his own mind.

His cad's moustache and smarmed-back hair readily identi-fied Graham Hill as the last English racing driver of the National Service generation. He had been a late starter, and it showed. In the mid-Sixties, while his younger peers were growing their Beatle fringes and experimenting with Bob Dylan caps, Hill still looked like someone who might know how to get hold of a fistful of petrol coupons or who could undo a reluctant popsie's four-hook brassière with a flick of finger and thumb. On the face of it, he was the heir to Peter Collins and Mike Hawthorn, those dashing Fifties aces with supercharged libidos. Like them, and like James Hunt after him, Graham Hill was loved by the crowds because he made it all look a bit of a lark, this business of life and death. And how could a man who painted his crash helmet in the colours of his old rowing club possibly be serious?

If you didn't know the real story, you'd think that Graham Hill had acquired his place in Formula One by accident, perhaps through bumping into some chap in a Home Coun-ties pub while he was at a loose end. But you don't become the only man to win two Formula One world championships, the Indianapolis 500 and the 24 Hours of Le Mans with a weekend hero's attitude and a spiv's instincts. Sure enough, despite the image, Hill's success was achieved through the application of persistence and hard graft. He began with no contacts and had no natural advantages – not even talent, according to his critics.

'I know it winds mum up when people say that,' Damon Hill observed. 'It's a big mistake to assume that dad was a bit of a . . . buffoon. Anyone who could win five times at Monaco must have had some sort of instinct.'

He was speaking on a dour December afternoon in 1992, on the day Frank Williams made the surprising announcement that Damon Hill had been nominated as the team's second driver for the following season, alongside Alain Prost. Inside the little terraced house in Bucharest Road, Wandsworth, the Hills' two small sons, Oliver and Joshua, were playing on the floor of the living-room. Georgie Hill, whom Damon met in 1981 and married in 1988, could be seen doing something domestic in the kitchen-dining area, knocked through like the similar homes of thousands of young professional couples in London. At thirty-two, Damon's salary had suddenly taken a leap from a test driver's pittance to £150,000 a year – another late starter! – but celebrity had yet to affect the life of his family.

That day the phone was ringing constantly with people who wanted to congratulate him and then jump straight into questions about the inner tensions set up by the perilous business of trying to emulate his late father, a proposition for which he seemed partially prepared. 'I just don't see it in those terms,' he said firmly. 'It would be a big mistake for me to do that. I'm not the same person as him at all.'

Same job, same instincts, same helmet. But, true enough,

one look was enough to show that he had inherited his mother's features rather than his father's. The face was softer, the smile gentler, the dark eyes entirely his own. But, sometimes, there was a look that could only have come from one place. And here he was saying that his mother was always telling him, 'You're just like your father.'

Fathers and sons: it's an old story in motor racing, where little boys are easily seduced by the noise and the shimmer. There are dynasties: the Brabhams; the Stewarts; the Andrettis. And, first of them all, the Ascaris of Milan.

Alberto Ascari was five years old in 1924 when his father, Antonio, propped him behind the huge steering-wheel of his Alfa Romeo, installed himself in the mechanic's seat and allowed the child to 'drive' around the new Monza track. A year later, after an accident at the Montlhéry circuit near Paris, the boy attended his father's funeral. But before he was out of short trousers Alberto was courting his mother's disapproval by playing poker to raise the money he needed to hire a motorcycle with which to repeat the Monza experience. Eliza Ascari sent her son away to boarding school to take his mind off the obsession, but he ran away and ran away and ran away again until there was nothing she could do but let him fulfil his destiny. In 1952 and 1953 he won nine grands prix in a row and two world championships; in 1955 he died while testing a sports car at Monza, taking the curve that was later named after him. His own son, Tonino, was twelve years old at the time. At twenty-one, against the wishes of his mother, Mietta, Tonino used his inheritance to begin a short racing career which reached its peak when he won the Italian Formula Three championship in 1964. Then, quietly, he retired.

'I found it hard to exist under the two strong shadows of my grandfather and my father,' he said many years later. 'If I were to succeed, people would say it was not because I was better than the others, but because I was my father's son. If I were to fail, then the dynasty was finished and I should not have attempted to continue it.'

Damon Hill was fifteen when his father crashed his Piper Aztec plane on to a golf course near Elstree on a foggy night in the winter of 1975, killing himself and five other members of his Embassy Hill grand prix team, including the promising young driver Tony Brise. They had been returning from a testing session at the Paul Ricard circuit, near Marseilles. Five months earlier, Graham Hill had announced his retirement from driving at the age of forty-six, soon after failing to qualify for the Monaco Grand Prix, a race he had won five times.

'You pretend it hasn't happened,' Damon Hill said, remembering his reaction to the bereavement. 'There's the shock and the numbness, but at the same time you half-expect him to walk in the door, as though he's just been away somewhere. And that, I have to say, is how I still feel, to some degree. He was such a larger-than-life man that it's difficult to imagine he's not around.'

It hadn't been at all bad, having a world champion for a father. 'It was fun, all the time. I don't really have clear chronological memories but I remember things like the old BRM transporter turning up at our house in Mill Hill, and going to racetracks like Brands Hatch when it was just a field with a few Nissen huts.' And the father certainly didn't discourage his son's interest. 'Put it this way, when I said I wanted a motorbike it wasn't long before I had one. It was for passing my 11-plus, actually. He was quite strict with us, but if you asked nicely you could usually get what you wanted. Oh yes, I was a spoilt child. I had everything I wanted.' Except, at the age of fifteen, a dad.

Bette Hill, his mother, was not a bit like Eliza and Mietta Ascari, so anxious to protect their sons from the perils of the track and guide them away from the possibility of meeting the same end as their fathers. She had been an integral part of her husband's career, encouraging him during the lean years and, stopwatch in hand, keeping the lap chart during the world championship seasons. When her son showed an interest in racing, she wasn't inclined to discourage him. 'At first she pushed me to go to college and learn some sort of discipline, like law or accountancy. I tried business studies, but I jacked it in after a term because I was thoroughly bored. In retrospect, I'd have liked to have gone to college and studied English, but at the time I wasn't sure what I wanted to do, except that I wanted to get stuck into something exciting. I think my mother accepted there was no way I was going to be forced into a square hole.'

During Graham Hill's career, and for some time afterwards, Bette Hill's pet project had been an informal club for the wives, girlfriends and widows of grand prix drivers. This was an era in which fatalities were relatively frequent. Damon Hill's wife knew nothing about motor racing when they met in 1981 but she came to share his enthusiasm and gave him unstinting support through the years of motorbike racing, when he was earning very little as a messenger. It was with a view to getting him into something safer than a bike that Bette paid for him to take a course at a racing school in France. But Damon lacked a mentor, a father. 'It's hard to find someone to replace your father,' Georgie said. 'The only one who really helped him was John Webb, who ran Brands Hatch. He gave Damon his first chance in Formula Ford. That was the only help he had.' But he fought his way up, eventually winning a seat in Formula 3000, the last step before Formula One, in 1989. His three seasons there were hindered by inferior equipment, which was also the case when he took a drive in his first Formula One team, the rapidly disintegrating Brabham organization, in 1992. But by then he was already into his second season as the Williams team's test driver, compiling more than two thousand miles a year evaluating the high-tech gizmos that took Nigel Mansell to the title, and providing the engineers with technical feedback accurate and reliable enough for them to support his campaign for full employment when Mansell announced his departure.

That morning, Prost had described his new colleague in *L'Équipe* as '*un garçon très "cool"*'. But at his own press conference, Hill characterized himself as 'charmless' and 'lacking the gift of the gab'. Whatever the motive, the attempt to distance himself from the collective memory of his late father was almost painfully artless.

'Obviously, I never got to know him completely,' he told me later. 'I just knew the family side. But I know that he really loved motor racing. It was his reason for being. And when the strain of running his own team and trying to drive at the same time became too much, he was very sad about it. There was a real sense of loss. But everyone else was relieved when he retired. I was pleased. I thought, at least he's safe. The irony is, of course, that he wasn't.'

*

Three years later, as the plane carrying Damon Hill cruised through the night to Lisbon, I asked him if he agreed with the basic Freudian analysis which said that, during a childhood spent watching his father from a distance, he was able to observe the difference between the public personality, the Terry-Thomas of the tracks, and the private man (far more demanding and difficult than the image suggested), and that he had become determined, consciously or more probably otherwise, never to put himself in a position where he might have to erect a similar façade. Hence his discomfort when faced with the notebooks and microphones of inquisitors, and with the basic requirement of Formula One that its insiders should be adept at the arts of evasion and deception. Hence, too, his admitted preference for testing Formula One cars, with its long periods of unrelieved, anonymous toil and its honest, certifiable results, over the glamorous business of actually racing them, when success and failure can be a matter of pure chance.

'You're half right,' he said. 'I'm not going to make any direct reaction to what you're saying about my father. But, certainly, I was backstage when I was growing up and I could see the show and all the tricks that were used to convince the people in the audience that what they were seeing was for real. There's a need to give the audience what they want, whereas I think for a long time I just pursued the goal of getting into Formula One, getting my hands on a vehicle and then doing as well as I could in the race. I just put blinkers on and let everything else take care of itself. But before I knew it I was in the spotlight and expected to perform other tricks that I hadn't learnt along the way.'

Hadn't learnt, or perhaps had chosen not to learn, out of

distaste for the whole superficial business? 'I wouldn't say distaste. I just didn't understand it. You don't really appreciate things until you've had a little experience of them yourself. It comes back to what we were saying about management. These days, drivers need to prepare themselves for being thrust into stardom and I'd never really felt the desire to have that kind of coaching. And so, I think, to some degree I'm a lot more up-front than many other people in the sport. What you see is what you get. And I hope that never changes, to be honest, because I think the public deserve that. If they're fed a constant diet of perfectly trained performers then the sport runs the risk of becoming less convincing.'

Something about Hill, something vulnerable, encouraged other people in and around Formula One to think they could get away with insulting him. David Coulthard, his team-mate during the previous season and his junior in both years and experience, felt at liberty to remark on his 'inconsistent' personality, an idea later picked up and repeated by Schumacher. Alan Jones, the plain-spoken Australian who won the world championship for Williams in 1980 and whose hundred-proof racer's instinct earned him a special place in the affections of Frank Williams and Patrick Head, summed up his view of Hill's widely debated qualities as a racer by saying that 'Damon either procrastinates for half the bloody race or runs into somebody's arse-end'. With only a few weeks to go before the start of the 1996 season, Head himself – the technical director of Hill's own team – made a pointedly dismissive comment about drivers with 'fragile egos'. Hill was not slow to defend himself, but there was a powerful sense that self-criticism came first, perhaps more painfully than he cared to let us know, and that devising a convincing response to the harsh words of others had not, hitherto in his life, been a priority. To some it comes naturally, others have to struggle to acquire the art and may never manage it.

Hill invariably came off second-best in the well-publicized mind games with Schumacher, which he attempted to dismiss as 'something to provide a little bit of spice to the circus. It's a bit like boxing. People will switch on if they think they're going to see two guys who hate each other's guts. But, sure, at times there's an attempt to play a bit of a psychological game. And, like advertising, it's difficult to prove whether it's effective or not. Sometimes it can be fun. Quite amusing. But I'll say one thing, there's no way you can stage-manage the performance on the track.'

As for Williams and Head, had they not borrowed from Enzo Ferrari the strategy of keeping their own drivers in a constant state of creative tension? 'That's a kind way of putting it. There are two ways to motivate people: positively or negatively. I don't need other people motivating me, I resist that kind of approach. I do not like to be pushed or prodded or intimidated. I go well when I'm enjoying myself, when I like what I'm doing and the people I'm doing it with, when we're all pulling together in the same direction and trying to achieve the same thing. But Formula One is much more complex than that, and I consider myself capable of handling all the various situations that come up. It's as challenging as the driving, to be able to stand your ground and survive in that environment.'

When I asked if he'd been able to make Williams and Head understand his point of view, he said briskly that he 'didn't want to polarize it around those two', and went on to describe how he split Formula One observers into two camps. You could simplify it, he said, by defining two views of the sport: the Senna view and the Prost view. 'In other words, some who regard it as no-holds-barred, anything goes, the only thing that matters is winning, and others who see it in terms of doing anything to win within what is permissible and what you feel is fair. Those two attitudes are quite distinct and you can go all the way back through the history of Formula One and find people who'd rather come second than do something they wouldn't feel happy with. To go further, some view the sport as a test of strength while others view it as an art.'

The previous year, he mentioned, he had been involved in a protracted dispute about what constituted a correct and legitimate overtaking manoeuvre. The regulations had said one thing, while certain drivers were out there doing something quite different. Hill, being a correct and literal-minded sort of chap, made overtures with the intention of getting everyone to agree on a common set of rules of engagement. This gave yet another opening to his critics, who muttered that a real racing driver wouldn't need a Highway Code in order to get past his rivals. 'I got involved in that and I found myself being accused of whingeing,' Hill said. 'But I just wanted to know what I was supposed to be doing, whether I could adopt a different approach within the regulations or not. And that's where I got a bit mixed up. Frank was extremely supportive the whole year. He gave me the right motivation at the right times. Patrick's approach is more attacking, I suppose you could say. But I know Patrick well and it's been a very successful operation over the last few years.'

They are, I said to him, a pair of unusually brilliant and

interesting men, a statement which made him laugh in an enigmatic sort of way. 'Yeah. True. Very brilliant and interesting men. And I have a lot of respect for them. But you can't afford to . . . well, I came into the team and I learnt things the Williams way. I had simply to follow instructions. But there comes a point where you know you're right and you have to insist on what you want. Otherwise it's too easy to fall into the trap of blaming someone else. I think we got a lot sorted out over the winter. Last year was a tough experience for everyone. In fact, we've had two tough years – you couldn't get a tougher year than 1994. We all wanted to win so much last year, so there was a lot of disappointment on everyone's part when we got off to a great start and then had a massive setback with mechanical problems. But there's been a big determination to understand what went wrong with our approach and what we have to do to put it right.'

After entering the team by the back door, as a junior partner first to Prost and then to Senna, he had not found it easy to establish his primacy, his right to the number one seat, once both of them had gone. 'I'd liken it to a parent coming to the realization that their child has grown up. A lot of parents find it difficult to accept that the child is no longer ten years old. That would be putting it too strongly in my situation, but it's a similar thing. I know that Frank is a perceptive person. He knows when a driver has matured and is ready to win championships. He knew when I'd be ready to win races, so I don't think there's a problem there. But, inevitably, there have been growing pains.'

Some of the pains had concerned Hill's remuneration, which reportedly had risen from £150,000 to £1.5 million to £5 million in successive seasons, after agonizing and protracted negotiations. And now Michael Schumacher was to earn £16 million a year at Ferrari. After a certain point, after you'd bought your three dream homes and your private jet and still the folding stuff came flowing in, weren't these sums really more of symbolic value than anything else? 'Yes. It would be easy to see it as simply an attempt to extract as much money for your own needs as possible, but it's not just that. The retainer that a team is prepared to pay for a driver is an expression of their desire for that driver.' And Schumacher's retainer, what kind of desire did that represent? 'Well, nobody knows the real figure. But it's stupendous.'

Is anybody worth that kind of money in this world? 'You get what you can. Sure, I'm on a lot of money. But I risk my life to earn it, and I can only do it for a short period of time. It's a big business, Formula One, and I certainly wouldn't be paid this sort of money if it wasn't there in the first place. It's more a measure of the value of Formula One than of anything else. OK, nobody asked me to do it, I did it out of choice, so it's a bit of a hollow argument to follow that you're risking your life so you must be worth this sort of money. A lot of people risk their lives for far better causes and for a lot less money. But it's still part of the equation, and it's part of the attraction as well. It makes headlines.'

Ferrari had courted Hill the previous summer, and he had responded. 'We had a number of meetings, and certainly I was intrigued by the idea because I'd spent three years at Williams and I could see that Ferrari were making progress. It would have been a new challenge, and who wouldn't want to drive for Ferrari? I mean, you shouldn't really allow yourself to get romantic about your job but when you're talking about Ferrari it's difficult not to take that into account.

So it was certainly a possibility, a lot more than just a rumour. And it was very flattering to be in discussions with them.'

Not many other top grand prix drivers would have been modest enough to formulate that last statement, but arrogance is not part of the Hill temperament, which is why his attempts at psychological warfare had been so unconvincing and so revealing. What people really like about sport, I said to him, whether they realize it or not, is the way it peels back the layers that are intended to disguise the essential components of a person's character. You can listen to a musician all your life and not have a clue about what he's really like. The same can go for your office colleagues. But sport discloses the shape and depth of character – even motor racing, where the competitors' facial expressions are hidden from view. 'I agree with that,' he replied. 'It's what attracts people. They like to see the discipline executed by its finest exponents, but they also want to see how different people react to the same situation. I wasn't happy with my own performance in some situations last year, to be honest. I've come to realize that however much coverage Formula One gets, it's only really a snapshot of your personality. There just isn't the time to go into great depth about any particular situation. So the ability to put things in a nutshell, to sum up what's happened as well and as simply as possible, is very important. That's not my natural character. I'd rather go into something in great depth than just roll off a one-liner and dismiss it. But it relieves a lot of the burden to be able to do that and forget it, because otherwise you're just dragging all this stuff around behind you.'

There is a danger in jumping to conclusions on certain matters, but on meeting Georgie Hill briefly three years earlier I had been impressed by her ability to share in the pleasure of her husband's success without being remotely in awe of it. 'She's an incredible woman. The first time I met her she was actually being taken out by a friend of mine. I tried out some of my best jokes on her but she didn't laugh. I was very impressed by this. She's the sort of woman who will not be messed about with. I admire her greatly for that. It can be hell to live with, of course, but stimulating.'

I said she seemed to be the antithesis of the Penelope Pitstop characters in evidence elsewhere, the ones with modelling contracts whose skills involve effortlessly transforming a start-line kiss into a photo-opportunity. 'Well, exactly. I think she sees through all that. She has a good sense of priorities. We discuss a lot of things and she's very much a part of the business. I had to teach her everything about motor racing but she's very well informed now and she enjoys it, too, although she's not starry-eyed. She's got a good head on her shoulders, she knows my moods and knows what to say to bring me back on line. It can have a very distorting influence, doing what I'm doing. Georgie's my datum, my point to which I refer back so that I don't go too far off track. In this situation, it's quite easy for that to happen.'

Damon's own childhood had conditioned his view of his role as a father. 'I'd say that's been the biggest pressure of all, since I'm so conscious of how childhood was for me and the fact that my father wasn't around. I can relate directly to my own children, so I'm determined to give them as much time as I can and pare the other things I do down to the bare essentials. I like Georgie to come to the races, but occasionally I prefer her to stay at home because I don't like us both being away from the children. And from time to time I like to take some friends along for a bit of a boys' weekend. She understands that.'

The previous three years in Formula One had taught him to be more efficient. 'I have less time for everything. It's a bit like going to university, I imagine. I've been going through a period of being taken away from home and being confronted by a great many new things. The learning curve has been steep but it's been very satisfying to tackle it. Not many lines of work give you the opportunity to measure your progress so immediately. And learning to juggle all the bits of it – family life, travel, fitness, talking to the press, being in a position of enormous responsibility – is something I've enjoyed.'

It hadn't always showed on his face. He had made mistakes, he could be infuriating. But it had been an odd sort of life, not one he'd asked for, in a way, and his struggle to match himself – his inner self – to its demands had been one of the most compelling features of Formula One in the mid-Nineties. 'A lot of the discomfort I feel is with myself as much as with anyone else,' he said. 'So I have to come back and have another go. I won't be able to race for ever. One day the music will stop and I'll have to get off and let someone else have a go, and when that time comes I want very much to be able to look back and say, "Well, I did everything I possibly could, as well as I could, and I'm happy with that, whatever the result may be." It would be awful to have to bear any other kind of feeling into old age. And much of my motivation is derived from that feeling as well, that I'm more frightened of not having lived life to the fullest than I am of dying.'

3

Jacques Villeneuve had barely lifted himself out of the cockpit of car number twenty-seven in Victory Lane at the Indianapolis Motor Speedway in May 1995 when a microphone was thrust at him and a voice asked how he'd felt as he crossed the finish line of the great 500-mile race, just twenty-four years old and the winner at his second attempt.

'Were you thinking about your father?'

'No! I don't see why I should have been thinking about my father! I don't race for him. I race for me, and for my team.'

The words came fast and even, and they didn't stop.

'Sure, he'd be proud of me, and it would be neat if he were here, but I don't see why I should be thinking of him. I know a lot of people would like me to say "I won it for you". But that would be ridiculous. It's not right to live in the past. If I'd started to race during his lifetime, maybe it would have been different.'

'And to have won with the number twenty-seven?'

'The number doesn't matter. What counts is that the team is good enough to win. For some people, the most important thing this season is that I'm racing with the number twenty-seven, but that's just coincidence. Last year I had the number twelve and my father finished second in the world championship and had some of his finest hours with that number. People only concentrate on twenty-seven because that's the number he had when he was killed. They'd like to see him brought back to life through that number. But that's not what I'm racing for.'

It wasn't Jacques Villeneuve's first win of the season and it wasn't the first time he'd been asked those questions. Four months later, when he wrapped up the Indycar championship, becoming the youngest man ever to win the series, they'd stopped asking about his father. But by then Villeneuve knew he was on his way to Formula One in 1996, which meant that he was in for another year of telling people that, no, he doesn't carry his father's memory around with him like a holy relic every time he steps into a racing car.

He was in the Williams factory having a fitting for the customized seat of his new car when I asked him more or less the same question, prefacing it with a sheepish disclaimer to the effect that maybe in a year's time we would be able to have a conversation without the subject coming up.

'Yeah, but it's O K,' he said politely, in his strange polyglot accent. 'I'm used to it. It's been more positive in that respect since I started winning races. The first time I was asked, it surprised me. The thought just hadn't occurred to me. I mean, I think about my father when I'm with my mother or my sister or with people who knew him when he was alive. But when I'm working, there's no room for that. I wouldn't be thinking about him at that moment if he were alive, so why should I think about him just because he's dead?'

It makes a great story, of course, and the prospect was for an even better one during the 1996 season, when the son of the great Gilles Villeneuve took his place in the Williams-Renault team alongside the son of the late Graham Hill: two examples of what the Italians call a *figlio d'arte*, a son of the art. Two highly professional young men forced – well, maybe not forced, exactly – into finding themselves with no choice other than to measure their worth against the reputations of their charismatic fathers. For Hill, the struggle appeared to be at least as intense as the one he had been waging against Michael Schumacher over the previous two years, and it seemed to have been largely responsible for the frequent and well-publicized disturbances in the balance between his skill and his self-belief. For Jacques Villeneuve, it seemed that such self-examination had barely begun.

'Look,' he told me, 'for sure I'm super-proud of my dad. Of course I am. But what exactly do they want me to do? Burst into tears at the thought of his memory every time I see the chequered flag? Ridiculous.'

The trouble was that his dad was the most beloved of all recent Formula One stars. Not, by any means, the most successful – Gilles Villeneuve won only six of his sixty-seven grands prix – but undoubtedly the most spectacular, and held in universal affection throughout those parts of the world in which Formula One has an audience. It was Gilles, the baby-faced little French-Canadian, who drove an unforgettable lap on three wheels after his left rear tyre exploded at Zandvoort in 1979 and who, in the same year, banged wheels with René Arnoux for the last three laps at Dijon in a bareknuckle battle for second place which had the crowd in ecstasy and the two drivers saluting each other's courage and chivalry on the slowing-down lap.

Whatever the race, and whatever his position in it, Gilles drove with his heart and soul. Born to race, brought up competing in snowmobiles on frozen lakes, he loved the feeling of machinery sliding underneath him; even in Formula One his car would spend most of its time in lurid powerslides that were usually caught at the last minute but which often took him beyond the limit of control. He was fearless, but he was also undoubtedly foolhardy, and he was killed at Zolder in 1982, still in a hot rage two weeks after his team-mate Didier Pironi had tricked him out of an important win at Imola.

It was Gilles' doomed flamboyance that did much to create the modern legend of Ferrari as a team condemned to endure a permanent agony of disillusion, of promise betrayed. And the number twenty-seven has since assumed a weirdly iconic significance; you will see them still at Monza and Imola, the fans with 'Forza Gilles' and the sacred number on their banners, daring his successors – René Arnoux, Michele Alboreto, Nigel Mansell, Alain Prost, Jean Alesi, Gerhard Berger, even Michael Schumacher – to wrestle with his inviolable memory. Such a fuss did Enzo Ferrari make of him that it is almost a surprise to enter the Ferrari family tomb in Modena and discover that there is no place within it for Gilles' mortal remains. Only Ayrton Senna's death, twelve years later, evoked similar emotions, similar visions – even in cynical hearts – of an unvanquished spirit racing on through the heavens.

When it became clear, in the middle of 1995, that the great romantic hero's son was heading for Formula One, Ferrari's interest was immediate. Jacques, however, was too shrewd to fall into the most obvious of honey-traps. It wasn't even a question of trying to avoid the comparison with a legend; it was a pure cold-blooded matter of refusing to settle for less than the best. He and his manager, Craig Pollock, went straight for Williams, the undoubted class of the field. They were encouraged by Bernie Ecclestone, who saw Villeneuve as perhaps the only man capable of mounting a real challenge to Schumacher's pre-eminence (and, perhaps, of reawakening North America's long-dormant interest in Formula One). A Silverstone test proved the young man capable of jumping straight into a Formula One car, mastering its sophisticated devices and lapping within a second of an established ace (Hill, in this case). Both sides took little time to make up their minds, which sent Williams' existing number two driver, David Coulthard, off in the direction of the McLaren team.

For Villeneuve, it was the next stage in the series of logical although not always obvious career choices that began soon after his father's death, when he decided that he, too, wanted to be a racing driver. After burying Gilles in his home town of Berthierville, forty miles north-east of Montreal, Jacques, his mother and his little sister Melanie returned to their home in Monaco, where Gilles had made his base after signing for Ferrari. At the age of twelve, Jacques was sent to school at Villars in Switzerland. There in the Bernese Oberland he honed a talent for skiing that had been sparked by his father's friendship with the downhill champions Steve Podborski and Ken Read, the 'Crazy Canucks' of the World Cup circus. A natural on skis, Jacques could have found his sporting destiny in downhill racing. But in his sixteenth year, on a family visit to Quebec, he took a summer course at the Jim Russell Racing Drivers' School at the Mont Tremblant circuit, where his father had briefly been a pupil. His mother, who had spent several years travelling around North America and Europe in a motor home while her husband pursued his career, wasn't keen but didn't stop him. 'She didn't really want me to race. She was hoping I'd do something else. I don't really think it's because she was scared that I'd get injured or anything. After all, for her it was a normal world. I think it's more that she was afraid I wouldn't succeed, and that the pressure would be too much. But she knew I was going to race and that there was no point in trying to stop me, because all it would have meant is that at eighteen I would have gone away from home and done it anyway. Now she's really happy because it's gone well.'

Two years after the course at Mont Tremblant he was out of his Swiss classroom and racing Formula Three cars in Italy, an apprenticeship which lasted three seasons before he accepted an offer to spend a year contesting the parallel series in Japan. 'That was like my university year. You know, like when you see a movie and kids are just having fun. In a way, outside the racing, I was living a little bit like you do at university, which I hadn't done because of the demands of racing.' It was in Japan that he bumped into Pollock, a half-Scot, half-Swiss in his mid-thirties who had been his sports instructor at Villars. Pollock, who had moved into the commercial side of motor racing, didn't recognize the long-haired youth at first. But Villeneuve told him of his plans and eventually persuaded him to become his manager. Together they devised the schedule that took the driver to North America for a reconnaissance year in Formula Atlantic, followed by two seasons of outstanding success in Indycars. Named Rookie of the Year for his second place at the 1994

Indy 500, the following year he ran a strategically brilliant race to scoop the million-dollar pot, despite a two-lap penalty for a technical infringement – making him the first man, as he said, to win the 500-mile race by covering 505 miles.

That opened the gates to Formula One, and he saw no point in delaying his entrance, although he was well aware that the last man to attempt a direct graduation from Indycars to Formula One had failed badly. Michael Andretti was the golden boy of the US series when he joined Ayrton Senna in the McLaren team in 1993. Despite being the son of a former Formula One world champion, and widely tipped for similar distinction, he never came to terms with the technology or, more particularly, the culture of the grand prix paddock, and was humiliatingly dismissed in mid-season. Villeneuve showed no fear of meeting a similar fate. 'The difference is that Andretti had lived all his life in the USA, and even when he was racing there he was still living in Pennsylvania and taking the plane on Sunday nights to go back home, so there's no way he could adapt to Europe. He couldn't get all the testing he needed, so he wasn't ready. He couldn't reach his own standard.'

Villeneuve, on the other hand, was already acculturated to the grand prix world. 'I've lived in Europe since I was six,' he said. 'Deep inside, I feel very Canadian. I'm proud of it. It's not something you can chop and change. But that doesn't mean my culture or my mentality are Canadian, or North American. I'm happier in Europe. I know it better and I feel better here.' The centre of operations would be a newly acquired apartment in Monaco, not far from the home where his mother, Joann, was bringing up a second daughter, Jacques' half-sister, aged three. 'My mother and I were very close. Lately I've been living in Japan and America and we grew apart a little, but we're a very close family.' His sister Melanie was living in New York and studying musical composition at NYU – another link with their father, who loved music and was a recreational trumpeter. The interest was also picked up by his son, who plays the piano and tends his CD collection – 10,000 Maniacs, the Cranberries, Erasure, various Japanese and French-Canadian bands – and calls music 'my drug'. It was also in the Principality that he met his girlfriend, Sandrine Gros d'Aillon, a communications and TV production student at university in Montreal; her family lives in Monaco.

Europe was where his father was best known and it was where Jacques himself would come under the most intense scrutiny he had yet experienced. Already people were saying that although the son might be fast, he hadn't inherited the irresistible recklessness that lifted Gilles beyond statistics and into immortality. 'On the driving side,' Jacques said, 'I think we're very different – from what I've seen on tape and from what I've heard people say. Although, of course, the cars were different then, and maybe if he were driving now he'd be more similar. I don't know and I don't really care to know. It's not important to me. What is important is that he was one of the best, and now he's a legend. That will always be there. Now I'm on my own road and I want to do it my way. If that's like him, great. If it's not, it doesn't matter.'

Too young to have known much about what his father was doing in the cockpit, later on he admired Senna and Prost, 'for different reasons, because they were entirely different drivers, but they were both impressive. It's difficult to judge from the outside, so I could be totally wrong, but Senna seemed to be very aggressive, very much in control and sure of himself, and he seemed to get more out of the car than the others. I'm not saying that includes Prost, because he got a lot out of the car as well. But Prost seemed to be a bit calmer and more strategic than Senna. He could be aggressive and set a quick time in qualifying, although he wasn't aggressive at all times – whereas Senna was aggressive from the first lap to the last. Even with a forty-second lead he would still be doing qualifying laps.'

So you don't just take the example of one person, your hero, and fall in love with everything about him? 'No. Even heroes will do something that isn't good in your eyes. Even the best drivers make mistakes.' Stupid question, of course. Too much of a realist to make an idol of his dead father, and perhaps having been made so by that father's death, how could Jacques install another driver in his place?

Somehow, too, the impression began to form at this point that perhaps giving entertainment to the spectators wasn't as important to the son as it was, or at least seemed to be, to his father. 'Not being sideways just for the sake of it, no. When you can see that a guy is coming back through the field or that he's driving a good strategy, yes. But when a guy's got a forty-second lead and he's still going sideways just for the sake of it, I don't think that's any use.'

Jody Scheckter and Patrick Tambay, respectively Gilles' team-mate and his successor at Ferrari, had helped Jacques' mother through the early years of her widowhood, advising on schooling for the children and so forth. Had Jacques sought or received advice on his driving from members of an earlier generation? 'I spoke with Tambay before I started racing but I don't think you can really learn from others, because everybody's situation is different. The only way you can learn is from your own experience. Someone can tell you something but when you're in the car how can you transfer what you've been told? Everything happens so quickly. You have to be able to understand your own mistakes, to feel what you can do to correct them. That's the only way to progress to the next level. Anyway, I hardly ever do what I'm told just because I'm told.'

His father was often criticized for losing races through rashness, for spending too much time entertaining the crowds and not enough time concentrating on the business of winning. 'I don't think he was doing it to entertain people. He was doing it to entertain himself, he didn't care what people thought. He would just go out there and go over the edge, and when he crashed a lot of people blamed him, but he didn't care. That was the way racing was for him.'

I told him that my own best memory of his father was of his least characteristic race, the 1979 Italian Grand Prix at Monza. Villeneuve and Scheckter both had a chance to win the championship: Scheckter if he won that race, Villeneuve if he won that and the two remaining rounds as well. Team orders dictated that whichever of them took the lead should hold it to the end. Scheckter got ahead at the start and Villeneuve, while clearly the quicker of the two, never budged out of his slipstream. When the two Renaults of Jabouille and Arnoux had retired, Scheckter was able to cruise to the title, unhassled by his team-mate. It was probably the most outstanding display of sportsmanship seen in Formula One since Stirling Moss testified to a steward's inquiry after winning the 1958 Portuguese Grand Prix, giving evidence which reinstated Mike Hawthorn's second place. Two races later, Moss lost the championship by a single point – to Hawthorn.

Jacques was eight when Scheckter took the title, but he was well aware of the story of Gilles' unselfishness at Monza. 'If my father had overtaken him, he could have won the championship. But he was a real racer: very clean and straight. He wasn't ever going to cheat. Not to copy my father, you know, but that's something I believe in as well. There's nothing to compare with being straight. What goes around, comes around. I still believe in those virtues.'

I observed that it would be a bit hard to imagine a place for that kind of sportsmanship in the Formula One of the Nineties. Only the day before we met, his own new team-mate had been holding forth in the newspapers about the need for the team to put its effort behind a designated number one driver – by which Damon Hill meant himself – rather than dissipating it on two drivers with equal status. 'There's no way I would race as a number two,' Villeneuve responded with some briskness. 'Although I don't want to be a number one, because I think the two drivers should always be treated at the same level. If you think that you're the best then you don't need the other driver to be a number two in order to beat him. If you believe in yourself, why should you bother with stuff like that? As a number two driver, everybody compares you with your team-mate. And everybody expects you to be slower because you don't get the same treatment. But if you are slower, everybody blames you. It happens all the time. The only reason I'm going to race next year and in the future is because I want to win. I want to be able to fight. So I want everything to be on my side. That doesn't mean I want more than the other driver. I don't really care, as long as I don't have less. That's all.'

But Senna had begun the business of establishing an advantage by insisting on the best equipment, the most attention and the newest modifications. Early in his career, he even vetoed a potential team-mate whose abilities would, in his estimation, dangerously divide the resources of a struggling team. Now Schumacher was adopting the same attitude. 'Of course, if there's only one piece [of equipment] that's made, you'd rather you had it than your team-mate,' Villeneuve said. 'And if one of you is leading the championship and the other one is nowhere, it's obvious who should get it. But if there are two pieces, you don't want to keep them both for yourself.'

All this stuff was much less political in Gilles' day. Or so we can tell ourselves until we start examining the circumstances leading up to his death, and the never-to-be-resolved rift with Pironi, who tricked his team-mate by overtaking against team orders when the pair of them were cruising to a one-two finish at Imola. Pironi was himself badly injured half-a-dozen races further into the season and died five years later in a powerboat race. He left small twin sons, born shortly after Villeneuve's accident, called Didier and Gilles. All sorts of memories are distorted by the passage of time, or erased altogether.

As Jacques Villeneuve sat in the cockpit of an FW 18 jacked up on the factory floor at Didcot, he certainly wasn't looking or sounding daunted by the prospect of Formula One. 'It's a step up on the technical side,' he said, glancing around the room, so antiseptically clean that you could have performed heart surgery on the floor. 'There is so much more money involved and the regulations allow you to do more stuff. All the teams make their own cars, so everything is being pushed to the limit in design terms – whereas in Indycars you buy a car from Reynard or Lola, who have to make something that will work for everybody, and then you see what you can do with it. You can't try weird stuff like you can in Formula One.'

He wasn't expecting more demands to be made on him as the driver. 'The design office is busier and they give you more bits to play with, but in the end they're either good or they're bad. Maybe it's easier to lose your way, but on the other hand when you do lose your way you have more options to try.' His first impression of Formula One had been that it was like 'a big, powerful, very fast go-kart. The Indycars are a little bit heavier, more sluggish. A Formula One you can play with more, throw it into the corner and slide a little bit. And everything happens extremely quickly.'

So far, it had been fun. 'But it really gets to be fun when you're on the edge, and I'm not there yet. At the end of my second year in Indycars, with a car that was a development of the previous year's model, it was just perfect. Doing those laps where the car just feels like it's on a razor's edge and when you're in a high-speed corner and the car reacts exactly as it should, that's a tremendous pleasure. The Williams is an unbelievably fast car but it's not the way I want it yet.'

He was going to miss the banked oval tracks of Indycar racing. 'I wouldn't want to be part of a championship that was just ovals, no way. But it's good to have a few of them. They're entertaining and demanding in the way you get your car set up. It's really interesting on that side. And in the race you're always in traffic, overtaking or being overtaken, running two or three side by side, and strategy gets very important. But if I were out there driving by myself I'd prefer a road course. And that can be a lot of fun, as well, when you're fighting against clean drivers, guys who are not going to bang your wheels and put you on the grass. When you find someone you can race with, you can spend three or four corners side by side, inches apart, and you know you're not going to go off, that's a lot of fun.'

After Senna and Schumacher started working out in the gymnasium, fitness became a fetish among Formula One drivers. Villeneuve, coming from the outside, had a fresh attitude to the question. 'You need to be fit, but it's not just about concentrating on one special movement, which is what people think. I don't do weights. I'll go into the gym if it's twenty degrees below outside, but I still won't do weights. What you need is to have great cardio-vascular fitness – good breathing, a strong heartbeat and so on. You've got to have strong enough muscles, but not too strong because then it takes twice as much blood and oxygen to feed them, which means you're going to get twice as tired. It's not like you're training for a sprint, it's a general fitness. Your neck will get tired but the more laps you do the stronger it gets. You sweat like crazy, of course. You can lose five pounds in a race, or more, you get short of breath and you're always under stress but you have to keep your mind clear so that you can work on strategy at the same time as pushing to be on the edge. So if you ski or you play tennis hard for two hours, that's awesome training. If you do that a lot, you're going to be fit.'

The team, he said, had made him feel welcome right from

the moment of his first test a few months earlier. 'They didn't treat me like a kid who could be put in the car for a few laps and then thrown away. Everybody was serious. I don't know if it's the same in other teams. From the outside, Formula One can look cold. Once you're inside the family, it isn't.'

The mechanics fiddled with bin liners and expanded poly-styrene bottles, making a mould for Villeneuve's customized seat. 'I want to fight with the leaders,' he continued. 'I don't want to sit here and relax and just learn my trade. I want to learn, of course, but I want to learn while I'm fighting. It's the best car and the best engine, so the team will be very competitive. I don't know 90 per cent of the other drivers and I don't know how the races happen. I know some of the circuits but not others. Personally, I believe I am up to it. I have confidence, so I want to be fighting for wins with the guys who are going to win the championship.'

People tell Villeneuve that his relationship with his father was a troubled one even in its brief span, that the adult put pressure on the small boy and made him so nervous that he could barely function when they were together. Villeneuve said he didn't remember that. 'I know about it because my mother told me but, personally, I don't remember. Maybe it's a blockage or maybe it's something I just forgot.' What did he remember about the relationship? 'Not much. There wasn't much of a relationship. I looked up to him because he was my father, but the few times I saw him we were on holiday or in the mountains for Christmas, stuff like that. And when you're a kid you have presents at Christmas, and that's all that matters. A few things I did with him, when we went out on a boat or in a four-by-four or on skis, it was a lot of fun. Always out over the edge. I remember that side, and that's all I remember.'

Damon Hill once said that he'd spent the years after the death of his father getting to know him, which seemed to be something the two Williams drivers might have in common, besides the colour of their driving suits. 'Yeah, probably true,' agreed Jacques. 'My father died when I was eleven. What do you know at that age? All you see is Father Christmas. The rest of the relationship is very important, but you just don't pay much attention – unless it's really terrible, of course, and I can't say much on that. I know more now because I've been told so much. It's as if people talk three or four times more about a person when he's dead. But I honestly don't know my father.'

There is a fine posthumous biography of Gilles Villeneuve written by a Canadian journalist, Gerald Donaldson, and widely admired for its honesty and accuracy. People who knew Gilles say that it gets him right, the faults as well as the virtues. It was published in 1991, but five years later Jacques had not read it. 'No. Well, the first couple of chapters. But since then I've been reading other stuff. It's not because I'm against him or anything like that. I just haven't read it. It sounds stupid. I know I should have. I've just never brought myself to read it, that's all. Perhaps I should, so that when people ask me questions about it, I'll know. But maybe I don't feel like reading a book about racing. You have so little time to do the things you really want to do.'

4

The old men stood together in the hard sunlight outside the farmhouse, bundled up in overcoats and scarves against the chill. These were men who remembered how the legend had been built, who knew the secrets of the big, dark old house in Modena's Piazza Garibaldi where Enzo Ferrari had lived and schemed. There were four of them, survivors from another time. Nello Ugolini, tall, white-haired and frail, known as Maestro when he managed the Scuderia Ferrari in the pre-war days, a yellow shield with its rearing black horse painted on the bonnets of Alfa Romeos piloted by the likes of Tazio Nuvolari and the rotund opera singer Giuseppe Campari. Next to Ugolini stood Sergio Scaglietti, an artist in aluminium who created the bodywork cloaking some of the loveliest Ferraris; from his factory, a few miles away on the outskirts of Modena, today's road cars emerged. Next to him, Gino Rancati, a television journalist who became Enzo Ferrari's confidant and amanuensis. And, lastly, Don Sergio Mantovani, the drivers' chaplain, who had said prayers in his dry, whispering voice for succeeding generations of Ferrari pilots, from the young Ascari and Villoresi through Castelotti, Hawthorn, Fangio, von Trips, Surtees, Bandini, Ickx, Lauda, Villeneuve and Scheckter – all the way up to the pair about to make their entrance this very day, in a ceremony instituted decades earlier by Enzo Ferrari. For these four old men, and for many others, the Ferrari *vernissage* had come to represent the annual triumph of hope over experience.

On this particular afternoon in February 1996, dozens of workers at the local ceramics factories had come out to line the bridges and fences separating the Fiorano test track from the main road between Abetone and Modena as the new Formula One Ferrari, designated the F310, sat glittering in the sun, its voluptuous scarlet bodywork shrouding the first ten-cylinder engine ever produced at the Maranello factory. The car was making its début a week later than promised, but it looked beautiful. In February, they always do.

Entering a specially erected marquee through an opening decorated with the emblems of the team's sponsors, the old men took their seats among the four hundred journalists and a hundred or so guests gathered to celebrate the unveiling. On the broad stage, two red Ferrari road cars faced the audience, on either side of a cluster of lecterns and microphones. In the front row of the audience was Gianni Agnelli, the silver-haired patron of Fiat, owners of 90 per cent of Ferrari, flanked by two younger men: his protégé, Luca Cordero di Montezemolo, and Piero Lardi Ferrari, Enzo Ferrari's son by his mistress, Lina Lardi.

Long discarded as unsuitable for the job of inheriting his father's oligarchy, but nevertheless still the holder of the 10 per cent of Ferrari stock not owned by Fiat, the gentle, forlorn Piero casts a lesser shadow over the empire than his long-dead half-brother Dino, whose memory was worshipped by his father. Outside the factory, a street has been named after Dino, who was training as an engineer when he died of kidney failure in 1956, aged twenty-four. At Imola, the racetrack is known as the Autodromo Enzo e Dino Ferrari. Successive generations of six-cylinder Ferraris have been known as Dinos, after Enzo's insistence that the boy dreamed up the idea of the engine. Piero, by contrast, received official acknowledgement of his existence only after the death of Laura Ferrari, Enzo's wife and Dino's mother. Now he has only a material inheritance and his father's strange, downslanted eyes; nothing of the myth attaches to him and he has no real function in the running of the business, although he has held various titles.

Instead Montezemolo, whose flamboyance matches Agnelli's own, was given the presidency of Ferrari, with a brief to revive the Scuderia's fortunes. What he needed to do was repeat his feat of the mid-Seventies, when Agnelli loaned him to Enzo Ferrari as manager of the racing team and, in partnership with Niki Lauda, he contrived a spectacular renaissance that brought them two drivers' and three constructors' championships. It also earned him a graduation first to the presidency of Juventus, Agnelli's football team, with whom Montezemolo won the European Cup thanks to the brilliance of such players as Michel Platini and Paolo Rossi, and then to leadership of the organization of Italia 90, the hosting of the World Cup – such an enjoyable event that the Italians even managed to swallow their disappointment when their own team went out in the semi-finals.

When Agnelli sent Montezemolo back to Ferrari in 1992 the company was in a bad way. Enzo Ferrari had died in 1988, just before the effects of the worldwide economic recession had become apparent. Among the secrets of the company's success was the exclusivity of its road cars, but the boom of the mid-Eighties had tempted Piero Fusaro, a

Fiat corporate figure installed as Ferrari's president following Enzo's demise, into allowing production to rise above the self-imposed limit of 4,000 cars a year. More than 4,700 were made in 1991. Then the bust came and the unthinkable happened: there were unsold Ferraris in the showrooms. In 1992, 3,500 cars were sold, and 3,000 in 1993. The company even invoked the Italian practice of *cassa integrazione*, a sort of government-sponsored breathing space which allowed them to close down production for a week, with the state picking up the wage bill. This was not unique among luxury car makers in the dark days of the early Nineties: in Germany even the Porsche management was doing something similar.

The race team, too, had fallen on barren times. Alain Prost had joined Ferrari from McLaren in 1990 and won five grands prix in his first season. But his arrival drove Nigel Mansell out of the team and then, in the following year, Prost alienated himself from the management to such a degree that he, a three-times world champion at the peak of his powers, was given the sack before the end of the season, joining a long list of illustrious drivers who had left the team in unhappy circumstances.

Montezemolo responded to the commercial crisis by cutting back road-car production to a maximum of 3,300 a year, a figure which ensured the restoration of the waiting lists so psychologically vital to a producer of low-volume exotic cars. On the racing side, he completely reconstructed the team. He brought back John Barnard, the English designer who had created the all-conquering McLaren-Porsche which gave Prost his titles and who had a brief involvement with Ferrari in the late Eighties. As Enzo Ferrari had done before him, Montezemolo bent to Barnard's wishes and allowed him to build a new research and development headquarters in southern England, on a five-year contract. He also hired Jean Todt, the tough little Frenchman who had started as a navigator in world championship rallying before managing Peugeot's successful sports car team. He gathered together the experienced Swiss engineer Gustav Brunner, the Dutch-Australian aerodynamicist Willem Toet and Osamu Gotu, one of the boffins responsible for Honda's hegemony in the late Eighties, who would work alongside the Italian engineers Claudio Lombardi and, later, Paolo Martinelli. He authorized the construction of a new wind-tunnel out of an annual budget said to be without limit but which, one way or another, probably amounted to £100 million a year. The determinedly multinational cast aroused a degree of controversy in the Italian media, as well as jealousy within the camp, but there could be no doubt that Montezemolo's ambitious hiring policy had created a far more formidable outfit.

But as the F310 made its first appearance on this spring-like day, Ferrari had still won only eight races in the first half of the decade. No Ferrari driver had won the world championship since Jody Scheckter in 1979. In five years together at Maranello, Jean Alesi and Gerhard Berger had won exactly two grands prix. The sole victory of 1995, Alesi's in Montreal, had been the result of a slice of great good fortune. Clearly, a final ingredient was missing. So Alesi and Berger were the casualties when Ferrari and the Philip Morris tobacco company, who had long subsidized the drivers' retainers in exchange for Marlboro logos on the drivers' suits and the bodywork of the most photographed cars in Formula One, agreed to pay Michael Schumacher, the reigning double world champion, $50 million over two years – or about 15 per cent of the team's alleged total budget – to bring his unrivalled speed and discipline to bear on the team.

When Schumacher appeared on the stage, however, with his new team-mate Eddie Irvine, alongside the unveiled F310, he maintained his shrewd policy of playing down the team's immediate ambitions. 'I know what people are saying,' he commented, 'and I'm not listening. I hope we're going to win a couple of races this season. That's the target, and then to be ready to challenge for the championship in 1997. This season I think we have to concentrate on developing reliability. Ferrari had thirteen retirements last season, and this is something we can't put right in just three months. I'm sure we'll be competitive, but I don't know if we'll finish all the races.'

His intelligent scepticism formed a considerable contrast with Montezemolo's bursting enthusiasm. The president bounded on to the stage and, encouraged by the presence of so many reporters and TV cameras, persuaded himself to issue a more bullish pledge of three grand prix victories in 1996, one more than the red cars had managed in the previous five seasons put together. His experience in football had perhaps convinced Montezemolo that while judicious understatement may be fine for Germans, the Italian people require bold promises, even if they come with the knowledge that disappointment is inevitable and tearful repentance will follow.

'If I say we'll win straight away,' Montezemolo said, 'and we stop on the first lap, there will be a lot of criticism. But even when Enzo Ferrari was alive there was a mixture of hope and caution, of guarded optimism and sometimes of outright pessimism. We know we have to improve. But the sun is out today, many friends are with us, and our aim is the championship. This year we hope to get closer, so that next year we can be in a realistic position to win. The new car is the result of three years of work. During that time we've also built a strong organization. We're grateful to Alesi and Berger, who drove for us in difficult conditions and always gave their best. But our goal is to win more. Now we have the world champion with us and we expect a lot from him. It is a new era for us. There is tension, pressure, enthusiasm.'

The cost of running Ferrari's Formula One team, he said, was paid equally by the profits from the sales of road cars and by the team's sponsors, among whom there were two new names to announce: the return of Shell, whose logo had last been seen on a Ferrari in the Seventies, and the arrival of Asprey, the Bond Street jeweller owned by a brother of the Sultan of Brunei. 'Asprey is one of the oldest names in the United Kingdom,' Montezemolo said. 'It is concerned with exclusive, top-level products, very close to what Ferrari stands for in the motor industry.' This was a shocking announcement only to those who knew that while Enzo Ferrari was alive no sponsors were allowed to put their names and logos on the car other than those who had made a technical contribution: the suppliers of petrol and oil, of brakes, electronics and tyres. The sole exception was Marlboro, which could be excused since Philip Morris paid the drivers' retainers. The nature of Asprey's technical input into the F310 was not explained.

'This will be a very tough championship,' Montezemolo continued. 'We have a lot of respect for all our rivals. But what I feel and hear around me at Ferrari is confidence.

Everything has been taken care of. We have tried to get the right people and to create the right conditions for their work. We thank *avvocato* Agnelli for being here. It's important for us to have our major shareholder with us. But now words don't count any more. What matters are deeds.'

Agnelli, who had driven himself from Bologna airport to Fiorano in a dark blue Ferrari with Montezemolo in the passenger seat, took the microphone. 'I must say that for me, today is a holiday,' he proclaimed, 'because I'm not going to have to talk about politics or economics, about the single European currency or the car market. On my way here I was thinking about the time when we started to establish this relationship, in 1968 or 1969. Enzo Ferrari had begun to negotiate an agreement with Ford for sports cars. But, at the last minute, he stopped the negotiations and the next day he called me. I told him, "Ferrari, don't worry, we'll make a deal." We at Fiat gave him some technical and financial support. Eventually we became the major shareholder. But he always ran the company.'

And now it had been restored to health and commercial success. 'We have sultans who buy our cars ten at a time. We also sell cars in Moscow and Beijing. The only thing missing is the world championship.' And this year, he said, the team had the means to achieve their aim. 'We have the personnel. We have Montezemolo, we have Todt, we have the best drivers on the market. Last year we had two excellent drivers, Alesi and Berger, but this year we have something more.' He looked across at Schumacher. 'We have a star.'

He followed the team, said the man whose political power had long been second to none in Italy, just like any other fan. 'The people who go to the races to support Ferrari have shown great patience for many years. Now is the time to repay them.' But he took the opportunity to deny widespread reports that he had issued an ultimatum ordering Ferrari to win the championship with Schumacher or face the possibility of a withdrawal from racing. 'We never set deadlines,' he said. 'I've learnt from Italian politics than a deadline is never really final.' And he was swept away to be helicoptered back to his discussions about the single European currency.

Todt took the stage, with Barnard and Martinelli alongside him. 'This is a moment of incredible emotion,' he said, 'because this car is the result of constant work by all of Ferrari's technicians over the past three years.' Principally it was the work of Barnard, who created the chassis at his studio in Surrey, and of the engine department, under Gotu and Martinelli. Invited to describe the new V10, Martinelli spoke of how, contrary to the views of those who claimed that Gotu's presence meant that it was merely a Honda with a Ferrari badge on it, this engine was 'truly part of Ferrari history, based on Ferrari culture'. Barnard, whose insistence on working from England was much criticized in the Italian press, had campaigned on behalf of the V10 configuration against the views of the traditionalists within the Ferrari hierarchy. Now he spoke of how the compact shape of the new engine had allowed him to create a more efficient aerodynamic package. 'I'm hoping it won't feel very different from last year's car as far as the drivers are concerned,' he said, 'because that one had good qualities in terms of driveability. This one just needs to be two seconds a lap quicker.'

'I had the good luck to work with Enzo Ferrari in the Seventies,' Montezemolo resumed, 'and I know the meaning of the Ferrari tradition. But I learnt one great lesson from him, and that was to look forward, not back. We should interpret our past, but not be the prisoners of it. Three years ago the Ferrari team was not up to date in terms of organization, method and expertise. To maintain the link with tradition may be the first goal. But the second goal is to create the Ferrari of the year 2000, with new methods and organization. If you look at our racing department, you wouldn't recognize it from how it was even two years ago. This means evolution, this means looking forward. And I'm very, very happy that Schumacher is with us. The fact that he is here and not elsewhere is a matter for satisfaction and confidence.'

When pressed, he stuck by his forecast of three wins, even allowing himself to speculate on the outside possibility of the championship. 'Scheckter won the title with two race wins. Niki won with two or three. Rosberg won with only one. So, who knows?' As Montezemolo spoke, Schumacher's face depicted a kind of half-amused disbelief that his president should be making pledges on behalf of an enterprise whose success would depend on a thousand factors, many of them as yet unidentified.

A couple of hours later, after most of the guests had left and the old men had been driven away, there were still a few dozen journalists waiting around the converted farm buildings to see if Schumacher would take the F310 out for its first spin. It was dusk when the noise of the engine cut the air. As the German reeled off half-a-dozen laps, the little lights on the cockpit instruments could be clearly seen and the glow from the carbon brake discs inside the wheel rims was weirdly bright as the car slowed for the bends. The new engine bellowed, its sound crashing off the walls of the nearby factories, but it was immediately apparent that it had lost the tearing screech of the old V12, a sound that enabled you to distinguish a Ferrari from every other car in the field before it had even come into sight and which, legend says, can be traced back to the day during the First World War when the young Enzo Ferrari, shoeing mules for the 3rd Mountain Artillery Regiment, was beguiled by the noise of the V12 engines in the Packard staff cars of the US Army. Or, in an alternative version told by Gioachino Colombo, designer of the first twelve-cylinder Ferrari engine, perhaps the inspiration came from the V12 of a Packard two-seater driven by Donna Maria Antonetta Avanzo at the sprint races held on the island of Fano in Denmark in 1921, and subsequently acquired in a swap deal by Antonio Ascari, Alberto's father. With Ferrari, you can never get away from the myth, which is the team's blessing and its curse. Anyway, out on the track at Fiorano the new V10 sounded like any other Formula One engine. Which was exactly the point, in that its inception was intended to provide Barnard with the same starting point as Rory Byrne at Benetton, Adrian Newey at Williams and Neil Oatley at McLaren. To that end, the sacrifice of a certain degree of romantic character represented an acceptable bargain.

'The V10 isn't far off the V12 now in terms of perform-ance,' Schumacher had said earlier. 'And since there's much more to come, I think we'll be a lot better off. I'm very happy with the situation.'

And, as Agnelli had said to Montezemolo before his departure, with a big smile and a wonderful fatalism: 'Let's enjoy this car today. After all, it hasn't lost a race yet.'

*

Above the cast-iron latticework of the gates to the family tomb in the cemetery of San Cataldo, a single name is carved: Ferrari. And, on either side, an epigram: *Ad maiora ultra vitam.* Towards greater things beyond this life.

Piero Lardi Ferrari's bodyguard turned the key to the gates, a gold bracelet jangling against the rolled-back cuff of his dark blue cotton jacket. From inside the tomb, an alarm sounded. He cursed lightly and turned the key again. Silence. The doors opened. Removing his gold-rimmed aviator sunglasses, the bodyguard crossed himself and stepped across the threshold into a hexagonal chamber.

In front of him was an altar, on which a heavy steel crucifix sat surrounded by four tall white candles. On each of the side walls, a large tablet of striated brown marble cut into an asymmetrical design bore the names, the dates and, according to Italian custom, the photographs of those interred: Alfredo Ferrari, 1859–1916; his wife Adalgisa, 1872–1965; their sons Alfredo ('Dino'), 1896–1916 and Enzo, 1898–1988; Enzo's wife, Laura, 1900–78; and Enzo and Laura's only child, a third Alfredo, also known as Dino, 1932–56.

Enzo and his father share one tablet. Enzo Ferrari was a man who, in his maturity, could write: 'The conviction has never left me that when a man says to a woman, "I love you", what he really means to say is, "I desire you". And that the only real love possible in this world is that of a father for his son.'

The bodyguard bent towards the tablet bearing Enzo's name and placed beneath it a pot of lilies on which he and I had split a few thousand lire at the roadside stall outside the cemetery. Then he settled himself in the doorway, arms folded, eyes hidden once more behind the aviator shades, facing out towards the vast acres of the principal cemetery of the ancient city of Modena, standing sentinel upon a legend.

5

A week after the launch at Fiorano, Giancarlo Baccini's mobile phone chirruped. Baccini, Ferrari's public relations man, was in the paddock at Estoril, trying to keep out the early-morning chill as he listened to the voice at the other end, calling from Italy to tell him that a fleet of road cars had been used to clear snow from the Fiorano track that morning, enabling Eddie Irvine to complete fifty laps in the F310 before it could be packed up and sent off to Portugal, where Michael Schumacher was waiting. The car had been late for its launch and now it was late for its first proper test. But Baccini was able to tell the waiting reporters that it would be on its way that night, aboard a specially chartered flight from Bologna to Lisbon.

Out on the track, Damon Hill and Jacques Villeneuve were completing their pre-season testing in the two Williams-Renault FW18s. Villeneuve had already logged more than 5,000 miles of familiarization during the winter, preparing for his first season in Formula One. Less than three weeks before the first grand prix of the year, in Melbourne, the English team was going about its business in an atmosphere of calm professionalism. 'Look at the Williams,' Baccini sighed. 'You do not have the impression that this is a new car. With us, everything is new.' Newest of all was Michael

Schumacher. Ferrari's latest and most expensive component was sitting on the pit wall, kicking his heels. Kicking his horrible clumping great black and white Nike trainers, actually: the product of an endorsement deal which put him alongside the likes of the tennis player Andre Agassi, the runner Michael Johnson, the footballer Eric Cantona and the basketball hero Michael Jordan in the dramatis personae of the American sportswear company's marketing campaign.

A couple of days earlier Schumacher had arrived at the Portuguese circuit to discover that the F310 was still at the factory, where Barnard's technicians were struggling to find a solution to a gearbox oil leak which had appeared at Fiorano while Irvine was running it in. So the world champion had jumped into a hybrid machine, a 1995 chassis equipped with the new engine, in order to use the time by finding out how the V10 performed. On his first day, the engine blew up. On the second, the car returned to the pits with flames, brown smoke and a peculiar acrid smell coming from beneath the rear panels. Before Schumacher could unclip his belts the fire marshals had put out the blaze and the mechanics were wheeling the car back into its garage, pulling down the door so that the damage could be inspected in privacy. Another blow-up, surely. Another set of embarrassing headlines in the Italian sports papers. No, no, Baccini insisted. According to him, the fire was merely the result of a broken exhaust pipe setting light to the car's carbon-fibre flooring. Hence, he pointed out, the peculiar smell.

A week after the gala launch of its new car, Ferrari's morale had plummeted back to pre-Schumacher levels. A visual comparison of the F310 and the FW18 showed that Adrian Newey, the Williams aerodynamics wizard, had found a more effective solution to the problems posed by the new safety regulations, which stipulated a higher cockpit surround to protect the driver's head. Whereas the Williams looked barely different from the previous year's car, the Ferrari had swollen around the cockpit area to such a degree that the driver appeared to be sitting in a Bath chair. The aerodynamic consequences promised to be damagingly significant. And the oil leak cast a shadow over the new Barnard-designed gearbox, made from carbon and titanium at an alleged cost that would be enough to run some smaller teams.

Already there was talk of going back not merely to last year's gearbox but to last year's engine, which Schumacher had praised during the winter. He had managed to score cheap psychological points over his predecessors, Alesi and Berger, by wondering aloud how they could have failed to win races with such a motor behind them. But the new chassis would not accept the old engine, being designed around the smaller V10. And the option of using last year's car in its entirety did not exist, since it could not be made to conform to the new regulations. So there was no alternative: the F310 had to be made to work. Once again, teeth were gritted in the Ferrari camp.

Further down the pit lane, another English designer mused on the problems confronting Barnard. Frank Dernie, formerly with Williams, Lotus and Benetton, now wore the uniform of the Ligier team. 'The problem we all face,' he said, apropos of the troublesome Ferrari gearbox, 'is that the technical regulations get tighter every year in order to reduce the performance of the cars, so there are fewer areas than ever for us to exploit. We're no longer allowed to do anything electronically, since the driver aids were banned, and we're no longer allowed to do anything interesting aerodynamically. You can make a gearbox out of composite materials but it's really something and nothing, almost an ego trip for the designer. There are some technical benefits, but whether you're talking about one-hundredth of a second or two-hundredths of a second in the course of a lap, I really wouldn't like to say. You could look at it on paper and determine a way to make a stiffer gearbox, but it would be very difficult to do it in such a way that you'd achieve a performance gain that wasn't negligible. And doing it would cost an absolute fortune. It's almost impossible to imagine why you'd want to do that, unless you'd been given too much money to spend.'

It's certainly true that Formula One cars have become closer together both in looks and technical detail. This is a phenomenon of the Nineties, created jointly by the increasing intensity of competition for the sponsorship cash and by the new computerized design facilities. After all, if you have one set of problems – a series of parameters defined by the regulations and the circuits – then designer A's computer is likely to come up with much the same solution as designer B's computer. And the designers are terrible copycats: if one of them comes up with a new idea (a raised nose, say, or a semi-automatic gearbox), the rest of them can't wait until they've got one of their own. That's why the cars all look alike, and why people who fell in love with grand prix racing in, say, the Fifties miss the days when you couldn't possibly mistake the Connaught streamliner for a Maserati 250F, a Scarab for a Cooper-Climax or a Mercedes for a Vanwall. Nowadays you need the fag-packet livery in order to tell them apart, unless you want to develop the sort of expertise that aircraft-spotters had during the war, when the ability to tell a Spitfire from a Messerschmitt from several thousand feet away meant the difference between life and death.

But if the cars were so similar, then at least the spotlight was being put back on the driver's contribution. 'I think,' Dernie observed, 'that the drivers are probably more important now than they've been for the last ten years.' Not just as racers, but as testers, which was where both Schumacher and Hill excelled, albeit in very different ways. 'Alan Jones was the best,' Dernie said, remembering his days as an aerodynamicist at Williams, when the Australian brought the team its first drivers' title. 'He'd tell you what the car was doing but he wouldn't make the mistake of trying to tell you what to do about it. No driver knows how to develop a car. Not even Niki Lauda. You only have to read his last book to know that. But Nelson Piquet at Williams and Michael Schumacher at Benetton had the right idea. And Michael, like Alan Jones, has a great memory.'

Dernie watched a Jordan mechanic hang out a signal to the circulating Martin Brundle. The Jordans and the Tyrrells had been setting good times. 'It's always difficult to assess what's going on because you never know at a test week. I've no idea who's been running realistic fuel levels to do proper race preparation and who's been running without ballast in order to do improper sponsorship negotiations. And some people still struggle to remember that it's on Sunday afternoons when you score points, not by getting a good mention in the press on the morning after a test day at Estoril. We won't be able to judge who's really quick until we're at the first qualifying session.'

*

The scene is like something from *La Dolce Vita*, transposed to the West End of London in the mid-Nineties.

A few minutes before midnight, as half-a-dozen policemen and a few security guards are keeping the jostling paparazzi and a handful of curious passers-by safely behind a temporary barricade, a procession of jovial men in evening dress and astonishingly thin women in shimmering cocktail frocks and four-inch pencil heels pop out of the front door of the Queen's jewellers to admire the low, scarlet machine parked at the kerb. Familiar faces – the restaurateur Terence Conran, the property developer Peter Palumbo, the broadcaster David Frost – pause on the red-carpeted pavement to oblige the cameras. A little way down the street, a flotilla of limousines wait, their interior lights softly glowing.

Eventually the photographers get the moment for which they've come. Two slim young men in red overalls and matching baseball caps appear from the entrance of the shop, accompanied by two models in long dresses. Behind them, Giancarlo Baccini lurks in a dinner jacket. The men look self-conscious as the models arrange themselves silently on the gleaming bodywork of the red machine while the flashguns flare.

'Michael! This way, Michael!'

'Over here, Michael!'

'Michael! Michael!'

Two or three minutes later, the photo-opportunity is over and the group breaks up. One of the men, Eddie Irvine, slips quickly through the door. But as Michael Schumacher turns to follow, he is suddenly engulfed by a small pack of men and women carrying notebooks, tape recorders and TV cameras. Pinned against the shop window, he answers the questions he has been asked a hundred times a day in the preceding weeks.

Such is the life of a modern grand prix driver. This one, anyway. In 1959, the American driver Dan Gurney earned $7,000 as a Ferrari driver, paid at the rate of $163 a week plus 50 per cent of all prize money. In 1996, Schumacher's income for the year, from all sources, was reliably estimated at around £25 million. And part of the payback for such exotic remuneration comes on nights like this. When the family of the Sultan of Brunei have decided that they want to contribute to the sponsorship of your team, ostensibly to promote the name of the Bond Street store they bought last year, then, if you are Michael Schumacher, you are expected to set aside your pre-season preparations, jump into a private jet, fly to London and put on your driving suit for a 'surprise' midnight appearance at the end of a gala fashion show.

'I've been in motor sport since I was four years old,' Schumacher had said in answer to a question about the amount of his retainer, 'and my intention is the same as it was then, which is to enjoy what I'm doing. Money is one aspect of that but sporting reasons are important, too. I had the opportunity to earn more money with another team, but my manager and I had dreamed of joining Ferrari for a long time. In four-and-a-half years with Benetton I'd achieved everything and I needed a new motivation. I've been very warmly welcomed into the team, but now we have to be realistic. I hope we're going to win a couple of races this season, that's the object. Then we aim to be ready to challenge for the championship next season.'

77

Given that he was costing so much money, he was asked, did he think the driver was a more important part of the package than the car?

'In my opinion, it's 50 per cent the driver and 50 per cent the team. I'm as much responsible if we have a technical problem as if I have a spin. You win together and you lose together.'

When Schumacher came into Formula One in 1991, his speed made him a sensation. Less than a fortnight after he had qualified in seventh position on the grid for his first grand prix, he had been poached from the Jordan team by Tom Walkinshaw, then the technical director of Benetton. Whatever it cost Walkinshaw to placate Eddie Jordan, he had pulled off the coup of the decade. Within three years Schumacher was winning the first of his two back-to-back championships.

He had looked good during his apprenticeship with the Mercedes-Benz sports car team, but the true dimension of his gift only revealed itself when he climbed into a Formula One car. After his sheer pace, the second thing people noticed about Schumacher was his confidence. It was not long before people were talking about him as a typical German: arrogant and ruthless, with a microchip where his sense of humour and his conscience should be. Somehow it all seemed to fit into a pattern when, in 1994, his team was suspected of using banned driver aids in the car which took him to the title. Even Hill succumbed to the temptation of falling for the stereotype when he described his rival as 'a bit of a robot' in an interview published just before the 1995 British Grand Prix, when their conflict was at its most bitter and personal. Hill insinuated that Schumacher had been programmed by the Mercedes team, intending a contrast with his own, more spontaneous, humanity.

Objectively, this hardly seemed fair. Who, after all, was more ruthless – on or off the track – than the posthumously beatified Ayrton Senna? After all, Senna thought little of lunging at an opponent while they were both doing 180 miles an hour, in the expectation that the rival would be intimidated into backing off. Nor was he above playing every political trick in the book in order to get his hands on the best car in the field. But Senna had a cool manner and a certain feline beauty that, in combination with his marvellous talent, brought him something rather distastefully close to worship from fans around the world. Schumacher, on the other hand, was the son of a former bricklayer who ran a go-kart track in Kerpen-Mannheim, a small town in an unprepossessing region of western Germany. The only similarity between his background and the Brazilian's was that both of them started at the age of four, in little go-karts built by their fathers.

Unlike the elegant Senna, Schumacher was a style-free zone. He may have been the last prosperous person in Western Europe to wear stone-washed jeans which rumpled around his ankles; his ski-jump chin gave him a concave profile that was a gift to caricaturists; and his neck, which – thanks to an unremittingly thorough fitness regime – seemed to go straight down from the sides of his head into his shoulders without tapering, added to the impression of in-elegance. Schumacher was a machine built for speed. When that speed gave him a victory, he celebrated with a million-watt smile, his fists pumping the air. Sometimes he leapt into the arms of Flavio Briatore, the Benetton team director, who adored such photo-opportunities. But if Schumacher had any deeper or more subtly shaded feelings, we were not allowed to see them.

So people outside Germany took Schumacher for a one-dimensional human being, that dimension being a combination of ambition and arrogance. But when he came into Formula One, joining first the Jordan and then the Benetton teams, he was forced to speak in a language not his own. With the engineers, that was fine. But with the media he needed to say complicated things sometimes without a good command of the necessary nuance or idiom. So his sense of humour – which may not be pleasing to the most sophisticated of tastes but does exist – seemed more ponderous than it really was. And his psychological games with Hill were occasionally conducted in language that may have been less subtle than he would have wished. In his other dealings he seemed as frank as it was possible to be, and a great deal more courteous than some members of his profession. He seemed, in fact, to be a thoroughly well-balanced individual. His parents were clearly an important part of his life, but never intruded upon his celebrity. After he had wrapped up his second world championship, he made what appeared to be a highly satisfactory marriage to a woman who shared his tastes. All very normal, all very unexceptional. But, you know, he's a German, and his head goes straight down into his shoulders . . .

Saliently enough, his beginnings were at a kart club named after Wolfgang von Trips, the German count who lived in a castle near Cologne and who, had he not crashed and died in his Ferrari during the Italian Grand Prix of 1961, would surely have become his country's first world champion that year. Von Trips was a classically handsome aristocrat with a smooth, calm driving style but, for all his success in the year of his death, he was by no means in the class of Moss or Clark. Schumacher, by contrast, came out of a blue-collar background with a divine talent. At six he was a champion at the club where his father supervised the young racers and repaired the karts, and where his mother ran a snack-food stall. His parents had little spare money, so his early days were sponsored by local businessmen: a carpet retailer and a slot-machine supplier. At school he was good at English, maths, football and judo, but he left at seventeen and went to work in a garage, where he became an apprentice mechanic, eventually passing a set of technical exams before his career as a professional racer began.

Like many drivers who begin racing karts in infancy, he had amassed an enormous store of practical experience by the time he reached the top level. So, after his speed and his confidence, the third thing that people noticed about him was his tactical brilliance: he won his first grand prix, at Spa in 1992, by out-thinking every other driver in changing conditions on a difficult track. And the fourth thing was his dedication, which showed itself in his willingness to shoulder the burden of developing a new car. In fact, he absolutely insisted on doing the donkey work. Schumacher's team-mates were lucky if they even got a seat-fitting, never mind a few laps in testing. One by one they fell into his shadow, and most of them were never quite the same drivers again. This was where his true ruthlessness lay and where, once again, he had taken Senna's example and refined it.

Senna's engineers used to say that his driving style was unique. They could show you the engine telemetry print-out which proved that in a corner he was constantly on and off the throttle, making small but extremely rapid adjustments even as he was going through a bend, where other drivers would try to maintain a constant throttle opening in a search for smoothness. Senna wasn't after smoothness. He wanted speed. In his own way, Schumacher drove in a similarly idiosyncratic style, unlike that of any other driver of his time. Going into a corner, he would habitually push the car fractionally over its limit before pulling it back and holding it on the edge of control. (This wasn't the same thing as the old four-wheel drift, as perfected by Fangio and Moss, who would break the adhesion of the tyres in order to make a car slide smoothly through the apex of a bend, its front wheels pointing against the direction of travel. The grip of modern slick tyres alone made that elegant, rather balletic technique an unfeasible proposition for Schumacher's generation.)

Although Schumacher denied it, he liked a car whose handling characteristics would strike another driver as unacceptably nervous. A car that twitched did not alarm Schumacher. Something in his brain, in the sensors measuring forward and lateral movement and controlling the balance between the two, enabled him to process an instant analysis of that twitch, to interpret it and to use his findings to stay closer to the edge. So, because he virtually monopolized the available testing time, he was able to develop the car in the way he wanted. And his team-mates, being more conventional in style, found the result almost impossible to get to grips with in the brief time they were permitted to test between race meetings. All of this was nothing more than a theory until, after he left Benetton, Jean Alesi and Gerhard Berger spent most of the 1996 season trying to get on good terms with the car that he had shaped over the preceding four seasons, and whose characteristics did not suit either of them at all.

So Ferrari knew that they were getting extreme speed, unshakeable confidence, undiminished ambition, high intelligence and unparalleled dedication for their £16 million a year. As Agnelli had said, now there could be no more excuses. It was not the twenty-seven-year-old Schumacher who would be on trial, but the venerable Scuderia Ferrari. The late completion of the new car meant that they were setting off for Melbourne knowing that the race would be little more than a development exercise. But if Schumacher succeeded in bringing them a happy resolution to the long struggle to restore the fortunes of the prancing horse, they would consider him worth every penny, and more.

6

Damon Hill left the shadow of the Williams pit and came over to talk. This was, in itself, unusual. Grand prix drivers live their lives in a constant state of social siege. During a race weekend, in particular, they are concentrating on trying to do their very complicated jobs while also juggling the necessities of being public figures and being required to give time to sponsors and fans. As a result they rarely make the first move, perfecting instead the art of the turned head, the glazed eye, the subtle avoidance. The best of them can bring it off without seeming rude. This was in Melbourne, four days before the first race of the season, and the atmosphere before the first race is usually slightly more relaxed. No one has yet discovered that his car, which went so well in testing, is in fact nothing less than a pig in race trim. No one has yet made an idiotic mistake or been humiliated by a rival.

I was wandering along the pit lane, having a look at the new cars on the afternoon before their first outing on the new Albert Park circuit. As Hill walked across to the tape barrier keeping the world at bay, there seemed to be something on his mind. While we were waiting for the plane to Estoril a few weeks earlier I'd given him a copy of my book about Ayrton Senna. There was a slightly more respectable reason for this than mere authorial egotism. In the course of writing it I'd had to make a lot of key deductions based on minimal evidence. Some of them were about the probable cause of Senna's fatal accident at Imola on 1 May 1994, others concerned what the team of Senna's principal opponent, Michael Schumacher, had been up to that season. The Italian judicial investigation was still examining the evidence, which meant that none of the principals of the Williams team had felt able to talk about the crash in any but the most general terms; the possibility of facing a charge of 'culpable homicide', an Italian version of manslaughter, sealed their lips. So since Hill had been Senna's team-mate and since he had taken on the burden of fighting Schumacher's Benetton for the remainder of the season, I was particularly interested in his response, even if he told me it was a lot of rubbish. The situation being what it was, I didn't hold out much hope.

Briefly, my conclusions on the crash were that Senna had gone off the road at 190 miles an hour not through driver error nor, in all probability, through the widely publicized fracture of the welded steering column – which was more likely to have been an effect of the impact rather than its cause. Some other failure of the car's systems had been to blame, and the small amount of evidence suggested that there may have been a sudden failure in the power-steering mechanism. And there was also enough evidence, technical and circumstantial, to suggest that Benetton had been using illegal driver-aid systems on their car, at least during the early part of the season.

The book had been well received, even though (or perhaps because) it was the only one of the seventy-odd Senna books published since his death not to contain a lavish spread of pictures. In fact, it didn't contain any pictures at all, since

I'd wanted people to buy it to read the argument rather than to drool over yet more glossy images of racing cars. But it had not been authorized or endorsed by any of the people mentioned in the text, which meant I had no way of knowing before publication whether any of the contentious material was accurate. So when Hill came over, I was a bit nervous.

'I read your book,' he said. 'Interesting. I enjoyed it.'

'Did I get it right?'

'Pretty well.'

I felt like jumping in the air and whooping. But he had something else to say, something that had a lot more resonance than a mere pat on the back.

'The bit I really liked was where you wrote about Senna leading the race at Donington, and feeling like he was all alone in the world. That's what leading a grand prix is like. You feel like you're the only person in the world. That's exactly it.'

And that was when I began to like Damon Hill a lot. Not because he had paid me a passing compliment but because his success had not made him too blasé to share with a near-stranger his precious and hard-won discovery that – in one significant way, at least – the reality lived up to the dream.

Hill's new team-mate was the sensation of the Australian Grand Prix. For all Bernie Ecclestone's confidence, no one had really known what to expect from Jacques Villeneuve. The memory of Michael Andretti's humiliation was still strong, and perhaps some of the insiders didn't want to believe that a young driver could come in and compete at the top level of Formula One straight away, no matter what his antecedents or his form elsewhere. At the Estoril tests, where his times were respectable rather than blistering, I had been struck by the verdict of Frank Dernie, watching from the Ligier pit. 'He's slow, isn't he? I mean, if you're going to be fast, you're fast straight away. If you go out there and do decent lap times and don't bend the car and improve gradually, you'll never be really, truly quick. If you're quick and you bend the car a lot, it doesn't matter. You can always learn to stop bending the car. But you can't learn to be quick. You either are or you aren't. But he's smart, and he can probably overtake, which is something that Damon's never quite mastered.'

At Melbourne, Villeneuve put his 5,000 miles of testing to good use and showed that he was really, truly, seriously quick. It helped that Albert Park was as new to the rest of the drivers as it was to him. That was one handicap removed. On the Thursday, after two hours of familiarization sessions on a track still slippery with dust and, as the drivers say, 'green', which means that the cars have yet to lay down enough rubber to make the asphalt really grippy, the rookie had the fastest time – a clear second ahead of his team-mate in the other Williams. On paper, since qualifying was still two days away, it counted for nothing. In the mind, it meant everything. If Villeneuve had entertained any doubts about his ability to do it, they were gone now. He knew. And so did his rivals – none more than Hill, who left the road twice during the day. Runner-up in the championship in the last two seasons, with thirteen wins in fifty-one grands prix, Hill went to bed contemplating the thing he had most feared – that his best shot at the title would be under threat from his own team-mate.

'I've been told that I'm the favourite for the champion-ship,' Hill had said at a small press conference on the eve of the first session, while Villeneuve sat a few feet away. 'But if it comes down to Jacques and me fighting for the title, at least that means it's going to the team. Right now we've got a bit of an edge, but it won't take people long to catch up. At the moment the gap is a slender one.' And he had spoken of the need to avoid the kind of confrontation that had scarred the previous season. 'Michael and I had a sort of physical attraction to each other last year. It would be great if we could steer clear of each other and have some good wheel-to-wheel action. I think everyone's clear now about what's permitted. But then the rules rarely make much difference when people find themselves in that sort of situation.' And what about a recent claim by Schumacher that other drivers would have done better than Hill in the Williams last year? He laughed, rather uncomfortably. 'I don't really want to comment on what Michael says. I feel good about racing, come what may.'

On the Friday, in the free-practice sessions, the two Williams cars were again fastest, but this time Hill was the quicker, by a quarter of a second. Afterwards Villeneuve made it clear once more that he had no intention of playing the faithful back-up man. 'There are no team orders,' he said. 'And there's no reason why either of us should slow down to let the other one past. We'll be fighting each other. But in a clean way, I hope.'

Only Giancarlo Baghetti, who won at Rheims in 1961 with a Ferrari and a lot of luck, had triumphed on his world championship début. Had Villeneuve contemplated the possibility of following him? 'Well, the speed is there. But that's not the way I'm thinking right now. I'm thinking about going quickly and fighting with the other guys at the front.'

He was enjoying Albert Park, a fast and sinuous three-and-a-half mile track within sight of the downtown office blocks and a five-minute tram ride from the beach, although there was a lingering threat of disruption to the race by an ad hoc group of environmental activists called Save Albert Park, already responsible for demonstrations in protest against the cutting down of several hundred trees to make way for the circuit, which winds around a man-made lake and is bordered by red gums, elms, palms and plane trees. The activists were promising to stage what they described as 'an international incident', although they pledged themselves not to endanger lives by interfering with the race itself. Nevertheless, rumours persisted of thousands of rabbits being let loose on the track. 'I think they've every right to be concerned,' Hill said diplomatically when someone asked him about the protesters. 'It's very important that we should not seem to be oblivious to what they're about.'

The track itself had been criticized by several of the drivers, who felt that some of the faster bends lacked adequate run-off areas, although they all recognized its particular character. Berger, the drivers' representative on track safety, described it as 'somewhere between a street circuit and a permanent track. It's quick and demanding, with some long straights and a variety of fast and slow corners.' Hill and Schumacher were among those who praised the challenge it offered.

'It's a long track, which is good,' Villeneuve said. 'It gives you the impression that you're going somewhere, rather than going round and round in circles. It's a fun track to drive on.' Since 'fun' is not a word that often spills from the lips of grand prix drivers, and since I had now heard Villeneuve use it in almost every sentence he uttered, it was becoming hard to deny a growing conviction that the rookie's refusal to be even slightly overawed by his new surroundings would be an influential factor when the field left the grid the following day, and perhaps on the season as a whole.

But no one yet really knew how he would cope. The Williams team's principals liked to put on an air of head-masterly puzzlement at his self-presentation and at his off-duty wardrobe – a mixture of untucked plaid overshirts, jeans and untied Timberland boots, accurately defined with wry amusement by Patrick Head as 'high grunge'. To Bernie Ecclestone, he was already the only man capable of challenging Schumacher in a straight fight, and therefore a prime box-office asset. The calculated informality of his appearance seemed designed to minimize the differences between the son and the father, to disguise the fact that whereas Gilles raced with his heart and soul but rarely with his head, Jacques seemed a much cooler and more calculating customer. And he was still having to cope with the same barrage of questions about his father that he faced on the Indycar circuit. 'I'm used to it,' he said at Melbourne. 'It doesn't disturb me. People want to ask me about my father and I'm sure that if I were doing their jobs I would want to ask as well. So I just answer for the thousandth time, always saying the same thing – that I'm my father's son, I always will be and I'm proud of it. But I'm on my own road.'

He was enthusiastic when I asked him about the ambience in the team. 'So far, it's great. I haven't seen anything bad. You hang out with who you want to hang out with and you don't talk to the people you don't want to talk to. I have no enemies yet. The team seems the same as the ones I raced with in Japan and America – normal people, very open, with a good sense of humour. It's not like they say in the press about Formula One, where everyone is mean and always putting pressure on the drivers and playing games. That I don't know yet. This is how it should be. Everybody has to trust everybody else, otherwise nothing good can be accomplished.' Of Hill he said: 'He's a nice guy. Everything seems to be all right. We haven't compared notes on our cars but our engineers have. I don't know about the other drivers. You could make yourself crazy worrying about that stuff. I just try to do my job.'

The following day he stunned everyone by putting himself on pole position, ahead of Hill, only the third driver to do so on his début, after Mario Andretti at Watkins Glen in 1968 and Carlos Reutemann at Buenos Aires in 1972 – both of them at their home grands prix, which Villeneuve was not. With ten minutes of the one-hour session to go, Hill had gone out and set the fastest time, looking businesslike. Three minutes later Villeneuve went out and beat it, leaving his team-mate no opportunity for another attempt. Hill arrived at the pole-position press conference in a state of something near shock, blinking and biting his lip. 'I thought I had it there for a little bit,' he said, 'but I got it taken away from me right at the end. I would have loved to get pole, obviously, but I'm not surprised because I've been watching Jacques in testing and he's obviously very competent at his job.'

'Before we got here,' Villeneuve said, 'I didn't expect this. But after Thursday and Friday we knew we could make it and we worked hard to be sure to get it.' Had he found it difficult to adapt to Formula One? 'Once you're in the car you don't think what series you're in. If you're used to going fast and being on the edge, it's the same thing.' Would there be some sort of first-corner pact between himself and Hill? 'If you agree between drivers, then one of them will just forget about the agreement.' And when he was asked how he would be approaching his Formula One début, he smiled and gave a short answer: 'Aggressively.'

Conflict exists at all levels of Formula One, and not just between the drivers or the teams. Max Mosley, the president of the FIA, motor sport's world governing body, chose the Melbourne race to reveal one such buried level by releasing a fat file of correspondence between his office and some of the drivers, including Schumacher and Hill, and their representatives, including the newly re-established Grand Prix Drivers' Association. Mosley's dismissive attitude to representations over safety, insurance and other matters suggested that he and Ecclestone, the man who turned grand prix racing from a semi-amateur sport into a global business, were concerned not to loosen their hold on Formula One in the face of a widespread realization of its current value.

It was not necessary to read very closely between the lines to recognize a move to pre-empt the threat of increasing participation by Mark McCormack's International Management Group, then representing David Coulthard and Johnny Herbert and also handling some of Schumacher's business affairs in collaboration with his own manager, Willi Weber. Among the documents was a pugnacious letter from the Grand Prix Drivers' Association to Mosley, accompanied by a draft of that letter faxed to the GPDA office from IMG's headquarters some days earlier – on the face of it, a clear indication of McCormack's prompting behind the scenes. Mosley's exchanges with Schumacher over the question of individual insurance cover for the drivers grew increasingly tetchy. One letter to the world champion showed the president adopting a dismissive tone which stopped just short of insolence; 'Please do not waste any more of my time with this question,' were his final words.

At Melbourne, Schumacher was clearly angry with Mosley's decision to let the world see correspondence on what he considered to be confidential matters. 'They were supposed to be private letters,' he said. 'But Max does that sort of thing. I'm surprised that he needs it, frankly.'

The last grand prix at Albert Park, exactly forty years earlier, had been won by Stirling Moss in a Maserati 250F, when the race was staged in conjunction with the holding of the Olympic Games in Melbourne. This time Moss was a guest of honour, doing demonstration laps in a 250F and in a Mercedes-Benz W196, of the sort he'd raced alongside Fangio in 1955. Many of us had never heard the sound of a W196 before. Its straight-eight engine gave a mighty roar as he brought it past the grandstands, although an official car in front prevented the sixty-four-year-old Moss from putting it through its paces. 'That bloody man,' he said when he returned to the pits, emerging from the cockpit in his white helmet and powder-blue overalls. 'I was dying to have a go, but he wouldn't get out of the way.'

The effects of the worldwide economic recession and of cold, hard commercial logic were evident when the grid formed for the grand prix. At the beginning of the Nineties, twenty teams were involved in Formula One, which meant forty cars battling for twenty-six places on the grid. In those days there were pre-qualifying sessions, at which the slower teams battled for the right to be allowed to qualify for the race. In Melbourne there were a mere twenty-two cars in all, entered by eleven teams. Assuming they all qualified within 107 per cent of the pole-position time, they could all start. Unsurprisingly, the two Forti-Fords, survivors of an age when some teams arrived with no greater ambition than to make up the numbers, did not make the cut, so only twenty cars were present when the race began.

But it only takes two crews to make a boat race and since there have rarely been more than half a dozen truly competitive Formula One cars in any one season, the absence of a few no-hopers at the far end of the pit lane made little difference to anyone except those who cherish the efforts of people trying to prove that it doesn't take £100 million a year to run a Formula One team. The people pleased by their absence were those who resented low-grade sponsors getting unearned TV time whenever their cars were lapped by the leaders – which, in the case of the Fortis, seemed to be every six laps, giving them more exposure than the honest toilers in the middle of the pack.

So twenty cars started the race, the smallest field for many years. For Ecclestone, the best news was that both Ferraris were on the second row, with Irvine surprisingly just ahead of Schumacher. A competitive Ferrari team would mean a successful season in audience terms, and therefore happy sponsors and broadcasters. But within a few seconds it looked as though the year had got off to the worst possible start when Martin Brundle, the oldest driver in the field, had the worst accident of his life. It happened on the third corner of the first lap, and there was a collective gasp and then a groan in the press room as we watched his gold-painted Jordan-Peugeot fly along the track, upside down at zero feet, before it started tumbling into a series of cartwheels, destroying itself in a cloud of dust and wreckage. You don't know what to do at moments like that. There isn't an etiquette, even in the press room. Do you turn away or carry on watching?

There were still clouds of dust in the air when the helmeted figure of Brundle emerged, held upright by a couple of officials but nevertheless clearly still in possession of his head, two arms and two legs. The cheer in the press room was succeeded by an astonished chatter as the TV cameras refocused on the Jordan, showing how it had been torn in two at a point just behind the driver's seat by the prolonged violence of the accident. Brundle said later that the whole thing seemed to have gone on for a very long time – long enough for him to think about the chances of surviving while trying to keep his head down. 'It just kept rolling over and over. And when I stopped, I could feel fluid coming out. I thought it was petrol but it wasn't, it was coming out of my drinks bottle. I was fine. When I got out I was, like, "Oh shit, that's made a mess of that." Half a million dollars' worth, or whatever, just history.'

His subsequent sprint up and down the pit lane, wearing thick flame-proof overalls in eighty-five-degree heat, was an heroic gesture. He was in search of Prof. Sid Watkins, the veteran Formula One medical chief. 'Two doctors saw me in the pits and said I was fine, but they wouldn't let me race until I'd seen Prof. Watkins and got his permission,' Brundle explained. 'Nobody seemed to be able to tell me where he was, so I went to where I thought he'd be but he wasn't there. Then I found out he was down the other end, so I had to run back up there. If I'd waited for somebody else to get him I'd have missed the restart. So I had to go and find him myself.' Watkins put his arm around Brundle's shoulders and listened to his plea. And when he cleared him to jump into his spare car and join in the restarted race, there was a moment of pure elation that went to the centre of the human spirit. Afterwards, Brundle effortlessly achieved the sort of matter-of-factness we are supposed to admire in our British heroes. 'If I'd lost consciousness during the accident,' he said, 'I wouldn't have got back in. But Sid's known me for a dozen years and when he saw me sprint 500 metres towards him he guessed that I was all right.'

The race had been stopped immediately after the accident. When it restarted, minus the Sauber of Johnny Herbert, who had been caught up in the incident, Brundle didn't really mind that for him it lasted only a few more corners. 'I caught the pack but my brakes were cold from starting the pits. Normally on the warm-up lap we're stamping on the pedal all the way round to get some temperature into them. They need to be up to about 600 degrees centigrade before they'll work properly. But when I came up behind Diniz and he braked early, I didn't have that luxury.' This time the accident was more banal in scale and much less expensive. But Martin Brundle had already done his job for the day by reminding those of us in the press room and the corporate hospitality boxes of the reality of what he and his colleagues were up to and why, really, when all is said and done, we were there to watch them.

Villeneuve had made a lightning getaway at the first start, while Hill had messed up. The Englishman did better the second time, slotting in behind his team-mate while Irvine and Schumacher held station behind them in the Ferraris. Schumacher took third place from his colleague on the second lap and the four cars maintained their positions for the first half of the race, with less than a second separating the two Williams, who eventually were more than half a minute ahead of the Ferraris. Villeneuve, the leader, exercised his prerogative to make his pit stop first. Hill followed him into the pits two laps later. What happened next set the competitive tone of the season.

When Hill came out of the pits, he found himself just in front of Villeneuve. As they dived for the first corner, Villeneuve's engineer, the highly competitive Jock Clear, pressed the radio button. 'There he is,' Villeneuve heard Clear shout. 'Go and get him!' Four corners later, around the back of the lake, he was back in the lead. Hill waited until his tyres were up to working temperature before counter-attacking at the beginning of the thirty-fifth lap. As he tried to dive inside his team-mate at the first turn, Villeneuve slid wildly on to the gravel. But instead of taking advantage of Villeneuve's mistake, Hill backed off and watched as the Canadian regained control and maintained his lead.

Hill's failure to seize the moment was an instant reminder of his crash with Schumacher at Adelaide in 1994 when he called it wrong, tried to overtake through a gap that suddenly didn't exist (for whatever reason), collided with the half-crippled Benetton and missed the championship by a single point. 'I thought Jacques had lost it,' Hill said. 'I thought he might catch me as he came back on the track, actually, at one point. I was going to go one side, but he started going back across the track so I had to lift off and, of course, when I got back on the power he was going straight again and off we went. It was a bit of a scary one, but . . . there were two or three other moments in the race when it got quite close, with back markers and things, but that's what it should be like if it's going to be an exciting race, and it certainly was.'

'I thought I was off,' Villeneuve said later. 'It was very bumpy. I was surprised that I was still going straight. And I was surprised that he hadn't gone by me.'

A few laps later, with Hill still less than a second behind Villeneuve, observers noticed that the white-painted parts of the bodywork of Hill's car were starting to be stained brown. Hill himself had been the first to spot the oil leaking from his team-mate's engine when a steady drizzle started to smear his visor. 'It was coming out of Jacques' car with about thirty laps to go. After the pit stops, really. Eventually it was down my neck, everywhere. I was worried that something would go bang and we'd both go off.' So he got on the radio and told the engineers, who had already noticed a slight abnormality in the Canadian's engine temperature. Soon the computer readings let them know that the problem was likely to be terminal unless someone was ready to make a tough decision.

That job fell to Patrick Head, the Williams design chief. Frank Williams had stayed at home in England so it was up to Head to tell their brilliant débutant that he could not follow Baghetti into the record books by becoming only the second man to win the first grand prix in which he took part – with the unique additional distinction of having done so from pole position. Head came to his decision after listening to the fervent lobbying of the two drivers' respective race engineers. For Hill, Adrian Newey warned that with the two cars travelling so close together a complete blow-up could release oil that would send them both into the scenery and leave the team with nothing at all. For Villeneuve, Jock Clear argued that Jacques had the race in the bag and could be left to make his own arrangements. Head looked at the readings, saw clear indications that Hill had been running well within his limits (in other words, that he was capable of going faster if necessary), and decided to tell Villeneuve to slow down and ensure a second-place finish. Somehow, though, the message on the radio didn't get through. Villeneuve continued at an unabated pace for a while, while Head shouted unavailingly through the intercom. In the end, on the fifty-third of the Australian Grand Prix's fifty-eight laps, Head ordered a sign to be hung over the pit wall, bearing the single word 'SLOW'. This time it worked. Villeneuve, who could also see the red oil pressure warning light coming on in the corners, eased up to let Hill by and then backed off to such an extent that he finished the race almost forty seconds back.

Had Villeneuve been ignoring the radio? 'Let's call that a team matter,' Head said, laughing. 'Neither driver has it in his contract that he has to give way to the other one. But, obviously, at the first race of the year the team is pretty keen to get a result in the bag. If there had been no technical problem I think I'd have had to let them get on with it. That doesn't mean to say we'll do the same thing all the time. After the pit stops I was a bit apprehensive about a couple of incidents between them and there was a big debate going on about whether we could slow Jacques down. He didn't respond . . . but he knew he had a serious problem that was going to stop him finishing the race by the time we actually asked him to move over.'

In fact, Head had gone to see Bernard Dudot, head of the Renault engine technicians, to ask what he thought about the temperatures, based on the information they were getting via the radio link to the sensors surrounding Villeneuve's engine. 'Bernard said they were happy with the temperatures and there was no reason to slow Jacques or Damon down just because of them. It's difficult. I know Adrian was agitated. He has been working on Damon's car this weekend and he was arguing that Damon had it well in hand and Jock Clear was saying Jacques only drives as well as he has to and that he had it well in hand . . . it's good, healthy stuff, you know. But Damon won the race and I would say one of the reasons why, if we did indicate to Jacques that we might want to slow him down, was that the data were telling us that Damon had been taking it easy after the pit stop. He was using few engine revs and driving very, very much within limits. I think he was sorting out how he was going to have a go at Jacques. Then he saw all the oil coming out of Jacques' car and he came on the radio. He didn't say, "Please slow Jacques down." He just said, "Jacques' car is pumping out oil, not just in the corners but continuously." We didn't do anything then, but when Renault told us that the oil pressure was dropping out in certain places . . .'

Head had also seen enough that afternoon to be able to figure out the shape of the season to come. 'I'd have to say we all know that we're going to be racing Schumacher and Eddie Irvine and others, but it's clear to us that Damon and Jacques are going to be racing all through the year. We don't have any fanciful idea that we can command the result, so we're just going to have to build the cars strong ... and by that I don't mean strong enough to bump into each other, I mean strong enough to be driven at the limit for the length of the race.'

In public, Villeneuve took his disappointment well. 'The win was there,' he said. 'We had a few more laps to go and it would have been a battle to the finish. I was happy until five laps from the end. The car was running strong, although I wasn't too pleased with my second set of tyres and I was sliding quite a lot more. Damon was very quick and always in my mirrors. Any time I opened up a small gap he would catch up again. It was fun, until I had to slow down. You don't see much in the mirrors but when I heard the team screaming on the radio for two laps I understood there was something wrong. And the red lights were coming on in the corners. I won't say I was robbed, because things like that happen. It happened to me today, it might happen to Damon another day. That's part of racing. The lap that it's important to lead is the last one.' It had occurred to him to keep his foot down and his fingers crossed, but only briefly. 'Maybe for half a second. But if your engineer comes on the radio and tells you to slow down, there must be a good reason – because he wants to win, too.'

Someone reminded Hill that he had just won his fourteenth grand prix, matching his father's career figure. 'It's a statistic,' he responded. 'He won fourteen grands prix but he managed to win two world championships too, so there's a way to go.'

'If you've got the breeding, the horse can run,' Stirling Moss said as the late-afternoon shadows dappled the paddock behind the pits after the race. 'And the breeding obviously showed through, didn't it?'

On his first day as a grand prix driver, Villeneuve impressed everyone. He may not have won the race but you couldn't go very far in the paddock without finding someone singing his praises. Moss needed no encouragement to continue. 'He proved today that he's a champion of the future,' said the man to whom fate wickedly refused the highest accolade. 'The fact that his oil pressure went down was just unfortunate, because it seemed to me that he was reasonably in control of the race.' Villeneuve had, Moss observed, 'pissed all over Hill' – which, coming from such a great driver, represented an extremely serious criticism of one Englishman by another.

'I was scratching my head a bit, to be honest, to see what could be done,' Hill said of the time he had spent behind Villeneuve, showing himself as decently incapable as ever of strategic fibbing. 'When you've got two guys in the same team racing each other you've got to have one eye on the overall result of the team. We had one or two moments, but we stayed away from each other. If I'd qualified on pole I might have had a better chance of being in front and not had the problem of trying to pass him. But I don't mind having someone to dice with. I quite like that. There were two or three chances when we came up to backmarkers and he left a bit of an opening, but I can't take a risk to pass him and then both of us end up crashing.' He had tried things like that before, with unhappy results. But, his critics were saying, a champion had to be prepared to take risks.

Head and Moss were unanimous in their praise of Villeneuve's precocious maturity. 'He's not like I was as a twenty-four-year-old,' the designer said. 'He's been out in the big bad world for a long time, looking after himself. I'm mightily impressed. Obviously he's very talented, although I'm not making any comparisons. We know Damon very well and we know how he responds to certain things. It's great to see that Jacques just loves his racing. He's got a grin all over his face and he loves all aspects of the process of qualifying, practising, sorting the car out, making his decisions, talking to people and the rest of it. It isn't stressful for him, it's natural. I think he'd hate to have a proper job. So he's a pleasure to work with. He's obviously big news.'

'He's completely dissimilar to his father in his personality on the track,' Moss added. 'His father had tremendous skill but he didn't think about it. I think Jacques has got his father's skill – when he was dicing with Damon, he didn't give an inch – but he's got an older head on his shoulders.' True enough. His father might very well have ignored the team's instructions and ended the race in a cloud of expensive smoke, probably within sight of the finish line, but he would have been in the lead when it happened, and that was all that mattered. Gilles Villeneuve did not care about championship standings or making sure that he scored a few points. He wanted to win every race and if, by the end of the season, he had won enough to take the championship – well, that would be nice. But it was not the point of the exercise.

Those were different times. Nowadays the title means everything, along with such considerations as ensuring enough screen time for your sponsors and learning to tell a convincing lie about the cause of your retirement when your engine, bearing the logo of a major motor manufacturer with market-share to defend, has just blown itself apart on worldwide television. Jacques Villeneuve had learnt to operate in that environment. How to ensure, for instance, that his sponsors received a mention at every opportunity: journalists sniggered when, instead of saying 'my car', he would invariably refer to 'my Rothmans Williams-Renault'. Still, at this stage practically everything else about him was enough to banish the cynicism that infects most of the people who spend a lot of time inside the Formula One paddock. Not so different from his dad after all, in that respect.

'Jacques showed today that he's a racer,' said Hill, generous in victory at the very moment of realization that he was in for another season of rivalry with his own team-mate. Was Villeneuve the moral winner? 'I'm sure you could argue that. But he knows motor racing and he knows that it's not quite like that. What goes around comes around. It's been a great race. I was with Jacques the whole way through, there was no one else near us. We've got every chance between us of bringing the championship to the team, and to one of the drivers, so I've got every reason to celebrate. It was a thriller, wasn't it?'

Surely, however, the team would have to think hard about imposing a tactical discipline on their drivers; after all, they had almost collided once during this race. 'I think we'll have to play that as it comes,' Head concluded. 'We're not in a position to be tactical: you win this time, he wins that time. It's not in a contract. The drivers drive for the team, they want to get results in their own championship, and it has to work out between us. But I don't think either Damon or Jacques is going to say, "OK, I'll play number two." We all know in the team, and everybody will be told, that our two guys are racing against each other.'

He hadn't forgotten 1986, he said, when Piquet and

Mansell were in contention for the title but fought each other too hard and let Prost through to win at the last gasp. 'We had great races that year, but we got it wrong. I don't think we'll make that mistake again.'

7

'You must always believe you will become the best,' Juan Manuel Fangio once said, 'but you must never believe you have done so.' His achievements made him a legend, but his modesty made him loved. The 1996 Argentinian Grand Prix was the first to take place since his peaceful death the previous summer, at the age of eighty-four. He died in Balcarce, which is about five hours' drive south of Buenos Aires, towards Mar del Plata. It was to Balcarce that he had returned when, a couple of weeks after his forty-seventh birthday, he decided that he was no longer capable of doing justice to his own talent and that he had seen enough of speed and the death of young men.

Retirement did nothing to dim his legend. Decades after their prime, the immortals can still change the mood of a room simply by their presence; think of Pelé, Ali, DiMaggio, Bradman. In motor racing it was Fangio. More than thirty years after he last acknowledged a chequered flag, fans who had never seen him in action would jostle to glimpse the unprepossessing little Argentine who, by most available yard-sticks, had been the greatest racing driver of all time. During his occasional visits to Europe to take part in anniversary celebrations, there were many who would rather watch Fangio in his seventies, the survivor of several heart attacks, tiptoe round a circuit in a restored museum piece than the present generation race at full throttle in their computer-designed super-machines. For his admirers, the 'Old Man' symbolized the heroic age when racing drivers went about their business in cork helmets, polo shirts, string-backed gloves and suede loafers, forearms bare to the wind, faces streaked with hot oil. It was an age when chivalry still played a part and when the physical danger was such that each race seemed to thin the ranks of the participants. Perhaps the two were not unconnected.

For all the affection lavished on him throughout his long retirement, Fangio was nevertheless a hard case, a professional in the post-war world of dashing amateurs. Although capable of kindness and consideration, he never allowed sentiment to obstruct his path. Sound judgement and mental toughness served him well throughout a career whose greatest triumphs – twenty-four grand prix wins in fifty-one starts, five world championships (still unmatched) in seven-and-a-half seasons – were achieved in his fifth decade, thousands of miles away from his homeland. But the bare statistics tell nothing of his extraordinary qualities, the combination of delicate virtuosity, carefully deployed aggression and mechanical sympathy that often allowed him to rise above unhelpful conditions, superior opposition or faulty equipment (and sometimes, being Fangio, above all three at once).

Fangio was born in Balcarce, a potato town, in 1911. Both his parents had their origins in the Abruzzo region of Italy. Juan's father, the accordion-playing Don Loreto, arrived in Argentina at the age of seven, becoming a stonemason and house-painter; his wife, Doña Herminia, a seamstress, produced six children, of whom Juan was the fourth. The young Juan was a good student who loved boxing and football. An agile inside-right, he was nicknamed *Chueco* – Bandy-legs – by his team-mates.

Argentina had held its first motor race in the year before Juan's birth. At the age of four he was enthralled by a neighbour's single-cylinder machine. At ten he was hanging around the garage of a Señor Capettini, fetching and carrying tools for the mechanics and driving a car, a chain-driven Panhard-Levassor, for the first time. At his father's wish, Juan was apprenticed to a local blacksmith but he soon talked himself into a transfer to Capettini's premises. There, and later at Miguel Viggiano's Studebaker garage, he learnt the intimate details of the internal combustion engine, such as how to profile a camshaft by hand and how to use a stone to grind a cylinder head. At night, after work, he began to modify machines himself. By his mid-teens he was also volunteering to deliver cars to customers and ascribed his famous skill in slippery conditions to his early experience of driving on muddy tracks, which encouraged him to acquire a delicate touch. At sixteen he briefly ran away from home to Mar del Plata, thirty-five miles distant, but was brought back by his father.

Soon afterwards, without telling his parents, he took part in his first race, as the riding mechanic in a four-cylinder Plymouth driven by one of Viggiano's customers. He performed a similar role the following year, accompanying his brother-in-law in a Chevrolet during a closed-circuit race in Balcarce. In 1931, however, Juan contracted pleurisy and needed a long convalescence with relatives in the countryside before, in 1932, he reported to the artillery barracks in Buenos

Aires for a year's compulsory military service. When he was able to return home he set up a garage with a friend, José Duffard, taking the first step in a long business career which ran in parallel with his life as a racing driver.

Races on the open roads were the highlight of Argentinian motor sport, and Fangio's first really significant result came with seventh place in the 1938 Gran Premio Argentino de Carreteras, over a route totalling 4,590 miles. His potential was now so obvious that the people of Balcarce clubbed together to buy him a decent car, a six-cylinder Chevrolet coupé. His first great win with the Chevrolet came in 1940, in the Gran Premio Internacional del Norte, which ran from Buenos Aires through Bolivia to Peru and back, a total of almost 6,000 miles in a fortnight, up mountain roads reaching 13,500 feet. Exhaustion and altitude sickness were enemies as formidable as the unmade roads. Victory in this, plus another in the Mil Millas Argentinas, made him the country's 1940 road-racing champion. He won the title again the following year and was beginning to grow accustomed to street parades in Balcarce when, in 1942, the war halted racing. He was thirty-one. For another sportsman these might have been the lost years of his prime, but Fangio was only just beginning.

With the resumption of racing in 1947, he was ready. That year, the Argentine Automobile Club invited two great Italian stars, Achille Varzi and Luigi Villoresi, to take part in races at Buenos Aires, the capital, and Rosario, the second city, 200 miles up the Parana river. The following year they returned, together with a third Italian, Nino Farina, and the French champion Jean-Pierre Wimille. Fangio began this series, known as the Temporada, in an old Maserati, but for the third race, in Rosario, he was offered one of a pair of Simca-Gordinis brought from France by their maker, Amédée Gordini. Fangio comfortably matched the performance of Wimille, a European grand prix star, in an identical car.

When Fangio arrived in Europe in 1948 with a delegation from the Argentine Automobile Club, Varzi and Wimille were among those who welcomed him. Fangio's only appearance during that trip was at Rheims, driving a Simca-Gordini at the French Grand Prix meeting. He failed to finish but the party returned home in possession of a pair of new single-seater Maserati grand prix cars. For Fangio, though, the year also held great sadness: he had been at the Bremgarten circuit in Berne when Varzi died under his capsized Alfa Romeo; and, while competing in the epic Gran Premio de la América del Sur in Argentina, he rolled his old Chevrolet, killing his co-driver and friend, Daniel Urrutia. Only three months later, during practice for the Gran Premio Juan Domingo Perón at Buenos Aires, Wimille was also killed.

That race was the first of the 1949 Temporada series, in which Fangio was to make his real impact on the Europeans. At the Grand Prix of Mar del Plata, driving the fast little Maserati 4CLT in front of 300,000 ecstatic fans, he beat Farina, Villoresi and Alberto Ascari in a straight fight. Now he was ready to take on Europe.

Within weeks he was leading the little Argentine team to victory in a grand prix along the San Remo seafront. It was followed by wins at Pau, Perpignan and Marseilles. So enthusiastic were his home fans that Perón's government bought him a new two-litre Ferrari, and he repaid his country's faith by winning his first race, the Monza Grand Prix, matched against Ascari and Villoresi in similar cars on a circuit that he had never seen before.

It was enough to attract the interest of the Alfa Romeo management, then preparing a team for the first world championship, to be held over a seven-race series in 1950. Fangio, Farina and Luigi Fagioli were their drivers and between them 'the three Fs' won all six European rounds in their crimson Alfettas. Fangio's victories at Monaco, Spa and Rheims gave him second place in the final championship table, just behind Farina. But the following season three more wins – in Switzerland, Spain and France – plus two second places gave Fangio his first world championship. He was forty years old.

Alfa Romeo, however, decided to retire from racing and during the winter Fangio accepted an offer to drive for Maserati. It was to be his worst season, thanks to the events of a June weekend. On the Saturday he was due to race a BRM in the Ulster Trophy race on the Dundrod circuit near Belfast, followed on the Sunday by his first race in the Maserati, in the Monza Grand Prix. After the BRM's retirement he flew from Belfast to Paris, there to be told that bad weather had ruled out all flights to Italy. Undeterred, Fangio drove non-stop through the night to Monza, just north-east of Milan, arriving two hours before the race was due to start. Although he had not practised, and was therefore not qualified to race, his fellow drivers immediately voted to let him participate. 'You look a bit tired,' Ascari told him. 'Oh, it's nothing,' Fangio replied. But after starting from the back row of the grid in an unfamiliar car, he misjudged the Seraglio curve on the second lap and woke up in hospital with broken vertebrae. It was the only serious accident he was to suffer in the whole of his European career, and it put him out for a year.

In 1954 Mercedes-Benz made their long-awaited reappearance in Formula One. Alfred Neubauer, their peerless talent scout, always hired the best, which meant securing the services of Fangio, who took the championship with a points total almost double that of the runner-up. The arrival of Stirling Moss in 1955 at least gave Fangio some competition, although Moss was generally content to follow in the master's wheeltracks, learning the finer points of racecraft in a sequence of one-two finishes. Fangio won in Argentina, Belgium, Holland and Italy. By contrast, at the British Grand Prix, Moss 'won' by a tenth of a second after ninety laps of the Aintree circuit. For many years Fangio did not reveal that he had run the race to the orders of the team management, which was looking for a public-relations coup in post-war Britain and had fitted Fangio's car with lower gear ratios, restricting his speed. In any case, the championship had already been decided in his favour.

Curiously, Fangio's finest drive of that season may have been among his least praised. In the Mille Miglia, the non-stop time-trial over public roads from Brescia to Rome and back, he finished second to Moss in a race that became recognized as the Englishman's greatest triumph. But whereas Moss enjoyed the prompting of a well-prepared navigator in the passenger seat of his eight-cylinder Mercedes 300SLR, Fangio accomplished the drive single-handed. And, for more than half the distance, on seven of the engine's eight cylinders.

At the 24 Hours of Le Mans Fangio's Mercedes was peripherally involved in the crash which saw the machine of his team-mate, Pierre Levegh, flying over an earth bank into a public enclosure, killing eighty spectators. Fangio and Moss, sharing a car, were leading the race when, at two o'clock in the morning, orders came from the team's Stuttgart headquarters to withdraw the remaining cars – a gesture of respect which also served as a partial safeguard against the consequent storm of bad publicity. The disaster bore heavily on Mercedes' subsequent decision to withdraw from racing.

Fangio, now forty-four, was contemplating retirement when a call from Enzo Ferrari changed his mind. Although they carried off the 1956 championship together, the relationship ended in bitterness and for the following season Fangio moved back to Maserati, whose 250F model, introduced in 1954, was reaching the peak of its development and now became the tool with which Fangio could demonstrate the most profound elements of his genius. Its superb chassis permitted the refinement of the high-speed cornering technique known as the 'four-wheel drift', in which the driver pushed the car just past the limit of its tyres' adhesion. It was a skill requiring enormous sensitivity and its masters were Fangio and his pupil Moss. Of Fangio's four grand prix victories in 1957, the greatest was undoubtedly the win at the Nürburgring, a fourteen-mile circuit around the Eifel mountains, whose 175 corners provided a test that revealed the relationship between the world champion and his Maserati as he caught and overtook the more powerful but less agile Ferraris of Peter Collins and Mike Hawthorn in an epic drive which set the seal on his legend.

It was his greatest grand prix victory and also his last. He had won five world championships but he entered 1958 with misgivings about prolonging his career. After missing the opening three races of the European grand prix season, he returned early in July for the French Grand Prix at Rheims.

As he went through his old preparation routine in his hotel room, he suddenly realized that 'racing had become an obligation. And when racing begins to feel like work, well . . .' After dragging his outclassed Maserati around in fourth place, Fangio discovered that Luigi Musso, a former team-mate, was dying in hospital after running off the track. The Italian, who was in financial difficulties, had needed the prize money and simply pushed too hard. For Fangio it was one accident and one race too many. Quietly, without fanfare, he returned to Argentina where he settled into the life of a garage-owner-cum-national hero. His Mercedes-Benz dealership expanded and he was often flown across the ocean to be the chief VIP at the company's functions in Europe. At home, his door was open; abroad, crowds attended him wherever he went.

His personal life was always something of a mystery: in his ghosted autobiography, published soon after his retirement from racing, he offered thanks to 'my wife, Andreina, for all she has done for me and our son Oscar'. They had married, he wrote, in 1941: 'She has not left my side since.' In the early Seventies, though, he described the relationship differently: 'We were not married, but we spent twenty years together. Then one day we had a discussion and she said, "If you don't like being with me, you may leave." So I left.'

Was he the greatest racing driver of all? His record says so but in motor racing, as in any sport, it is impossible to draw exact comparisons. If we say, as some critics would, that he was merely the shrewdest (which is beyond dispute) and not as divinely gifted as Nuvolari, Rosemeyer, Moss,

Clark or Senna, then how do we explain the incandescent virtuosity of his drive against the odds at the Nürburgring in 1957? All we can say for certain is that Fangio raced against the best of his time and beat them. And became, in the process, the embodiment of his sport.

During his prime, telegrams and newspaper cuttings reporting his triumphs had been posted in the shop windows of Balcarce. When he retired the townspeople built a museum in his honour, installed in an elegant turn-of-the-century building and mostly dedicated to the cars he raced and the trophies he won. Some of them were on view at the Buenos Aires autodrome during grand prix week – the track on which he won the race four years running.

Behind the main grandstand his compatriots queued up to view the Model A Ford he raced in the Thirties, sometimes using the pseudonym '*Rivadavia*' – the name of his football team, itself named after a hero of the Argentine revolution – to hide his identity from disapproving parents. Next to the old Ford stood the red Volpi-Chevrolet, a well proportioned but mechanically crude local copy of a single-seater Maserati. Since such expensive European machinery was beyond both the geographical reach and the financial means of a driver like Fangio during the immediate post-war years, he had used the Volpi in the Mecánia Nacional series in the late Forties. And next to that an even more mythical machine: a big, pale green 1940 Chevrolet coupé, of a type familiar from the Hollywood thrillers of Hawks, Ray and Tourneur. This was the car, paid for by the people of Balcarce, in which Fangio won the Gran Premio del Norte and the Mil Millas Argentinas, fearsome events lasting several days in which the competitors were required to navigate open mountain roads that were often no more than rough tracks, chewing coca leaves to ward off altitude sickness. I thought of that later in the day as I listened to Hill, Schumacher and their colleagues complaining about the current circuit, earnestly describing the difficulties they faced when confronted by a little bit of dust and a handful of bumps no more than half an inch high.

No, you're right, that isn't fair. But one of the things that was lost from the grand prix world many years ago was an appreciation of its roots in the open-road races, from town to town, of the pioneers. When Fangio competed at Rheims or Spa-Francorchamps, it was on public roads – closed for the duration of the meeting and with a few straw bales at the corners, but still recognizable as highways. These grands prix provided a clear link with Fangio's own background in the great South American road races and with their European equivalents, such as the Mille Miglia or the Targa Florio, a race through the mountain villages of northern Sicily.

That connection had come to mind in Melbourne, when Villeneuve said he liked the track because it was long and it gave him a sense of going from one place to another, rather than being on a kind of roundabout. For sports cars there remains the 24 Hours of Le Mans, albeit in a somewhat emasculated version, and Formula One retains the race around the tax haven of Monaco, deplored by some people as a foolish anachronism yet which manages to inspire a thrilling race year after year. But what has happened, in general and over a long period of time, is that the tail has wagged the dog: the circuits have been adapted to suit the changing technology of the cars, compounded by an increased awareness of public safety and, as the carnage of two world wars recedes from living memory, a modified valuation of the individual human life. No bumps, no dust, no surprises. Yet for people of a certain romantic temperament the temptation is always to disparage one's own era in comparison with the past. No doubt sometime in the next century future generations of grand prix fans will come across Hill's machine in a display of historic machinery in a paddock and will peer at it with the same sense of awe and wonder that overwhelmed me as I looked at Fangio's big green Chevrolet.

I felt the sensation even more strongly a couple of days before the race when I was walking through the Galleria Pacifica, a shopping centre in downtown Buenos Aires, and came across another exhibit sent along by the Balcarce museum: a Maserati 250F purporting to be the one in which Fangio won the German Grand Prix of 1957, when he showed the full measure of his divine virtuosity. The 250F was probably the most beautiful racing car ever built and, since fewer than thirty were made, their rarity value is immense. Many replicas have been openly created – and some unacknowledged fakes – while genuine cars have been reconstituted to resemble more famous ones. Just as there are probably a thousand white Fender Stratocasters with left-hand stringing and certificates saying that Jimi Hendrix set fire to them at the Monterey Pop Festival in 1968, so there must be several 250Fs with a yellow band and a number one painted on the nose. For sure, the one in the Galleria Pacifica wasn't the real thing. Its chassis plate bore the number 2518, which actually belonged to a car completely destroyed in a fire at the factory in 1956. Fangio's Nürburgring car was 2529 and it is to be found in a European collection. But this one had been got up to look near-perfect, with its long nose and elegant tail. As it sat proudly on a small dais, the object of semi-curious stares from people moving between the clothes shops and the fast-food court, I thought that in this context its authenticity didn't matter a bit. The people of Argentina deserved the original, but if they couldn't have it then this was the next best thing. Anyway, it was nice to sit and look at the car and think for a moment about what had been achieved in something very much like it.

On Sunday, an hour before the race, the organizers unveiled a plaque to Fangio at the circuit, which is named after his friend and rival Oscar Galvez. Galvez was a gifted driver who won many of the long-distance races and competed brilliantly against visiting European stars in Argentina but who remained behind when Fangio went off to make his reputation in Europe. To open the ceremony another of Fangio's cars, the Mercedes W196 of 1954–5, was pushed silently down the main straight and past the grandstand by four mechanics in spotless white overalls decorated with the manufacturer's three-pointed star. The car, a sister of the one driven by Moss at Melbourne a month earlier, certainly looked very striking and it seemed a pity that they didn't fire up the straight-eight engine and perhaps ask José Froilán González, Fangio's contemporary and fellow countryman, to drive a lap or two in it. But somebody said that, as a sentimental gesture, the immaculate silver car would never be started again because they wanted Fangio to have been the last man to drive it; a bit like leaving Churchill's War Room or Noël Coward's study at his house in Jamaica the way they were, as if the occupant had just popped out.

Someone more cynical claimed that the thing simply wouldn't run and, anyway, González was stuck in the traffic jam outside the circuit. (When he eventually arrived it was hard to recognize the figure so familiar from the photographs of forty years earlier: he had lost several stone since the days when he overflowed the cockpit of his Ferrari and was known as the Pampas Bull.)

Alain Prost attended the little unveiling ceremony, as did Bernie Ecclestone, who is a romantic about motor racing underneath the surface and who saw Fangio drive many times in the Fifties. But none of the current drivers was there. They're an unsentimental bunch, understandably enough, and tend to leave that sort of thing to the rest of us, but I thought they could have made an exception for the only man to win their championship five times. Senna, I felt, would have made the time to pay his respects, had he been alive, because he would have been aware of the special thread connecting him to the great man of a previous generation.

Still, I was glad that if one engine had to be running in the pits as Fangio's old car was wheeled past, it should come from the McLaren pit, where the present-day Mercedes engineers were poring over their laptops and fine-tuning Coulthard's car, oblivious to the little ceremony. Perhaps, after all, the man we were honouring would have preferred that. Life going on, work being done, a race to run.

The eyes of Michael Schumacher stared down from a huge Marlboro billboard over the teeming Avenida del Libertador like those of Scott Fitzgerald's Dr T. J. Eckleburg, but it was Damon Hill who imposed his presence on Buenos Aires over the Easter weekend. After Melbourne, Hill had scored a more impressive victory at Interlagos, perhaps the best of his career, leading the Brazilian Grand Prix from start to finish in dreadful conditions, putting on an utterly convincing display of wet-weather driving while others, notably Villeneuve and Alesi, were caught out. The winning streak – counting Adelaide at the end of the previous season, he had now taken three races in a row – seemed to have given him a serenity missing from his mood during the bitter rivalry with Michael Schumacher which had previously threatened to define his career as a racing driver.

The first practice sessions in Buenos Aires saw Schumacher doing his best to let Hill know that he was still around, despite having to cope with a new Ferrari which was still clearly deficient in some of the basic virtues. 'They look like a proper racing team,' Patrick Head had said in Melbourne. 'And despite the fact that they got their car ready pretty late, they're obviously the most serious opposition team. It's very early days for them. I don't think we'll be resting.' Hill, too, had been impressed: 'They're competitive and they'll be a threat.'

The old Buenos Aires autodrome, built in the Fifties, had been modified and resurfaced since the last grand prix was held there in 1981, but there were significant bumps caused by ridges running across various points of the two-and-a-half mile track. Martin Brundle came back to the pits shaking his head. 'I think they've been laying cables under the track,' he said. 'We were going into the turn at the end of the straight with the ride height set at 2.7 millimetres. If you try to run a high-tech car on a track like this, it doesn't take much of a bump to throw you right off.' At the corner after the pits, where not one but two bumps, thirty metres apart, preceded the apex, every car behaved differently. Most of them were in various kinds of trouble as they came off the brakes and turned into the corner. The Fortis juddered horribly, the Saubers lifted their noses, the Footworks just looked undriveable. The crowd thronging the grandstands hummed with anticipation whenever a car approached; each time one of them bounced off the usual line and flicked into a spin, they roared their delight at the entertainment.

They didn't get much from Williams, whose FW18s contrived to appear as smooth and unruffled as if they were still using the computer-driven active suspension which had smoothed out all the corrugations, even those measured in millimetres, earlier in the decade, giving Mansell and Prost a magic-carpet ride to the championship. The Ferraris, on the other hand, looked as if they were being driven by racing drivers. Schumacher's red car slid and bucked on the very limit of control, and sometimes well beyond it, as the world champion demonstrated his virtuosity. The drivers were talking about how the F310 would play tricks in the middle of a corner, suddenly switching from oversteer to understeer and back; and in the practice sessions down at the first turn you could see the way Schumacher would drive around the car's bad habits, forcing it to do things its nature resisted. That was what Senna used to do: the emotion was visible in his driving, and now it was visible in Schumacher's.

In Hill's corner of the paddock, a hat trick of wins had clearly had a relaxing effect. 'I feel good,' he said. 'I went to Rio after São Paulo and had a great time there for three days. I played tennis and golf, did some windsurfing – enjoyed myself, basically, with a view to coming here and enjoying myself even more, if I can. And there's no reason why I can't.' He had learnt, he said, how to switch off between races. 'I didn't spend too long thinking about motor racing. But now I'm here my mind's on the job.' But he remained prudently unwilling to overstate the case. 'I'm mindful of the fact that I've had three grand prix victories on the trot and, statistically, it gets more difficult to keep that up the longer you go on. You're going to have mechanical failures during a season, you're going to have things that put you out of a race. You can only go on for so long before something like that will stop you. Right now I'm in a situation where I can return to Europe still in the lead of the championship, even if I don't race here, but that's not what I really want. I want to go back to Europe with an even bigger lead.'

Nigel Mansell's record of five wins at the start of a season had not, he said, crossed his mind, although he showed himself aware of the record books when he remarked that the only man to have won more than five consecutive grands prix was the late Alberto Ascari, also the son of a famous father, who won no fewer than nine in a row back in 1952–3. 'Those things are interesting,' Hill said, 'but you've got to isolate each event. As far as I'm concerned, I haven't done anything and I haven't got anything. I'm treating this race in exactly the same way as the first race or the last race. Nothing before or what happens in the future is going to affect this result. You start from scratch every time you go to a race.'

Was his new-found calm the cause or the effect of those three wins? That was the big question. 'I think it's a bit of both,' Patrick Head observed with typical candour. 'You can be serene if you're in a strong position, but I think he's worked very hard over the winter to put himself in that position. The car's obviously pretty sound but he's fitter than he's ever been and you can hear on the radio that he's less bothered about what Schumacher and the others are doing on the track. We all had a bit of a drubbing last year. We went away and tried to look after our bit and I think he went away and did some thinking about his bit. At times in the past, and particularly when he's under pressure, he's been uncertain and unconfident about what he wanted. He's got himself well organized now. He sits down and has a good, clear think about what the car is doing before he opens his mouth and starts talking. But the test comes when somebody comes back at you. There's a hell of a long way to go in the season so the question is, will he be serene when Ferrari or Benetton get their cars right?'

Hill had won in Argentina the previous year, one of the four victories that made him runner-up to Schumacher for the second time. Now, thanks to the mechanical superiority of the Williams over its rivals, he had a good chance to become the first man since Fangio to win twice in a row in Buenos Aires. But the history of the event was evoked in a more disturbing manner when, during the first practice session of the meeting, Gerhard Berger came round Turn Five at about 150 miles an hour in fourth gear to discover a dog crossing the track ahead of his Benetton. An hour later, the Austrian could laugh about it. 'It must have been Schumacher's dog,' he said, referring to Flea, a mongrel which had attached itself to the world champion and his wife Corinna in the paddock at São Paulo a week earlier. Generating enormous publicity, the couple were said to have spent something like $40,000 in veterinary and quarantine fees and on the air fare to take the animal with them to Argentina. A small brown and cream creature, it now looked neat and tidy enough to have been ordered from a catalogue, possibly even the one that detailed the products available from the newly launched Michael Schumacher Collection. The dog that crossed Berger's path, however, was reported not to have been wearing a paddock pass. Nor, really, was it a fit subject for humour. Although the driver could be forgiven for cracking a joke to ease his tension, the consequences of a collision could have been nothing short of horrendous.

The incident raised the spectre of the death of the great French driver Jean-Pierre Wimille back in 1949, the year before the world championship began. Wimille, twice a winner at Le Mans before the war, was killed during practice for a grand prix in Buenos Aires' Palmero Park. Because the race was taking place in a residential district of the city, the practice sessions were held soon after dawn to minimize disruption to residents and the business traffic. Some said Wimille was blinded by a shaft of sunlight coming between the trees; others claimed he had swerved to miss a dog. Crowd control was a perennial problem at races in Argentina during the early post-war years and in 1953 the *autodromo* itself was the scene of one of the worst crashes in motor racing history. A crowd of 100,000 lined the verge of the circuit, with only mounted police to hold them back, when Giuseppe Farina came round a corner to find a child running across the track. Farina, the first world champion of the modern era, avoided the child but ran into the spectators, killing a dozen people.

But Hill was less worried about encroaching spectators and livestock than about the pronounced bump on the back straight. 'I'm worried about my crowns,' he said, rubbing his jaw after coming in with the fastest time of the day, a fraction ahead of Schumacher. 'You whack your teeth together going over the bumps, and that's a bit uncomfortable.'

A week before Argentina I'd been telephoned by someone called Rachel Huggard, one of Hill's public relations people. She was calling on his behalf, she said, because he'd read the piece I'd written after the interview *en route* to Estoril and he was upset by the reference to him refusing to have his photograph taken by a fan in the airport departure lounge. I'd said in the piece that it had made me want to kick him. Pelé, I wrote, had never refused to have his photograph taken, and he was a man revered by princes and peasants alike. That analogy arose from direct experience, since I'd come across Pelé waiting for a car outside a hotel in Chicago just before the opening match of the 1994 World Cup and I'd asked him for an autograph. He'd inquired if I wanted it dedicated to someone and I'd said to my son, please, so he asked his name and wrote: 'To Jack. Good luck, Pelé.' Then I watched as he posed for snapshots with two German fans, making sure they got exactly what they wanted, putting his arm round them to make a better pose. Yes, he's retired, which can make people behave more generously and yes, he's renowned as a world-class PR man, but on this particular occasion he didn't have to do any of it since no one else was watching, and certainly not with such charm and care for people he had never met and would most likely never meet again. I also wanted to make the point that celebrity seemed to be making Damon Hill behave in certain ways that were not true to his essential nature.

Well, I told Rachel Huggard, I just wrote down what took

place and what I thought about it. She said that, according to Damon, that was not what had happened, and if it had it was because he was concentrating on our interview. 'Damon says that he wasn't rude to the man and he only did it because he was trying to give you his full attention as he knew that time was limited.' No, I told her, the interview hadn't started. We were chatting about music at the time, as I recalled. I was struck by the brusqueness of his response to the fan, which seemed to be both out of character and in keeping with the curiously awkward image he presented to the world. I suppose, if I'm honest, I have to say that it fitted the little theory I was constructing. But was I supposed to ignore it? I said that if he wanted to argue about it he should call me himself.

When I saw him in Buenos Aires, I raised the matter. 'It was a bit below the belt,' he said, 'and anyway, I met Pelé last week and he wouldn't give me an autograph.' Ho, ho.

Before the race there was some discussion about the status of the Grand Prix Drivers' Association and about the fact that Villeneuve had not yet signed up. Either he was trying to assert his independence or he was acting on the instructions of Bernie Ecclestone, who had godfathered his contract with Frank Williams and had never been keen on the equivalent of player-power finding its way into Formula One.

Villeneuve's team-mate was in no doubt of the organization's value. 'I'm a keen supporter of the GPDA,' Hill said at a press conference. 'I think it's a good thing. Its intentions are important for Formula One, including giving the drivers' perspective on safety issues, and if we can continue to work like that with the FIA . . .' But surely the FIA, someone said, doesn't recognize the GPDA. 'Nevertheless the FIA has sought the views of drivers over the last year in order to improve safety. That's a good measure of the respect that there is between the two parties. Things are going in the right direction. Safety has improved, I'm confident of that. It'll never be completely safe, as we know, but drivers are in a unique position in that they're the only people who can give their perspective from the cockpit. It's just not possible to look at it on a map or go round in a road car and see exactly where the danger spots are. It does require going round in a racing car.'

Did he expect the GPDA to get official recognition? 'I don't want to say any more on the matter. Things are progressing well. There's a lot that still needs to be discussed.' Was the GPDA weakened by the fact that it was not a closed shop and that at least one driver was known not to be a member? 'Every driver's free to choose. If people feel that something can be gained from being part of the GPDA and contributing to the discussion, they're welcome to join. It would be nice to have everyone, but it's not a Union and no one's going to be forced into joining.'

His hat trick of wins, someone observed, suggested that the team had been sandbagging in the pre-season tests, disguising the true potential of the FW 18. 'No, I'm always trying to prepare the car and myself for the season and I did a good job in the tests. The most important thing was to do laps to get reliability, and we did that. There's always a danger that if you go testing and try to disguise things you can end up fooling yourselves. I haven't been up to any tricks. There's a big difference between testing and racing, I'll just say that.'

*

Only ten cars finished the race, which was held in hot and dusty conditions. Hill, maintaining the immaculate form of the practice sessions, made a perfect start, holding Schumacher at bay as they contested the first bend. Villeneuve fared less well. His clutch slipping as he tried to leave the line, he saw the Benettons of Alesi and Berger roar past. By the time the field had sorted itself out he was a potentially disastrous ninth, and beginning the long haul back towards the leaders.

As Schumacher failed to make an impression on Hill, Villeneuve's brisk progress through the field became the main focus of interest in the early stages, climaxed by a powerful rush down the inside of Coulthard to claim fifth place on the ninth lap. When Hill extended his lead to six seconds, Schumacher tried to break the stalemate by taking on fuel and tyres first, a typically inventive decision by the man who had been the first to work out that such flexible strategies could be decisive in modern racing. And he got his reward. When Alesi came out of the pits a lap later, the world champion had the big crowd cheering as he squeezed the Ferrari past the Benetton into the first turn.

But the race really came alive on the twenty-seventh lap when Luca Badoer, apparently nudged by Pedro Diniz, turned his Forti over on the inside of the turn behind the paddock and could be seen crawling out of the inverted car. The machine did not seem to be in a particularly dangerous position but the race director sent out the safety car to sit in front of the leader, allowing the field to bunch up and costing Hill the margin he had so assiduously built up. Now Schumacher, Alesi and Berger were right back in his mirrors. If the use of the safety car had been imported from American racing in order to inject new interest into a race that was in danger of boring the casual television audience, it was doing its job here.

The field was still circulating gently three laps later when Diniz's Ligier, which had just left the pits, burst into flames around the back of the circuit, fuel having escaped from the breather valve. The car spun to a halt and the young Brazilian emerged from a ball of orange flames, miraculously unscathed. On lap thirty-three the pace car left the track and again Hill held a narrow lead for several laps before Schumacher returned to his pit at the end of the fortieth lap, resuming the race in eighth place. Alesi got his revenge when, emerging from his own second stop after having to restart his engine, he dived inside Schumacher at Turn One. But when Barrichello and Herbert also swept past the Ferrari, it was evident that trouble had struck Schumacher. At the end of the forty-sixth lap he headed for the pit lane and drove straight into his garage. Later it emerged that a piece of debris had struck his rear wing, creating a pronounced instability. Replacing the wing, a team spokesman said, would have taken too long.

Hill, too, suffered from handicaps but managed to overcome them all – the artificial shrinkage of his lead, a disturbed stomach and the loss of radio communication with his engineers, which meant that all signals had to be transmitted via the old-fashioned board hung over the pit wall. But the race went smoothly enough to give him a comfortable twelve-second cushion over Villeneuve by the time it ended. Villeneuve's second place provided the Williams-Renault team with their second one-two of the season, as well as reaffirming the internal order of supremacy in Hill's favour.

This gave him a perfect thirty points for the season to date, an eighteen-point lead over Villeneuve and twenty-six points more than Schumacher.

'It's a great result and a fantastic day,' Hill said. 'It can't get any better than this. The competition's getting closer all the time and there will be some fantastic races to come.' His sixteenth grand prix success had brought him level with Stirling Moss's career total. He welcomed the statistic. If he had been trying to suppress thoughts of the title, they would be difficult to keep out of his dreams now.

8

It was at Imola that we saw both sides of Hill's ability to cope with media pressure. His run of victories had come to an end two weeks earlier at the Nürburgring, the first race of the European season, where he made a poor start from pole position and finished fourth, giving Villeneuve the opportunity to confirm his early good impression by taking the first grand prix victory of his career. And the rookie had done it in style, by holding off a late assault from Schumacher's Ferrari. He had been impressing the team by his aggressive and adventurous approach, even when they didn't necessarily agree with his firmly expressed opinions on technical matters. It was enough to put the pressure back on Hill, almost as if those four wins in a row had never happened.

Cornered by a group of reporters at the back of the pits after the Saturday morning practice session for the San Marino Grand Prix, Hill was asked by Ted Macauley of the *Mirror* if he was looking for revenge (over Villeneuve, presumably). It was a question clearly designed to generate a tabloid headline. 'Only against you, Ted,' Hill replied, as quick as you like, getting a good laugh from a bunch of people who appreciated him going along with the game. But at the formal press conference later in the day he was invited to describe his response to the criticisms that followed his defeat in Germany. 'I didn't read them,' he said testily. Then, after a moment's pause, came the unwise addition: 'But I did have a good fish and chip supper on Monday night and I saw some of them then.' This time there was no answering warmth.

What we saw in that exchange was the awful result of the destructive force exerted on prominent British sportsmen by newspapers whose editors demand stories of conflict in which all emotions are heightened until they are caricatures of the original impulse. Hate, rage and fury are the key emotions. Among those also subjected to, and damaged by, the process have been Ian Botham, Paul Gascoigne, Will Carling, Linford Christie and Mike Atherton. Apologists for the technique would say that these people would never have been such heroes without the tabloids and would further claim that the sportsmen often connive at their own downfall, either by saying or doing stupid things or by taking the tabloids' money for writing a bylined column. Damon Hill, it seemed to me, had done nothing to deserve being dragged into this cartoon world. But there he was, and there he would stay for the rest of the summer.

When the Formula One circus arrives at Imola, thoughts turn to Ayrton Senna. And since the judicial investigation into Senna's death had yet to publish any findings, there was all sorts of speculation. Some people felt that if the men who designed and built Senna's car were to be charged with manslaughter, it would mean the end of motor racing in Italy because no team would want to take the risk of having an accident and facing criminal proceedings. An end to

Formula One racing at Imola and Monza seemed a terrible thing to contemplate.

This being Italy, there were already several hundred fans in the grandstands opposite the pits at the Autodromo Enzo e Dino Ferrari when the cars went out for the first time early on Friday morning. Their banners had been attached to the railings and there seemed to be a remarkable unanimity of thought. Gerhard Berger, they had decided, was their love-object. The banners, some illustrated with carefully painted likenesses of the hero and a few of them decorated with pink hearts, came straight from the Mills and Boon school of copywriting: 'Gerhard Berger always and forever'; 'Crazy Gerhard Berger Fan Club Italia'; 'Gerhard continue to warm our hearts with your smile'; 'Gerhard look at the sky it's the only thing greater than you'; 'Forza Gerhard: Con Ayrton e Roland'; 'Gerhard we are always with you'. No one else got a look in, really, although there were token signs of encouragement for Schumacher, Hill and Alesi.

It's funny to think of Gerhard Berger as Formula One's senior pro. He always seems more like the last echo of the days of the playboy pilots, guys like Alfonso de Portago and Peter Collins who didn't let marriage to movie stars or heiresses cramp their style. After all, he's the man who taught Ayrton Senna how to laugh. But at thirty-seven, and with almost 200 grands prix behind him, that had become Berger's role. Times have changed, and so had the man famous for putting itching powder down his rivals' fire-proof combinations, for dropping Senna's carbon-fibre briefcase out of a helicopter and for letting loose a couple of dozen frogs in his team-mate's Australian hotel room (and then, when Senna had found and removed them all, saying something like

'Only another twenty to go – and have you found the snakes?'). So what is the life of a racing driver like in the era of corporate sponsorship packages and vertically integrated marketing campaigns?

'The driver's function is still the same,' Berger said, sitting in the Benetton motor home. 'It's to drive the car as quickly as possible. But the work has changed. Motor racing got more professional, as we know. It became more expensive. That meant increased sponsorship and bigger companies coming in. It's not a small club any more, it's a highly professional marketing instrument of huge multinational companies. And that's altered how people have to behave.'

The Austrian has altered less obviously than most. In the present-day paddock, an ambience permanently crackling with the static of psychological warfare, he is a notably relaxed presence. He speaks rapidly and crisply and is known to be unafraid to tell uncomfortable truths. He is his own man. While most of his rivals are rushing from motor home to garage, eyes down, desperate to keep the news of a technical breakthrough from their team-mates, Berger is more likely to be found propping his lanky form against a pile of tyres, shooting the breeze with a friend and casting an eye over the talent.

There are many stories about Berger and a lot of them involve women. When he and Senna spent three years together in the McLaren team, and were therefore usually booked into adjacent hotel rooms, they were both accustomed to being approached in the lobby by hopeful girls. Not wanting to seem disobliging, the monastic Brazilian would indicate his interest and give them a room number, which turned out to be not his but Berger's. A satisfactory arrangement all round.

So it's still possible for a chap to have some fun? 'Yes,' he said, with a hint of a grimace, 'but you have to be a bit more careful. I don't think that the race weekend is the right time to have big fun any more, because people would think of you as not serious.'

Berger was born in Wörgl, a small Tyrolean town in the valley below Kitzbühl. His father had started his own haulage business, which gave Gerhard an early intimacy with motor-ized transport. But his first experience of going fast was on skis. By the age of twenty he had a job running an offshoot of his father's company. He also had a daughter, Christina, by a girlfriend. Saloon cars and Formula Three led him to a Formula One début in 1984 at his home track, the formidable and much missed Österreichring, where he drove for ATS, a small team financed by a German manufacturer of road-car wheels.

His career has since included stints with Arrows, Benetton, Ferrari and McLaren, and it is perhaps the most eloquent tribute to his temperament, as well as to his talent, that he was invited back for a second spell at Ferrari and then made a return to Benetton. More usually a driver completes his contract with a team in the knowledge that they have learnt enough about him never to want him back in one of their cars again. But Berger has always been not just a fast and consistent driver but a good fellow to have around.

He is a professional racing driver who keeps his life and his work in proportion – although the severest critics might say that a bit less of a sense of proportion and a bit more obsession would have brought him a better reward than nine grand prix wins and two third places in the championship. He is serious enough about his job, however, to have become visibly agitated when his return to Benetton did not go smoothly in the early months of 1996. For, if Berger helped Senna locate his sense of humour, the favour was returned in full when Senna taught Berger what it means to be a racing driver. When he arrived at McLaren, Berger had won races and was known to be quick. Sharing a team with Senna, he learnt exactly how quick he was, and what it would take for him to become quicker.

'I think this was one of the times when I felt naïve,' he said, looking his interrogator in the eye rather than using the thousand-yard stare that most drivers affect. 'Because I'd already had many team-mates, people like Michele Alboreto, quick guys, and I never had a problem beating them. So, I thought, what about Senna? Beat him. But then I understood quite quickly that he had some special qualities.'

There were some straightforward problems. For a start, McLaren expected the 6 ft 1 in. Berger to fit a car tailored to Senna and his previous colleague, Alain Prost, both of them several inches shorter. It took the team more than a season to get around to alleviating the terrific discomfort in which he was required to do his job. Nevertheless, it was a while before the whole truth dawned. At the Senna–Berger level the game is as much about psychological supremacy as technical advantage. It must have been hard for Berger to admit that someone else was better than him. 'For me, no,' he said, quite sharply. 'I think you can always find somebody who's doing something better than you, so I don't have any jealousy. If I see somebody better it just motivates me to try to see what is he doing and try to do it the same way.'

The first thing he learnt from Senna was the right preparation away from the cockpit. 'I saw that his physical condition was very strong, so I had to start training. I had good natural fitness but I needed more. Then I saw his detailed work on the technical side, so I started to learn how to do that. But he had some special concentration that was better than any other driver. I was never able to do that the same way and I don't think anybody else in Formula One could, either.'

Before his partnership with Senna, during the first of his two spells at Ferrari, he shared a garage for a year with Nigel Mansell, with whom he had little in common beyond the basics of their profession. 'I think Nigel had already had some bad experiences with team-mates, so he didn't trust people at all. He tried to do everything for himself. At the time I thought it was wrong. Now I understand because I know that he'd been with [Nelson] Piquet before and things hadn't worked out well.' He had compliments, nevertheless, for Mansell's attributes as a racing driver. 'What was always great was his fighting. Physically he was not trained, but he was strong.' And, once he returned to Williams, a worthy world champion? 'Yes. I don't think he was good like Ayrton Senna or Alain Prost. But I think he was a quick driver, and a fighter.'

Since 1993, first at Ferrari and then at Benetton, Berger's team-mate had been Jean Alesi, the Frenchman of Sicilian ancestry, five years younger and originally expected to assume the favourite-son role at Ferrari left vacant by the death of Gilles Villeneuve in 1982. Like Mansell, Alesi had a driving style far removed from Berger's, which has made their presence in the same team sometimes problematic for their engineers, who favour a single solution to a single problem yet found themselves needing to develop the same car in two directions at once to satisfy two sets of requirements. With Senna, life was easier. 'Our styles weren't the same, but they weren't far apart. We could drive the same car. Now Jean's changed his style, so it's not such a big difference.'

When he returned to Ferrari in 1993 it was for a bigger retainer than anyone except Senna was then receiving. The team was on the floor and they were ready to part with around $10 million a year in order to put his experience alongside Alesi's fire. 'My job was to try and get a structure into the team – and in the second and third years we got back among the top teams. I don't want to say that it was just my work, some other people did a fantastic job – but I spent day and night thinking about it.'

Berger thinks of the first of those seasons, when the team was struggling with a computer-controlled active suspension system, as his worst ever in racing. 'We just couldn't get the car working properly.' At Estoril there was a particularly terrifying moment. As he was coming out of the pits after a mid-race tyre change, the computer went haywire. Instead of blending into the traffic the Ferrari went directly across the track into the barrier, just missing a line of cars coming by at 180 miles an hour. Two years later, with Schumacher's arrival confirmed, he declined the team's invitation to stay on and moved, with Alesi, to Benetton. 'It was difficult. They offered me a lot of money and were pushing very hard. But I was tired. I couldn't cope any more with trying to think about the strategies, about the technical side, about the personal relationships. I appreciated what they did, I had a good time, I was paid well, they liked me and I liked them.

But I wanted to go back to a team where I could just concentrate on the driving. And that's exactly what I have here.'

Inevitably, a number of commentators speculated that after the Senna experience, Berger had made the decision to leave because he didn't want to face the challenge of another super-quick team-mate. Not at his time of life, and particularly not a driver he was said to dislike as a man. 'No, I nearly stayed exactly because of the challenge to drive with Schumacher. But I just said, "Shit, don't look at Schumacher. You want to win races, be consistent in races, finish races. Which teams can give you this? At the moment, Williams or Benetton. So try to get a place there. Maybe being ahead of Schumacher in the same car would give you a special feeling, and it would certainly make him feel bad. But, at the end of the day, it's all for nothing." '

It was during Berger's first spell with Ferrari that he walked away from one of the most lurid Formula One accidents of the modern era. At Imola in 1989 his car was doing something like 180 miles an hour when it hit the wall at the curve called Tamburello and exploded in a ball of flames. Thanks to amazingly rapid and efficient rescue work by the fire marshals, he got out with nothing much more than scorched hands and the memory of coming close to death. 'It was very hard for me. If you're even a little bit normal, a situation like that stays in your brain. Before, I was happy to take risks. Even if the risk couldn't influence the result, I took it because I needed the adrenalin and I loved to be sitting there thinking, "Ah, I just spun through three-sixty! Good fun!" Then I started to tell myself, look, it's not so good if you do that and touch the wall, because you're going to end up injured or maybe paralysed. Afterwards, I got myself to the position where I could think, "OK, I'll take the risk if it's going to affect the result and if the result is important, like winning the race or getting on the podium. But don't kill yourself in free practice on a quick corner in the rain." ' Did it, then, slow him down? 'It's impossible to say. But if it made me slower, I must have been fucking quick before . . .'

What it certainly did was increase his general awareness of safety and his sense of responsibility, which came to the fore when Senna was killed four years later at the same curve. Berger took a central role in reconstituting the Grand Prix Drivers' Association, which had been originally created by Jo Bonnier and others in the early Sixties as a means of persuading the circuits and the team owners to consider measures to reduce the risks. Now, following the deaths of Senna and Roland Ratzenberger in the same weekend, the GPDA recreated itself principally in order to monitor the reconfiguring of circuits to cut out corners like Tamburello, which offered little hope of survival in the event of a crash. 'I'm not really interested in a lead role,' Berger said, 'but I like to see the drivers fighting on behalf of each other. I think the governing body should listen to the drivers because we're the ones who are sitting in the cars, and we have a different view.'

It was a view he had already enjoyed for ten years, during which he had continually been ranked among the handful of genuinely fast drivers. Yet he had never won more than two races in a season or finished higher than third in the championship. In the latter stages of his career, this dis-appointing record seemed unlikely to be improved much – and particularly not in the light of the troubles he was experiencing with Benetton, where the car developed by Schumacher turned out to be virtually undriveable by his successors. 'It's very simple,' he said. 'If I've finished third or fourth in the championship a few times, the reason is that I wasn't better than third or fourth. It's all bullshit to start talking about how I had this problem or that problem. It doesn't count. To be three or four times third to the world's best drivers is not something to be ashamed of. At Ferrari, Mansell was physically stronger than me and I was on antibiotics because of the accident [at Imola]. But in qualifying I was usually in front of him. Then he went to Williams and he won nine races in a season and became world champion, and therefore one of the greatest drivers of all time. The luck I never had.'

He got married a couple of years ago to a Portuguese woman called Ana; they have a baby daughter, Sara. Like most of the drivers, he calls Monaco home. After twelve years in Formula One the championship remains his motivation, although there is inevitably a sense that time is getting short. Already this was not shaping up as a promising season, having begun with a virus that wouldn't go away and continued with problems in making the car work the way he wanted, rather than the way Schumacher had liked it. For all the warm encouragement of the banners opposite the pits, people in the paddock were starting to say that he might be nearing retirement. 'Nobody likes to see the end of their career. But honestly, yes, I know there are two or three years and not much more than that.'

And which year had he enjoyed most? 'Oh, 1987, with Ferrari.'

In 1987, the Ferrari myth was still a living thing. The Old

Man was going to the office most days from the big house in the Piazza Garibaldi, still a year away from death. He watched on TV as Berger won the last two races of the year, at Suzuka and Adelaide. When Gerhard went back to the factory after a race, old Enzo would take him for lunch at the restaurant across the road, Il Cavallino, and ask him about the girls.

'In 1987 I went to the circuit in the morning, not knowing which set-up I had on the car, and I'd put it on pole or lead the race.' He smiled, more to himself than at me. 'I didn't know what I was doing but I was always in front. And I was so young and free in my mind that I didn't even know I was happy.'

A Ferrari was fastest in the unofficial practice sessions at Imola on Friday, and all seemed right with the world to the thousands in the grandstands. Michael Schumacher's labours appeared to be ensuring that Gianni Agnelli's investment would bear fruit and that the plot of the Formula One season would be following the script. At the Fiorano test track on Wednesday, Schumacher had completed seventy-three laps behind the wheel of the F310, a car now four races old and still in the early stages of its development. The titanium gearbox had been restored at the Nürburgring, along with the suspension and aerodynamic parts that went with it; Schumacher described it as 'a bit of an improvement'. He was trying various aerodynamic modifications intended to improve the car's handling and to ease the flow of air to the engine. The work took all day and was watched by Eddie Irvine, who was rapidly discovering what Nelson Piquet, Martin Brundle, Riccardo Patrese, J. J. Lehto, Jos Verstappen and Johnny Herbert could have told him, which is that to sign up as Schumacher's team-mate is to take on the hardest job in sport. Almost the hardest non-job, in fact, since lengthy periods of enforced inactivity are an unspoken condition of employment. And Irvine's empty day at Fiorano was typical of his season up to that point. Having begun the year by outqualifying Schumacher in Melbourne and finishing third in the race behind the two Williams cars, he had fallen behind to the extent that he was now virtually expected to be slower than the double world champion by a second and a half per lap.

That was no surprise, probably least of all to Irvine. When Schumacher made his Formula One début five years earlier it was immediately clear that he was blessed with the sort of natural speed seldom given to more than one driver in a generation, and which will one day put him alongside Ascari, Fangio, Clark and Senna in the pantheon of post-war greats. Pretty soon it also became obvious that he believes no team can run two cars at the highest level of competitiveness, which is the only place he is interested in being. His answer is to bend the team to his will, forcing it to concentrate all its efforts on him. Since he is both the man most likely to bring them the best results and utterly constant in his readiness to work the same hours as every other member of the team, they do this willingly. No mechanic minds putting in an extra effort for such a driver, and Schumacher had quickly commanded the devotion of a Ferrari crew weary from many years of frustration. By Imola, Jean Todt was already describing Schumacher as a 'reference point' for the team. What the team manager meant was that Schumacher was providing his engineers with the sort of consistent technical feedback that enables them to make meaningful adjustments to the thousand-and-one things that affect a Formula One car's performance. 'He's very professional,' Todt said. 'Everybody is keen to work with him and to help him succeed. So we concentrate on the testing with Michael, and Eddie doesn't complain.'

For confirmation of Schumacher's effectiveness it was necessary only to look at the plight of his old team. By their own former standards, Benetton were performing miserably. In Friday's practice, Alesi and Berger finished thirteenth and fourteenth. Even when the Benetton was a bad car, as Schumacher's was at the beginning of 1995, he never allowed it to look as bad as that, never less than competitive. Now the team had a development of last year's chassis, a development of last year's all-conquering Renault engine (still all-conquering in the Williams chassis), the same engineers and management. Only the drivers were different. So it must be them. Neither Alesi nor Berger, it seemed, was capable of driving the team as well as the car, of pushing the engineers towards the necessary technical solutions. So what did that say, in retrospect, about their three troubled years together at Ferrari? Was the problem not the team, as everyone imagined, but the drivers? And after wondering about that, perhaps it was legitimate to ask – as Flavio Briatore no doubt had, probably waking in a sweat – whether Benetton would have repeated their championships of 1994 and 1995 in 1996 had Michael Schumacher chosen to remain with the team rather than accepting the challenge offered by Ferrari.

But his move enabled us to make a further discovery about Schumacher: that he is also a brilliant politician who understands the place of realism in public rhetoric. Talking at Fiorano about his heroic second place behind Villeneuve at the Nürburgring the previous Sunday, he first expressed his pleasure at the result but quickly added a qualification: 'It has to be said that if Damon Hill hadn't experienced problems I would have finished not second but third.' The tone of this was consistent with every pronouncement he had made since signing his Ferrari contract the previous autumn. Understanding the emotional volatility of Ferrari's home public, knowing how unhappy they felt at the brusque removal of the highly *simpatico* Alesi and the loyal Berger, and how suspicious they were of his own perceived arrogance, he chose a modest approach. Underplaying the team's prospects ensured that necessarily gradual progress should not lead, as it so often does in Italy, to frustration and eventual disillusionment. Wisely, he appeared to stay out of the team's internal political struggles and look like he was just getting on with the job, not being lured into indiscretion. Again in Imola he was saying that the team was not yet ready to win. A place on the podium, he claimed, was the best he could hope for on Sunday. The time for victories would come in mid-summer. Until then, the fans must show patience and understanding.

On race day the local voodoo was running at full throttle. In Imola's elegant Piazza Matteoti there was a display of old cars centring on the very first Ferrari, the graceful 815 sports model raced by the young Alberto Ascari in the 1940 Mille Miglia, its carefully restored maroon coachwork and silver wire wheels glinting proudly in the sunshine. A mile away, across the turbid Santerno river, Don Sergio Mantovani, the drivers' chaplain, arrived at the track from Modena to hiss

God's blessings upon the home team. And minutes before the start of the race a shirt-sleeved Piero Lardi Ferrari, the Old Man's only surviving son, took his seven-year-old nephew – another Enzo – on to the starting grid to meet the drivers of the bright red cars, like a deposed monarch revisiting the land he was not strong enough to hold.

None of it worked. An hour and a half later, as Damon Hill stood on the podium acknowledging the applause for a convincing victory over the entire Italian nation plus Michael Schumacher, it was clear that he felt he had done more than merely win another race. He had answered his critics.

The amazing thing is that he should have been made to feel the need. In terms of sheer statistics, he was already up there with the very greatest British racing drivers. Hill had won seventeen of his fifty-six grands prix, compared with Mansell's thirty-one from a hundred and eighty-seven, Stewart's twenty-seven from ninety-nine, Clark's twenty-five from seventy-two and Moss's sixteen from sixty-six. And to anyone who thought it was because he was in the best car, it could be firmly pointed out that the instinct for getting yourself into the right team is as much a part of being a champion racing driver as the ability to drive the thing at the limit for an hour and a half on a Sunday afternoon. Fangio's entire career was a demonstration of that.

Hill had learnt to operate within his limitations. He had also enjoyed a certain amount of good luck, but he had worked for it. The run of victories was the reward for diligence, patience and planning, to which his contribution had been vital. 'It's good to get things back on track,' he said after the race, referring to the mistakes which had relegated him to fourth place at the Nürburgring the previous

Sunday, and for which he had been severely criticized. It may seem curious that a man who can lap somewhere like Imola at an average speed of a hundred and twenty-five miles an hour and race wheel-to-wheel with Schumacher or Alesi should not be built to withstand mere journalism. Hence the resentment that was continuing to colour his behaviour. Even after starting the season with four wins in five races, he was not at ease with his success. But in the San Marino Grand Prix, Ferrari's home race, faced by 130,000 paying customers desperate for his rival to succeed, he did the only thing an Englishman can do in such circumstances: he put his faith in his own grit and professionalism. He was not taking his victories flamboyantly, but now he was certainly taking enough of them to make us take him seriously.

9

'There was a girl with pale pink lipstick,' Stirling Moss remembered. 'She used to sit outside Oscar's Bar, by the side of the track going down from Casino Square to the station hairpin. It was opposite the Metropole Hotel, where I stayed every year. They gave me a 20 per cent discount. Anyway, I noticed the pale pink lipstick and I used to wave at her every time I went past.'

Moss won the Monaco Grand Prix so many times that he made it look easy: three wins in seven starts, and he was in the lead on each of the four other occasions before some sort of misfortune struck. (Later, Graham Hill was to win the race five times out of seventeen, but both of them were eventually topped, statistically speaking, by Senna, who triumphed six times in ten years.) But once in a while the opposition made the Englishman work. When his obsolete Lotus beat the entire Ferrari team at Monaco in 1961, skill and racecraft were his only weapons. 'It was rather like a fighter plane being chased by a superior enemy and being saved by dodging into clouds,' Denis Jenkinson wrote that night in his race report for the magazine *Motor Sport*. Moss drove lap after lap right at the limit, without a moment's relaxation, 'having no time to waste on waving to his friends . . . holding off the inevitable by sheer brilliance.' The photographs of Richie Ginther being lifted out of his Ferrari's cockpit after two hours and forty-five minutes spent chasing the Lotus's tail are classic studies of sporting exhaustion. Even the normally unemotional Moss, holding Prince Rainier's cup as the British national anthem played, felt 'the old eyes prickle'. It was, he thought, the greatest race of his life.

Thirty-five years later, it is fashionable to be cynical about Monaco's annual race around the houses. This is the one race to be sure to take the sponsors to: a table on the terrace of the Hôtel de Paris during practice; a party on somebody's yacht at the point where Alberto Ascari's Lancia somersaulted off the track and into the drink in 1955; a balcony suite at the Hermitage for the race, overlooking the entire harbour; champagne and a flutter at the Casino's *salon privé* and, with any luck, a flash of pale pink lipstick should be enough to get a signature on next year's contract. If all that doesn't work, nothing will. And anyway, even if you can ignore the thrusting and pouting ranks of Eurotrash, where's the racing? The circuit is so narrow and the cars are so wide that you can't get a clear lap in practice, and if you're not on the front row then you just haven't a prayer, old boy . . .

'Nonsense,' Moss said. 'In my time, Monaco and the Nürburgring were the real drivers' circuits. OK, it's a bit different now. What we drove were basically road-racing cars, whereas today's cars are developed for the track – and they're a lot wider, although the track's been widened, too. But it's still a place where skill can make up for technical deficiencies. If there's anywhere a car's shortcomings can be negated by skill, Monaco is the place.'

Funny things happen at Monaco. A procession often turns

into a drama. This can happen right at the beginning, as with the multiple crash at the old *tabac* bend on the opening lap in 1951, when Fangio guided his Alfa stealthily between the wrecked cars of Farina, González, Fagioli, Rosier, Trintignant, Rolt and Gerard, and through a river of petrol from ruptured tanks to take the first of his two victories. Or it can happen right at the end, as Jack Brabham found in 1970 when a last-lap charge by Jochen Rindt so disconcerted the most streetwise of racers that he went off the road at the final corner, the old gasworks hairpin.

The names have gone. The railway station has been replaced by a Loews hotel. The unsightly gasometer disappeared many years ago and the hairpin is now called after a restaurant, La Rascasse. The tobacconist is still there, but hidden away now under the scaffolding of a giant grandstand shrouding the old pits. Nevertheless the circuit's unique appeal has something to do with the fact that nowhere else are grand prix drivers confronted with a test so precisely resembling that faced by their pre-war counterparts. Steel barriers and advertising hoardings apart, when Michael Schumacher and Damon Hill roar up the hill and into Casino Square, the sight is the same one that greeted Rudi Caracciola. When Jean Alesi's car goes light and twitchy and then squats and snakes under acceleration down the narrow, bumpy chute to the Mirabeau, he is sharing a sensation known to Robert Benoist. True, if he then goes wide at the Loews' hairpin he will hit not a straw bale, a bit of baroque plasterwork or a pedestrian but a firm steel barrier such as one might find dividing the carriageways on an *autoroute*. But it remains a place that could make even the proverbially prosaic Nigel Mansell, describing the sensation of coming out of the tunnel backwards at a hundred and something miles an hour, sound as lyrical as a mid-Fifties playboy.

Monaco is not usually dangerous. Plenty of cars end up in the guard rails but the track has proved lethal only twice. In 1952 the temperamental, stubble-chinned Luigi Fagioli, the winner in 1935 but by then fifty-four years old and past it, lost control of his borrowed Mercedes sports car in the tunnel, smashed into a stone balustrade and died in hospital three weeks later. And twenty-nine years before Schumacher took pole for the 1996 race in his Ferrari, his predecessor Lorenzo Bandini, the handsome young favourite of every Italian race fan, turned over at the chicane on the eighty-first lap, landed on top of the straw bales and perished in the ensuing inferno, which was seen around the world on live television. The following year the race distance was reduced from a hundred laps to eighty and straw bales were never seen at a grand prix circuit again.

Modern grand prix drivers don't generally go a bundle on history. It's possible that none of the 1996 entry even knew the name of the first winner of the race, back in 1929. His team-mates weren't much the wiser. The name on the entry list was 'Williams'. Just that. No first name. That was how he identified himself when he raced as a member of the Bugatti works team in the late 1920s. William Grover, which turned out to be his real name, was a figure of mystery. Some said he was a rich amateur, others believed him to be a chauffeur in Paris. We know that his father was English and his mother French. The research of the journalist Joe Saward uncovered the information that in 1942, having enlisted as a driver in the Royal Army Service Corps, his perfect French attracted the interest of the newly formed Special Operations

Executive which recruited him, trained him in the techniques of undercover warfare and parachuted him back into France, where he landed at Le Mans, near the site of his second French Grand Prix victory. Thereafter he built a sabotage network in Paris, to which he recruited two more great French drivers, Benoist and Wimille. But in 1943 the network was uncovered by the Germans and Grover was tortured at Gestapo headquarters in Paris before being executed elsewhere, probably at Sachshausen concentration camp. Benoist, who escaped, was recaptured the following year and died at another camp, Buchenwald.

When 'Williams' won the first Monaco Grand Prix, he picked up a few thousand old francs for his efforts. Like Moss, he would have paid his own fares and hotel bills. Schumacher, leading the field round the parade lap in 1996, had just taken third place in the annual list of top-earning international sportsmen published by *Forbes* magazine, his £25 million a year putting him just behind the boxer Mike Tyson and the basketball genius Michael Jordan. What linked him to his predecessors across the generations was that narrow road up the hill from Sainte-Dévote and the skill and courage needed to hurl a car blind through the left-hander past the Casino entrance into one of sport's great amphitheatres and then back down the snaking hill to the seafront. It would be nice, but probably unrealistic, to imagine that sometime during the afternoon a driver would spot a flash of pale pink lipstick.

Schumacher put the Ferrari on pole for the second race in a row and no one was in any doubt that the achievement owed more to his innate brilliance than to any inherent quality of the car, which was still being subjected to revisions between every race. After hitting the barriers and putting himself out of Thursday's free practice, there were three minutes of Saturday's qualifying session to go when he beat Hill's time – itself a second faster than the 1995 pole figure – by half a second, a margin recalling Senna's supernatural qualifying performance on the same track in 1988, when the Brazilian found himself going so fast that he had to stop. Schumacher didn't have Senna's way of intellectualizing the experience, of examining the metaphysics of a fast lap, but there wasn't much doubt that he could drive himself into the same zone, where speed became something supernatural.

In the time left, Schumacher ran another lap that was almost as fast and then toured round accepting the applause of the many Italians and Ferrari fans of other nationalities in the crowd, just as Jean Alesi had done the previous year. Unfortunately, Schumacher stayed on the racing line, which meant that as Gerhard Berger came out of the tunnel on a hot lap and prepared to take the chicane, he found the Ferrari bumbling along on the piece of road he required. Berger tried to take avoiding action, spun the Benetton, and was going backwards as he shot past an astonished Schumacher. Mika Hakkinen, who was also on his best lap, was slowed by the incident. 'There are some forms of behaviour which are acceptable in grand prix racing,' Ron Dennis, Hakkinen's boss, said, 'and some which are not. I don't think doing a lap during an official qualifying session, waving to the crowd, is behaviour befitting a world champion.' No, but you could see the temptation, giving that he was driving a Ferrari, the Italian border was only a few miles away and Monaco was the circuit that probably offered him the best chance of booting the difficult F310 to a victory in the first half of the season, since it might minimize the car's defects. And Schumacher was properly contrite. 'It was purely my fault,' he said, words which are not often heard from a Formula One driver of any era.

In the paddock, where the trucks and hospitality tents are packed together on a strip of land next to the harbour, John Barnard talked quietly to his fellow Ferrari engineers, having arrived from the Ferrari design and development centre in Surrey in time for the qualifying sessions. Barnard, forty-nine years old, had long been thought of by the Formula One world as a genius. He created the McLaren-Porsche MP4/2 which took Niki Lauda and Alain Prost to their world championships in the mid-Eighties before moving to Ferrari for his first spell (when Prost came within an ace of the title) and then on to Benetton, where he worked with Tom Walkinshaw to revive the team. He was tempted back to Ferrari in 1992, just as the Benettons were turning the corner, but after four years of his second spell with the Italian team the jury was still out on his current standing. In recent years his cars had not looked right or worked properly on their first appearance and had been subject to revision throughout the season. Some said that Barnard had lost his touch, and that by shutting himself away in his carbon-fibre tower in Surrey he had lost contact not only with the Ferrari people at Maranello but also with current Formula One practice. In Barnard's view, the ability to communicate with the technicians in Italy by computer in real time was as good as standing next to them over a drawing-board. He didn't need to go across the road to Il Cavallino with them for a plate of lunchtime pasta in order to get the job done.

Nevertheless, whether he liked it or not, he had become part of a grand tradition of Ferrari designers which began with the likes of Aurelio Lampredi, Vittorio Jano and Gioachino Colombo and stretched into the Sixties and Seventies with Carlo Chiti, the designer of the famous 'sharknose' Ferrari which carried Phil Hill to the world championship in 1961, and the studious Mauro Forghieri, who drew up the blueprints for the cars with which Niki Lauda spearheaded the renaissance in the mid-Seventies. Enzo Ferrari's first designers were his cronies; they are in the old black and white photographs of the test days at the long-demolished Modena Aeroautodromo, in rakish hats and overcoats, bending over the bonnet of a 425 or a Dino 246 to admire the architecture of its front suspension or the perfection of its row of carburettors, usually with a priest loitering in the background.

Barnard's world is different. No impromptu arias are sung while his technicians peer at their blinking screens and no one spills red wine over his pristine keyboard. But Formula One races are not run on computers. The car has to be driven by a human being and Barnard was quite ready to pay tribute to the difference Schumacher's presence had made to Ferrari. 'Any time a driver brings the kind of commitment and speed that he brings, it reflects all around the team,' he said. 'And it's always easier when you're working from the front. You have to look back at the other guys who've been like that. Senna and Prost, for instance. It's the ability to concentrate the mind so much on the job in hand that everyone around him has to follow in the same way. It's hard for the rest. He's giving so much concentration all the time that the rest of us have to do the same for five or six days a week on a regular basis, and that makes it pretty tough. But when you start to get the results and you qualify on pole, that provides the incentive to keep going. And if we have a win, the morale will lift some more. It will just self-generate. It's more than simply a question of whether he gives us good technical feedback, which he does. It's a kind of a mental attitude, a total commitment. Technical knowledge isn't so important. To be honest, his knowledge of the car – what to do with it and what reactions the car will have – I wouldn't say they're super-special. They're like those of a number of good drivers I've worked with. But he has this innate ability to go quickly, which means he's able to concentrate on what the car is doing a lot more. That means that he can recount clearly every corner around the lap, exactly all the way through each corner, and this feedback is clear and sharp. It's what all the really good ones have got. Alain Prost was the same. You could talk about something a week after it had happened and he'd still give you the exact picture. It's that ability to use a lot of mental capacity to concentrate on all the other things that are going on while you're driving quickly that makes them extra-good. Prost had a very different driving style and when I worked with him we had much less telemetry and information-flow going on. There was more need for the driver to input the feeling and the information. Today we have all the telemetry and the electronics so we can look at what the car is doing ourselves. Those things develop and make each period different.'

My next question was not the most tactful one to put to the designer of the F310, even when it had just claimed pole position for the Monaco Grand Prix. Did he agree that part of Schumacher's special talent was the ability to drive over or round a car's basic faults? 'Yes, up to a point. There are a lot of circuits on which you can't do that. Some you can. But I suppose the thing about him is that he drives the car in such a way that there probably aren't many drivers who could get into his particular car and drive it at even half the speed he does. That's the way he drives it and the way he wants the car to work. It's hard to determine how big his ability to cover up problems on the car is because we're not driving it, so we can't actually see how big the problems are. But he certainly has the ability to drive a car which is what we call very loose, where the back comes out easily. He has an ability there that you would have to go a long way to match. It's car control, innate feel, reactions.'

A team that is on the up and up always looks well organized. But the Byzantine nature of the Ferrari team's internal structure had been such a focus of debate for so long that it looked as though the work done by Montezemolo and Todt to streamline and simplify it was at last bearing fruit. From the outside, though, it still looked complicated. 'Everybody talks about the organization, but it's not that different from before,' Barnard said. 'The fact is that my parameter in anything, any time I get involved with a team, is that you have to make the quickest car you can, quicker than everyone else. And once you've done that the other things fall into place. A lot of the problems that might be huge problems when you're struggling in the middle of the field suddenly become a lot smaller when you've got something that's quick. And when you've got a quick driver and a car which is reasonably quick as well, it makes many of the other things a lot less of a problem.'

Like a lot of the cleverest people in Formula One, Barnard has an enigmatic manner. It was impossible to know from his demeanour whether he was enjoying the day, the meeting or the season any more than he had enjoyed the troubled years that preceded it. Did something like Schumacher's pole position make any difference to his state of mind? 'Not really, no. My own commitment is something I generate within myself, and I've done it for too long now to go with the ups and downs. If I did go with the ups and downs then I'd have been out of it a long time ago. My side is the technical side. To keep going, I have to have my own goals and targets – even my own disappointments – and effectively keep them within myself. It's nice when you're up there and in the front, but that's what we're here for. So let's not wave and shout and jump up and down, because that's where we should be.' And how would he feel tomorrow if his much-criticized creation won the race? 'I'll be pleased, but I'll still be in there on Monday morning as usual, so it won't make too much difference to that.'

Forgiveably enough, the driver himself was a bit more emotional. 'Yes, it's surprising, even for me,' Schumacher said after the session. 'This morning I was six-tenths of a second off the pace and I was struggling to think how I could make it up. But obviously the track has got even better and when I had my new tyres it was quite early in the session compared to the other guys.' Half a second is a phenomenal margin, though. 'Yes.' Would he be able to repeat that everywhere, after this? 'I will try, yes.'

Something of Schumacher's acuity and decisiveness came through when he talked about how he had aborted the second of his three runs during the qualifying hour. 'We made a set-up change and it didn't work so I came straight back in. I saw my section times were down.' Meaning he had spotted, on the digital read-outs built into the thick upper rim of his squared-off steering wheel, that he was slower at the intermediate checkpoints and had decided to abort the effort in order to conserve laps and tyres. 'We were just trying something different but we made a little final change and that did it.'

The whole of Italy wanted to know if he could win the race. Did he believe the car had the necessary reliability for a race in which attrition often played a major role? 'I think we do. We've done a race distance at Imola with the new engine, everything was fine, and this circuit is usually a bit less hard on the engines so I don't expect any major problems.' And the controversial high-tech titanium gearbox? 'They always crack, but they last the race.' There was laughter. The world champion had made a joke. 'It's not the gear-changes, it's the force which goes into the gearbox from the bumps and so on. And they've done a great job on resurfacing here, so I don't expect anything worse than Imola. We've done a lot of work on the brakes and on the clutch. The effect is that we've significantly improved our start perform-ance. We were nowhere at Nürburg and Imola. We've found the reasons for this. I mean in 1994 in Benetton I did my best starts ever, and I've gone a good step beyond this. So I think the start should be good for tomorrow.'

This was a significant statement for two reasons. First, Schumacher's rocket-like starts in 1994 had been achieved with a Benetton which was widely suspected of carrying a variation of the outlawed traction-control system, matching engine revs to gear changes as the car left the start line. So if the Ferrari had managed to improve on the performance of that package, this was big news. Second, Schumacher's optimism was a contrast to the way he had previously dealt with the natural enthusiasm of the Italian fans by carefully underplaying the team's prospects. And he was willing to go further when he was asked if he felt confident for the race. 'Yes,' he said. 'I'm surprised about it myself. I came here with slightly higher expectations, but they were obviously right down after the Thursday practice. Now they have come back up again. So, looking good for tomorrow.'

Only three cars were left running at the end of the 1996 Monaco Grand Prix, and none of them was driven by Damon Hill or Michael Schumacher. Run on wet roads and punctuated by frequent incidents, the race produced a first victory for Olivier Panis, who ended a fifteen-year drought for the Ligier team and became the first Frenchman to win this almost-French race in a French car since René Dreyfus in a Bugatti in 1930. The results sheet made the race look like a throwback to the days when its particular demands and the mechanical fragility of earlier generations of racing cars meant that in most years fewer than half-a-dozen cars saw the chequered flag. Second this time was David Coulthard's McLaren-Mercedes, only five seconds behind Panis when the race was stopped after reaching the two-hour limit, with Johnny Herbert's Sauber-Ford half a minute further back in third.

Panis, a twenty-nine-year-old Grenoblois whose talent had been evident since he arrived in Formula One two seasons earlier, started the race from fourteenth position on the grid and deserved his win. Anyone who had watched the morning warm-up from the barrier on the outside of the Casino Square had a hunch that it was on the cards, since the harsh ferocity of the Mugen-Honda engine was matched by the verve and obvious commitment of Panis' driving as he topped the times for the session. In the race itself, inevitably he relied to some extent on the misfortunes of others, notably that of Hill, who was in complete command of a race that meant a great deal to him when his engine blew just after half-distance. Hill's path had been cleared when he made a much better start on the wet track than Schumacher, who had won the race in the previous two years but must have been regretting his words about the new clutch when he found himself a distant second going up the hill to the Casino. Clearly annoyed at himself for wasting the advantage of pole position in front of tens of thousands of German and Italian fans, the world champion pushed too hard and made a misjudgement less than a minute into the race, clouting the barrier at the downhill right-hander after the old station hairpin. Again, however, he made no bones about accepting the responsibility. 'I made a mistake at the start,' he said, 'and I made a mistake here, too. I'm very sorry for the team and angry with myself.'

Seizing the opportunity as the world champion began to walk back to the pits, Hill pulled quickly away from the two Benettons. Behind them a degree of carnage spectacular even by Monaco's standards removed more than a third of the field of twenty-one cars within the first five laps. Three cars – the Minardis of Giancarlo Fisichella and Pedro Lamy, who ran into each other, and the Footwork of Jos Verstappen – had failed even to get round the first corner. But Panis was already catching the eye. While others were simply trying to avoid the guard rails, he went past Brundle, Hakkinen and Herbert in the space of fifteen laps – all the more remarkable since he was also having to cope with a car made heavy by a full tank of petrol, a risky strategy aimed at saving time by making just one swift pit-stop. Meanwhile, Berger retired with a broken gearbox, giving third place to the surviving Ferrari of Irvine, who was holding up a queue of nine cars covered by less than eight seconds with a display of obduracy that eventually degenerated into sheer pig-headedness. Frentzen was the first to lose patience, breaking his front wing against Irvine's rear wheels at Sainte-Dévote and stopping for a replacement.

Hill had built up a lead of twenty-three seconds over Alesi by the time he headed for the pits, allowing him to resume only just behind the Frenchman. Within two laps the Williams, now fitted with slick tyres to suit the drying track, had repassed the Benetton and was drawing away again. Panis was up to fourth, only to find that it was his turn to be blocked by Irvine. The blue of the marshals' warning flags suddenly seemed to have taken on a distinctively French tint, but Irvine remained insensible to their urgency. Panis, sensing the chance of a good finish, decided not to wait. Coming down to the station hairpin he ran down the inside of the Ferrari, nudging it into the barriers. Irvine limped back to the pits and had his nose section changed. But before the Ferrari could wreak further damage, Hill's hitherto untroubled progress had come to an end. On the fortieth lap, the red oil-pressure light winked a warning. Halfway through the tunnel the next time round, a cloud of smoke deprived him of certain victory in the race his father won five times. As he climbed out he clasped his gloves to his helmet in a gesture of despair. 'It's been a long time since an engine let me down,' he said later. 'It was all going brilliantly. Our strategy was perfect.' So ended the Williams team's six-race winning streak.

Renault's own run of sixteen victories for their V10 engine looked like being extended as long as Alesi was in the lead, and for the next twenty laps he seemed likely to redeem a terribly disappointing start to his first season with Benetton, comfortably keeping ahead of Panis – who had spun, without damage, on Hill's engine oil – until his rear suspension failed. Thereafter Panis, Coulthard and Herbert needed only to steer clear of danger, which meant avoiding Luca Badoer, who was fined $5,000 for sending Villeneuve into the barriers and out of fourth place with eight laps to go, and Irvine, who spun at Schumacher's black spot and took Salo and Hakkinen with him.

The Ligier crew were justifiably delirious as their car crossed the line. Brought into Formula One in 1976 by Guy Ligier, a former rugby union international who had driven a Cooper-Maserati and a Brabham in a dozen grands prix in the mid-Sixties, they became loved for two reasons: for their *joie de vivre* particularly when contrasted with the corporate seriousness of their rival compatriots at Renault; and for their original number one driver, the enthusiastic Jacques Laffite, who gave them their first victory only a year after their arrival in the top flight. But after that bright start their subsequent fortunes had been less buoyant. At one point it seemed that only Guy Ligier's personal friendship with François Mitterrand ensured them access to Renault's engines, and it was with those engines in mind that Flavio Briatore bought 85 per cent of the team from its founder in

1994. The following season, the Renault engines had been switched to Briatore's Benettons while the Ligiers were having to make do with their seventh different brand of engine in twenty years – although, since it was the powerful Mugen-Honda, that was not exactly a disaster. And with Briatore came Tom Walkinshaw, who switched from Benetton to Ligier on the understanding that he would soon buy the team from its owners. But Guy Ligier's eventual refusal to part with his 15 per cent, at least on terms agreeable to Walkinshaw, led the Scotsman to end his involvement altogether, moving his attention to the purchase of the Arrows team. And while Walkinshaw had laid the foundations for a Ligier renaissance, at Monaco the team personnel were able to celebrate their victory as a predominantly French affair.

Panis took his lap of honour with a large tricolour flying from the Ligier's cockpit. This is the sort of gesture that Ayrton Senna and Nigel Mansell used to make, but it was outlawed after someone realized that not only did the driver have to stop to collect the flag, but someone had to jump over the barriers in order to give it to him. Nobody, however, was in the mood to press charges against Panis on a day like this. His victory was unlikely to affect the higher narrative of the championship battle, but it had made its own sweet little bit of history.

10

For Silverstone, you need to pack both the quilted anorak and the sunblock. This is the spiritual home of British motor racing, a disused Second World War bomber base on a Northamptonshire plateau where the weather can move from hailstorm to heatwave and back in the course of a single midsummer morning. Even after almost half a century of top-level motor sport, nothing looks quite permanent. The grandstands are made of scaffolding, the corners are regularly reprofiled and the bridges to the infield area are moved. It would only take a gang of workmen a week or two, you feel, to put the place back into the shape it was in when the B17s thundered down the runways.

Before the war, British motor sport made its headquarters at Brooklands, where wealthy amateurs bounced around the steep banking in their Bugattis and Bentleys under a famous slogan: 'The right crowd, and no crowding.' Located in suburban Weybridge, in the Surrey stockbroker belt, it created an ambience of Pimms blended with Castrol R, with a cast of characters including the American millionaire Whitney Straight and the English playboys Woolf Barnato and Tim Birkin. Had it survived, had a slice not been taken out of the majestic banking during the war to lengthen a runway for an aircraft testing centre, it would, in all probability, have established itself alongside Wimbledon, Henley, Royal Ascot and the Lord's Test in the English calendar of summer sport. But the war came and what happened to British racing in the aftermath was to change the face of Formula One.

During one of the practice days preceding the 1996 British Grand Prix, a small press conference was held to launch a report into the success of the British motor sport industry. Produced by the Institute for Public Policy Research, a left-wing think tank, it had been funded by Paddy McNally's Allsports Management, the company which sells advertising space on the hoardings around the grand prix circuits. In front of a minute audience, including the President of the FIA in lonely majesty in the front row, the sixty-page publication, titled *Playing to Win*, was summarized for the benefit of reporters by one of its co-authors, Dr Beverly Aston, a lecturer in finance and business strategy at the University of London.

First she described the scale of the industry's success. In 1995, she said, 633 British firms had been involved in the motor racing business, from eight Formula One constructors to twenty-eight suppliers of data acquisition equipment via six manufacturers of nuts, bolts and fasteners and one company making rod ends. Their turnover was conservatively estimated at around £2 billion, about 40 per cent of which came from exports. Then she described the origin of that success, tracing it back to the very different scene of the immediate post-war period when Germany, Italy and France were still the dominant powers in motor sport, as they had been between the wars. The key was the establishment of the 500 and 750 Motor Clubs, bodies made up of men who wanted to build cheap racing cars and discovered that the best way was to create a home-built 'special' by putting a chassis and a body around an engine taken from a British motorbike or a small family saloon such as the Austin Seven or the Ford Popular. There was no shortage of ingenuity, and they were keen to share their growing expertise. 'Many men under the age of forty had spent the preceding six years making, maintaining or operating fighter aircraft, military vehicles and weaponry,' the report said. 'The 750 MC's formulae were aimed at those who already owned the relatively inexpensive and basic Austin Seven, or could lay their hands on the parts. The Austin Seven was treated as a grown-up Meccano set which, when stripped down, served as the basis for a sports, trials, sprint or rally car. The handling of the original model was so diabolical that even a novice could make improvements.'

Since racing over public roads was illegal on mainland Britain, these would-be racers were forced to devise their own venues. Fate presented them with a selection of newly abandoned airfields across the country: Silverstone, Snetterton in Norfolk, Thruxton in Hampshire, Castle Combe in Wiltshire and Goodwood in Sussex, and lesser known or shorter lived ones such as Brough in Yorkshire, Stapleford in Essex and Greenham Common in Berkshire. All the organizers of the early post-war meetings needed was a few straw bales, a selection of flags and a rudimentary Tannoy system. Yet it was these humble airfields which, quite fortuitously, provided the impetus for the major cultural change which the British 'special' builders were to instigate.

In continental Europe, racing had started at the beginning of the century with a series of great city-to-city marathons over open roads, and the sport had retained its links with those early days. Even in the Fifties, some of the grands prix were still held on public roads specially closed for the occasion: Monaco, Spa-Francorchamps in Belgium, Pescara in Italy, Oporto in Portugal, Rheims and Rouen in France. Permanent circuits created between the wars had been designed to incorporate features that made them resemble natural highways, such as the gradients and the 175 corners, lined with trees and ditches, of the Nürburgring in Germany, or the partially cobbled surface of the great high-speed circuit in Monza Park. Endurance, too, remained a factor in these contests, an echo of the days when races were held in order to prove not just the speed but the reliability of cars which were still close to the models that ordinary people could then go out and buy for themselves. European manufacturers continued to build their racing cars with these historic echoes in mind: they needed to be rugged enough to withstand unpredictably bumpy surfaces, sometimes featuring kerbs, tramlines and manhole covers. Thanks to the airfields, this was not the way of things in Britain's emerging amateur racing scene.

'Club racing on smooth airfields fostered a new and different approach to race car design,' Dr Aston wrote. 'UK club constructors built race cars around proprietary engines. When a reliable engine was found a racing formula tended to develop around it. With the output of the engine fixed, although some modification may have been possible, the bulk of the engineering effort focused on squeezing competitive advantage from adjusting the weight and size of every other parameter (chassis, position of engine, suspension, transmission, brakes, wheels and so on). Winning races with an underpowered engine, offset by an ultra-light car with independent rear suspension, was viable in the UK because racing took place on smooth surfaces.' Dr Aston drew a parallel between the British motor clubs, with their hosts of enthusiastic young amateurs, and the Homebrew Computer Club of Stanford University in Palo Alto, California, where in the Seventies an informal atmosphere encouraged independence of thought and action, providing the spawning ground for Bill Gates and Steve Jobs, respectively the founders of Microsoft and Apple Computers. The first three key graduates of the 500 and 750 Motor Clubs were a trio who went on to exert remarkable influence within their field: John Cooper, Colin Chapman and Eric Broadley.

Grass-roots networking enabled these men to sell their expertise to those who admired the success of their early one-off designs. One-off became two-off, then series production. Ideas were tried and discarded or adopted with great rapidity, thanks to the availability of the best sort of laboratory: races every weekend at the new airfield tracks. John Cooper, who built more than a thousand motorcycle-engined 500cc Formula Three cars in the Fifties, was the first to break through into the world of commercial success. His little half-litre cars were as light as possible and their Norton or JAP engines were placed between the driver and the rear axle. When Cooper moved up to Formula Two, and eventually to Formula One, he held on to his principles. His cars remained light and nimble, thanks to the balance achieved by the location of the engine.

In 1958, with the aid of a subtle pit-stop strategy, Stirling Moss won the Argentine Grand Prix in a tiny Cooper, beating the Ferrari team with a car powered by a two-litre

Coventry-Climax engine adapted from a fire-pump motor. The Italians thought it was a fluke. When a former dirt-track driver from Australia called Jack Brabham won the world championships of 1959 and 1960 in John Cooper's cars, they began to realize that something significant was taking place. By 1961, Ferraris were rear-engined. And so, for ever more, was every other Formula One car, including Colin Chapman's Lotuses, masterpieces of lightweight construction which were to carry off six drivers' world championships for Jim Clark, Graham Hill, Jochen Rindt, Emerson Fittipaldi and Mario Andretti. Eric Broadley's Lolas did not have such spectacular successes in Formula One, but their founder was a better businessman than either Cooper or Chapman and success in other types of racing, notably at Indianapolis, permitted his company to remain so active into the late Nineties that it was able to announce a projected return to grand prix racing.

The motor clubs also produced the brothers Costin, the brilliantly original aerodynamicist Frank (who drew the shapes of the Vanwall and the Lotus XI, two outstandingly beautiful and effective racing cars of the late Fifties) and Mike, a co-founder of the company that, in 1967, launched the three-litre Cosworth DFV engine – a landmark design which, in return for Ford's investment of a mere £100,000, powered a variety of cars to more than 150 grand prix victories. Behind them came a generation including the engine specialist Brian Hart; the South African designer Gordon Murray, author of Nelson Piquet's lovely title-winning Brabhams; Tony Southgate, designer of the Le Mans Jaguars of the late Eighties; and Adrian Reynard, whose cars were to dominate a variety of single-seater categories around the world in the Eighties and Nineties. Generations begat further generations – Patrick Head and John Barnard, the two most gifted racing car designers of the Eighties and Nineties, both cut their teeth at Broadley's Lola factory.

The history of the sport was playing into their hands. Big crashes at Le Mans in 1955, when more than eighty spectators perished, and in the Mille Miglia in 1957, when the Marquis de Portago's Ferrari ploughed into the crowd, killing another fifteen people, aroused concerns about the security of the public. The deaths of many Formula One drivers during this period – Alberto Ascari, Eugenio Castelotti, Onofre Marimon, Harry Schell, Jean Behra, Peter Collins, Luigi Musso, Chris Bristow, Alan Stacey, Wolfgang von Trips and others – concentrated the governing body's mind on the safety of the pilots. The era of the open-road races was over. No more Pescara, Oporto, Rheims or Rouen. The emphasis was on specially designed, permanent circuits devoid of the sort of features that had once given each track its character. No accident could be allowed to start with a car losing control by hitting a kerb or getting stuck in a tramline. Now the circuits were to have uniform safety fencing, uniform medium-speed corners and a uniform lack of natural features. And they all, even the surviving road circuits like Monaco and Spa, had new surfaces made of silky-smooth, high-grip bitumen, which handed a decisive advantage to the light-weight British cars.

'By scaling up light cars,' Dr Aston wrote, 'the UK club constructors were competitive in Formula One, despite an underpowered engine, because minimal size and weight had been central to the design.' The veteran constructors, such as Ferrari and Maserati, found it hard to adjust their thinking to the new concepts. Steeped in their own traditions, used to manufacturing the engine and gearbox as well as the chassis, they lacked the flexibility to compete with the quick-minded inventiveness of men who were used to using outside expertise where necessary, pushing their external suppliers to raise their own standards. That inertia survives today in the problems of internal organization which continue to affect the fortunes of the Scuderia Ferrari, for all their talented employees and virtually unlimited budget. The British were light on their feet. A man like Colin Chapman could back his own sudden technical hunch, lifting the phone to get someone to make the necessary part by the next day. At Ferrari, everything took an age because it had to pass through an entire political process, subject to personal and departmental power plays (and, until his death in 1988, to the Old Man's whim).

The universal adoption of disc brakes, independent suspension, the monocoque chassis and the rear-engine configuration was the responsibility of the British. By contrast the Mercedes-Benz W196, which steamrollered all its rivals in 1954 and 1955, also bristled with technically adventurous features; yet it turned out to be almost the last of a line. The future was elsewhere, across the Channel, to such a degree that even Mercedes, when they returned to Formula One in the early Nineties, could not escape the British influence.

When Mario Illien, a Swiss engineer, wanted to create a company to build racing engines, he set up Ilmor in Brixworth, near Northampton. Before long Ilmor was building engines with the Mercedes-Benz name inscribed on their cam-covers. These engines were put first into Sauber cars, then into McLarens in Europe and into Penskes in America;

all the cars carried the Mercedes three-pointed star on their noses. When I asked Norbert Haug, who was running the Mercedes competition programme, whether Mercedes had any technical involvement in the engine, he replied: 'What is Ilmor? What is Mercedes-Benz? Ilmor is Mercedes-Benz, there is no difference. So you could say that all the input is Mercedes-Benz. We formed a partnership that works. Nowadays the seats in your car are fitted by another factory and you're doing a joint venture with them. I think the right way to go, as a global player like Mercedes, is to form partnerships. You don't have to prove that your piston was built in Stuttgart-Untertürkheim. You just have to prove that your system works. You can have an engine partner in Brixworth and a chassis partner in Woking and another one in Poole. We're convinced that's the way to go.'

So you could say that the really significant moments in the rise of the British motor racing industry came when the Vanwalls beat the Ferraris and the Maseratis in 1957 and 1958; when the Coopers and Lotuses revolutionized racing car design over the next ten years, setting the patterns for the future; and when Mercedes-Benz, a company which had exerted absolute domination over grand prix racing in the Thirties and the mid-Fifties with cars built and designed by German engineers and technicians at the company's headquarters in Stuttgart-Untertürkheim, came back to Formula One with an engine built in Northamptonshire and a chassis constructed in Surrey.

The underlying paradox is obvious. How on earth could the British motor sport market generate such booming success and establish such pre-eminence at a time when the country's mainstream motor manufacturing was being systematically destroyed? How could an industry that produced world-beaters like Chapman, Cooper, Costin, Williams, Head, Dennis and Barnard allow – for example – the companies that came together in the successive forms of the British Motor Corporation, British Leyland and the Rover Group to be driven so far into the ground that their remaining constituent parts had to be sold off to BMW of Germany, Ford of America and Volvo of Sweden? The answer must be that the Chapmans and the Heads could not have put up with the intellectual constriction of a great nationalized conglomerate, with its bureaucratic inertia and (in the Sixties and Seventies) its crippling warfare between lacklustre management and destructive unions.

Philosophically, Formula One racing is the antithesis of the command economy; its technical geniuses owe their freedom of thought and movement to a belief in competitive autocracy that runs right through the sport. What a waste, though, that the sum total of the legacy of British motor racing to its parent industry amounts to little more than the Cooper and Lotus badges on lovingly preserved thirty-year-old Minis and Cortinas. And nowadays even that little gift goes abroad: the Williams badge is on a Clio produced by its engine partner, Renault.

Yet the strain of genius survives and flourishes, strengthened by example. For contrast, ask how many Italian constructors have established themselves in Formula One since the retirement of Maserati almost forty years ago. What happened to Tecno and Alfa Romeo? Why has a Minardi never come close to winning a grand prix, after more than a decade in Formula One? Where are the cars of Enzo Osella, Gianpaolo Dallara and Guido Forti now? Can the

Benetton-Renault, entirely built in England and France, really be considered an Italian car, as its entry form states? From time to time British constructors have also disappeared, big names like Lotus and Brabham succumbing to natural selection along with the tiddlers such as Pacific, Simtek and Hesketh. But they are always replaced, and the British presence continues to define the technology of the game.

Look around the paddock. Look at Patrick Head, who works back in England at a desk beneath a picture of his father racing a Cooper-Jaguar in the Fifties. Look at Ron Dennis, who began his career as a mechanic, built a company called Project Four that became strong enough to take over the ailing McLaren team and went on to win a series of crushing world championship victories with Lauda, Senna and Prost, and who now sits down at the negotiating table with the chief executives of multinational businesses and dreams of creating a technology park incorporating a sort of Harvard Law School for young boffins. Look at Ken Tyrrell, a Surrey timber merchant who is now the doyen of the paddock, even though his last grand prix victory came in 1983, which means that his cars won twenty-three races during his first thirteen years in Formula One – and none at all in the subsequent thirteen years – yet who survives, thanks to the ability of his engineers and to the FOCA bonuses. And look, of course, at Tom Walkinshaw.

Amid the bustle and posing of the Formula One paddock, Walkinshaw is not one of the more obviously charismatic figures. As the photographers press around Ferrari's visiting royalty, Gianni Agnelli and Luca di Montezemolo, or Benetton's flamboyant Flavio Briatore, a small, square, deceptively soft-spoken Scot who wears the same uniform as his mechanics can go about his business largely unhindered. In fact, Walkinshaw is one of the sport's hard men, a scrapper and a grafter whose location at the humble end of the Silverstone pit lane in 1996 was sharply at odds with his twenty-year record of success in motor sport. This condition, in his view, was merely temporary.

Walkinshaw, a multi-millionaire from his varied business dealings, is an interesting combination of racing nut and wheeler-dealer. The major manufacturers who have benefited from long-term partnerships with his engineering company appreciate his understanding of business philosophy as much as his knowledge of suspension geometry. He talks their language. His conversation is full of formulations – 'core pools of competence' and 'proper business structures' – which might seem oddly suited to his background as a former driver of racing saloons.

A Jim Clark fan in his boyhood, he had progressed through an apprenticeship in the Scottish club racing scene and was already well known as a hard and highly competitive driver when he founded Tom Walkinshaw Racing in 1976. He admired the genius of Colin Chapman, the 'pure' designer, but also the business methods of Roger Penske, the American team boss whose success and ability to develop relationships with his sponsors led eventually to a seat on the main board of Philip Morris. From the beginning, TWR was a vehicle for forming partnerships with major manufacturers who wanted to benefit from the publicity associated with a successful racing programme but lacked the specialist knowledge to make themselves competitive. Walkinshaw would supervise their racing projects, taking the shells and engines of their production cars but then subjecting them to the expertise of his own staff of engineers. BMW and Mazda were his initial clients and in his first year he drove a BMW to victory in the Silverstone Six-Hours race. Similar victories and several touring car championships came his way before he began a relationship with British Leyland which saw a TWR Range Rover win the Paris–Dakar Rally in 1981 and then, a year later, the beginning of the Jaguar project. Walkinshaw built racing Jaguars for ten years, during which they won the European touring car championship and, twice, the 24 Hours of Le Mans – a race with a special place in Jaguar's mythology, since they had won it five times in the Fifties – *en route* to capturing the world sports car championship. TWR built Jaguar's XJ 220 'supercar' and entered further saloon car racing partnerships with General Motors and Volvo.

But Walkinshaw had always kept the top rung of the racing ladder in view. He maintained an interest in single-seater racing by running a Formula Three team, allowing him to keep an eye on new driving talent, and in 1991 he acquired a significant shareholding in the Benetton Formula One team, of which he became technical director, with a brief to establish the team among the front-runners after several seasons of mediocre performance. It was Walkinshaw in two of his incarnations – the perceptive talent scout and the merciless predator – who engineered the lightning coup that brought Michael Schumacher to Benetton within days of his grand prix début for Jordan in 1991, and Walkinshaw in a third guise – the shrewd organizer – who put in place the team of engineers (Ross Brawn, Rory Byrne and Frank Dernie) that was to be responsible for giving Schumacher the machinery with which he won two world championships and nineteen grands prix during his four-and-a-half seasons with the team.

Yet sharing a team with the Benetton family and Flavio Briatore, the team's managing director, did not satisfy Walkinshaw's ambitions. In 1994, after Briatore had added 85 per cent of the shares in the Ligier team to his personal portfolio, Walkinshaw moved over to become technical director of the ailing French team with the promise that he would eventually be able to buy not just Briatore's holding but also the 15 per cent retained by Guy Ligier, who had founded the team in the Seventies. Typically, Walkinshaw took a core of his technical personnel over to the new team, building a car for the 1995 season which closely resembled that year's new Benetton – thus drawing charges from other teams of illegitimate co-operation between the two concerns, which would constitute a breach of the sporting regulations. Walkinshaw managed to satisfy the governing body that no rules were being infringed and it soon became clear that TWR's involvement was reviving the team. But the project went sour at the end of 1995 when Ligier's sudden refusal to sell his shares frustrated Walkinshaw, who was only interested in 100 per cent control.

When Briatore agreed to take back his majority holding and look for another buyer (who was to appear in the shape of Alain Prost, at the head of an all-French consortium), Walkinshaw reset his sights. And so, early in 1996, he spent £6 million on buying the Arrows team – which had been in existence since 1978, racing continuously in Formula One without managing to win a single grand prix. Confusingly, and for reasons to do with an old sponsorship deal and the regulations restricting name-changes, the cars were now called Footworks, but Walkinshaw was buying the company from the men who had founded it and run it for eighteen years.

It might seem a lot to pay for a team that had spent almost two decades trundling around in midfield, but for the new owner this was simply a convenient method of acquiring not just his own team but the benefits enjoyed by an established outfit. These arrived principally in the form of transportation subsidies handed out by Ecclestone's Formula One Constructors' Association according to a formula which, for many years, was a better-kept secret than the latest Benetton transmission software but which took into account the duration of membership of the organization. 'The financial side to it is reflected in the price you have to pay,' Walkinshaw observed. 'The people who ran the team knew the value of the FOCA benefits. You don't get anything for nothing. But I think to take over a team that's been part of the establishment for quite some time has a benefit that's intangible.'

The poor competitive state of the Footwork cars represented no deterrent; that could be fixed, as Walkinshaw had fixed such things many times before. 'Basically it didn't make any difference how Arrows were competing,' he said a few days before the British Grand Prix, looking thoughtfully at the large Japanese koi carp gliding listlessly around the black-tiled pond set into the floor of his office at the team's new headquarters. Hidden away down a country lane a few miles north-west of Oxford, this old British Telecom training centre was rapidly being transformed into a high-tech, high-security, low-rise, low-profile research and development centre to match the Williams or Benetton facilities in the same part of England. 'What we were looking for was a core pool of competence in the team, which Arrows had. It was a small team so you can work with the best of those people and add to them whatever is necessary to win a championship.'

When it came to adding to the pool, Walkinshaw had plenty of his own competence upon which to call. TWR was employing 1,300 people on a variety of race-team projects, which included operating Volvo's successful racing car programme in Britain, a similar project for General Motors in Australia, a British Formula Three team and a large engineering consultancy which designs road cars for mainstream manufacturers. A month before Silverstone, one of his sports car designs, commissioned by Porsche to fit around their engine, gave him another Le Mans victory.

So he was not in Formula One merely to make up the numbers or to pick up the travel perks. When he took over Arrows he thought it would take him three years to transform it into a championship-winning team. But if such a swift transformation were possible, did it mean that Formula One is actually a softer target than its top people would like us to believe? 'Well,' he said, 'I went into Benetton at the end of 1991 and restructured that team when it was little better than Arrows is at the moment. I put a lot of our people from TWR in and built it up and we won a world championship within three years, with Michael Schumacher. That team had a lot of good commercial backing, but we had to restructure the entire engineering side.' He was on the way to doing the same thing with Ligier, after only a year in charge, when the plan to buy the team collapsed. 'That was a complete no-hoper outfit but we turned it round and got a lot of momentum going.' A few months after he had left, the team took its first win for fifteen years at Monaco.

How had he felt when Panis took the chequered flag? 'Good and bad. To take Ligier, which was no better than Arrows, to turn it round, motivate everyone and eventually get a result at Monaco ... we'd got a lot of momentum going, so it was disappointing when we had to pull out for political reasons in France. But you have to be philosophical and get on with something else. When it came to it, Guy Ligier didn't want to be out completely and started stirring up a lot of nonsense and it just ended up a complete mess. Formula One is too difficult a business to get yourself involved in a whole lot of stuff that weighs you down and prevents you from delivering what you should when you should. I took the decision that we were never going to win a championship carrying that amount of baggage.'

So Walkinshaw started again, moving his little band of technicians and engineers on to the next task. 'We still have the engineering and we can put it into Arrows. The challenge now is to raise the money from outside to fund it. With any team it takes you three years to deliver a championship because you've got to get a certain critical momentum going. You can win the odd event a lot sooner than that, but to get everyone in the team to a level at which they can stand the pressure so that they react and behave in the correct way when they're going head to head for a championship, that takes time. In my experience it takes two years of hard work.'

When the Ligier deal fell apart, he decided that he didn't want to waste another year. 'The first year with any team is a construction year, so there's little chance of being successful. I wanted to get on this year and build up in order to be fully competitive in 1997. When Arrows were on the market it made quite a lot of sense for us to take them over and start all the reconstruction, putting in a proper infrastructure and so on. This is our reconstruction year, if you like.' In terms of personnel, he made an analogy with football or rugby teams. 'Individually the players could all be the most talented in their positions, but you've got to get them to work together, each changing slightly to accommodate the next guy. We have to educate the staff in our philosophy and help them understand why we want things done a certain way, to help them deliver their full potential. You only need one guy to screw up a pit stop and it can cost you a championship, no matter how good your driver is. There's very little we can do this year other than begin to educate the staff. Our effort is going into designing the car for next year.'

His habit had been to move about a dozen key people from his organization into any new Formula One project. 'They're not necessarily the same people and we don't always leave them there. The first priority is to start putting a proper business structure in, proper processes for manufacturing, quality control and so on, so you can start to get a reliable car. Then when it's reliable you can start to go looking for the performance. We have quite efficient processes, which are all based on road car systems, and I think to a great degree it explains the reliability that our cars have enjoyed. If you're looking at designing a road car you have to make sure that you have the proper system to analyse every single component and control it from the initial drawing to the final version and its use. We implemented those systems in our sports car programme when we were doing endurance racing and they paid off. I put them into Benetton when we restructured the team in 1992 and we were the first team for about thirty years, I think, that scored points in every single championship round.'

There would probably be other changes, starting in the cockpit. Walkinshaw hoped to hire an experienced driver to work alongside a younger man. 'If we can generate the funding that I hope for, I'd be wanting to have an established driver. I think there'll be a few on the market at the end of this season. What you'd get is stability: been there, done that, doesn't get fazed. That can keep the younger driver on the straight and narrow and he can then deliver the speed he's capable of.' At that stage there was no indication that the next world champion might be on the market, or that Walkinshaw might be in a position to attract his services.

The search for a new main sponsor was among his priorities. 'It's not easy to generate the sums of money necessary to run a Formula One team these days. And it's particularly difficult for teams from the middle to the back of the field, because if you're spending substantial sums of money and wanting pretty guaranteed success, it's essential that you establish yourself as a solid runner quickly. But different manufacturers put in different sums of money. When we did sports car racing we won three world championships for Jaguar and I reckon the budget we ran on was, at the most, about a third of the other manufacturers we were racing against and beating. I often think that having a small budget focuses everyone's attention on the priorities, to get value for money on your research and development. Unlimited funds are not always the best thing to have. Look at some of the best funded teams in Formula One, they're the ones that are delivering the least result.'

There was also an interesting little argument going on

over whether Walkinshaw would be allowed to change the name of the cars. Arrows was the original name, but it had changed to Footwork when a Japanese sponsor came in and injected finance in 1991. Now the team was called Arrows, but the car was called a Footwork. It would have seemed sensible for Walkinshaw to change the name on the nose to TWR, but he was restrained by a rule which said that all FOCA teams had to agree to such a switch. This had been devised to prevent buccaneers coming in and taking advantage of the travel subsidies available to old-established teams, but when McLaren's Ron Dennis explained his opposition to Walkinshaw's desire to change the name he advanced a reason that had to do with tradition and the desirability of maintaining names familiar to the public. Coming from Dennis, who swims and survives in the shark-pond of free-market capitalism, that seemed odd. 'I got a letter last week,' Walkinshaw observed, 'which said that Ron's agreed to sign the letter consenting to a change of name. I personally don't see the sense in forcing a team to have the name that it's had for twenty years if someone else wants to fund it and take it forward. I think the team should be allowed to call it whatever they want. They own the brand and if they think it's no longer worth anything and they want to put a new one on it, that should be their decision. I don't think other people should be allowed to influence that. It's a commercial decision about a company asset and you should be allowed to do what you will with it.'

Other changes in prospect for Arrows included a switch to tyres made by the ambitious Japanese Bridgestone company, representing the first challenge in several years to Goodyear's monopoly. There would also be a brand-new chassis and a new engine from a supplier as yet unidentified. The engine market had just been thrown into turmoil by Renault's announcement that they would be leaving Formula One at the end of 1997, and Walkinshaw's long experience of collaboration with major manufacturers had given him a particular insight into their strategic thinking. 'Renault have enjoyed enormous success over the last decade,' he said, 'but the more success you have, the less impact it has. Once you've been winning regularly it's only big news when you fail to win. It rebounds on you after a while.' Mercedes-Benz, for instance, withdrew in 1955 after two seasons of virtually unbroken victories. They pulled out partly because they had achieved their publicity aim, but also because they were worried about the effect on their image of the Le Mans crash, in which one of their cars had caused carnage. (In contrast, Ferrari did not pull out of racing after the Mille Miglia crash two years later, despite pressure from the Vatican – thereby demonstrating the philosophical difference between a company that races in order to advertise the road cars which are its real business and one that sells its road cars in order to fulfil its destiny, which is to race.) Renault, too, had previously ceased to run their own grand prix team in 1985 for negative reasons, when their thirsty turbo engines kept running out of petrol. Television pictures of a stranded yellow car with the maker's name in large letters on the engine cover, together with a commentator's words about uneconomical Renaults, were damaging to the company's image.

This time, however, the withdrawal appeared to have been caused by a surfeit of success. 'Maybe they've decided to pull out for a period of time in order to be able to come back in and get full credit for their achievements,' Walkinshaw said. Other manufacturers, such as Audi and Volvo, had been sniffing around Formula One and he didn't think they would be put off by Renault's announcement. 'It won't encourage them any more, either, because there's very little difference now between the top engines. It's the package of the car, the engine and the driver that's delivering the results. Anyone who aspires to winning grands prix has to have a plan to put that complete package together, not just to supply an engine to somebody.'

Walkinshaw thought, however, that the significance of Formula One to major manufacturers might be changing. 'It's going through a transition,' he said. 'A few years ago it was the pinnacle of technology and a lot of manufacturers were interested in being involved because of the speed of the technological development. For various reasons, a lot of them cost-driven, Formula One has been trying to redefine itself and it's not quite clear at the moment what message it's sending out to the industry. It hasn't been helped by the recession. Everyone is analysing their investment much more closely. I think we've got to get back to a clear direction. Do we really want to display our competence in developing and exploiting new technology, or is it just to be a show? And, if it is, what do you need for it to be a show?'

The change of emphasis, or perhaps the uncertainty, seemed to have been introduced at the end of 1993 when the new generation of complicated and highly expensive computerized driver aids such as traction control and active suspension, most of them devised by British engineers, were outlawed. 'The ban may have been introduced with the right intentions,' Walkinshaw said, 'but it raised the question: is Formula One changing its direction? People in the industry are looking and waiting to see the fallout of all that before they commit the substantial sums of money necessary to become involved in it. It's not just engine manufacturers, it's on every level of the suppliers who are using Formula One to develop their new technology rapidly, in a way that was having a massive benefit to the motor industry. If there aren't the freedoms, and perhaps the best reasons in the world are behind them not being there any more, that opportunity is now denied them and that causes everyone to re-evaluate whether they're getting benefit from their investment.'

Only 10 per cent of Walkinshaw's business is now directly connected with racing; his operations around the world include such projects as the design of the Aston Martin DB7 and a company set up with Volvo to design and build 'niche' vehicles. But the reputation accruing from TWR's racing success is what makes all this possible, and his own explanation of his personal motivation takes account of that combination. 'On the technical side you're looking to determine the maximum you can take out of the car and deliver your team a competitive package. At the same time you're conscious that you have to put on a good show because that's what the public and the media want. So there's always a balancing act. That's always gone on, it's no different now from how it's been for the last twenty years. But I like the technical aspect and what can be extracted from the rules and regulations, the car and the technology to deliver a winning package.'

None but the fittest survive in Formula One. At Silverstone in 1996, even in the reduced twenty-car field, hardly anyone noticed the Footwork-Harts of Jos Verstappen and Ricardo

Rosset, trailing in the wake of Hill and Schumacher. Next year things would be different. After all, would anyone want to bet against the man who dreamed up the 170 miles-an-hour Volvo?

Walkinshaw looked across at the sullen shoal of koi carp, which the Japanese cherish as a symbol of good luck. 'They aren't doing too well,' he said. 'They may have to go.'

Tony Blair was on the grid at Silverstone, posing by Damon Hill's car on pole position and chatting to television reporters, making himself visible in the run-up to the 1997 British general election. But if he needed a reminder not to count his votes before they were cast, and then to stay calm and wait for a recount, he was given one when Jacques Villeneuve trumped his team-mate at the start and pulled out a winning lead. Hill, who had come into the race on an overwhelming tide of patriotic support and optimism and with a lead of twenty-five points in the championship, retired before half-distance, spinning off into the gravel trap at Copse Corner when a front wheel-nut worked loose. Villeneuve, taking his second victory of the season, reduced Hill's lead in the world championship standings to fifteen points, with six races to run. In second place, nineteen seconds behind Villeneuve's Williams-Renault, came Gerhard Berger in a Benetton-Renault, with Mika Hakkinen's McLaren-Mercedes a further half-minute back in third. For both men the race represented a welcome upturn in a dismal season, while the two Jordan-Peugeot drivers, Rubens Barrichello and Martin Brundle, were happy with fourth and sixth respectively, sandwiching David Coulthard's McLaren.

To all intents and purposes, the race as a spectacle lasted

a few hundred yards that separate the start line from Copse Corner. In the twenty seconds or so that it took the field to arrive at the fast right-hand bend, all the meaningful overtaking was done. On the start line, Hill could not match his engine speed to the bite of his clutch and the adhesion of the part-worn set of tyres that he had chosen. As wheelspin robbed him of momentum, Villeneuve shot past on the inside, followed by Hakkinen. 'We'd planned to get the jump on Damon,' Jock Clear, Villeneuve's race engineer said with evident satisfaction. When asked what had caused Hill's bad start, Villeneuve remarked: 'I don't care what caused it. I was just happy about it.' Behind Hill, Schumacher also faltered momentarily, allowing Alesi to zip by with such speed that the Frenchman's Benetton was also past Hakkinen and challenging Villeneuve by the time they arrived at the braking point for Copse Corner.

Schumacher, meanwhile, had found his way by Hill and was in fourth place, behind Villeneuve, Alesi and Hakkinen as they crossed the line at the end of the first lap. While Villeneuve disappeared into the distance, the rest squabbled among themselves. But as they went into the third lap the world champion's race was over. Suddenly Schumacher found himself able to select only sixth gear, and although he had managed to finish second in Barcelona two years earlier with only fifth gear at his disposal for most of the distance, this time the challenge was too great. Three laps later, less than ten minutes into the race, he was joined in the Ferrari garage by Irvine, who was reported to have suffered a broken differential bearing. Thus the Ferrari nightmare, which had featured a full set of ignominious retirements in the previous two grands prix, reached a new pitch of intensity.

The myth of the great Enzo is so potent that it deceives many people into believing that the first forty years of the Ferrari story must have been a tale of unbroken success. Wrong, to say the least. Ascari's steamroller championships of 1952 and 1953 were followed by a decline so vertiginous that by the end of 1955 the team was in danger of going out of business and was saved only by the decision of the Italian government to hand over to Ferrari the remains of the Formula One team launched at the beginning of that season by Lancia, which had subsequently gone bust. Lancia's lovely D50, slightly modified, was the basis of the car which took Fangio to the championship in 1956, reviving the team's fortunes. Again, in 1973, the cars and their results were so appalling that Ferrari was reduced to sending a single entry to the British Grand Prix. One of the ugliest and least efficient Formula One cars ever seen, it was qualified a pathetic eighteenth by a disgusted Jacky Ickx, who hauled it round to finish eighth in the race but would probably rather have stayed at home. Still, the total embarrassment of that performance led directly to the inauguration of the Montezemolo/Lauda era, helping to create the subconscious belief in most grand prix fans that somehow, someday, the Ferraris would always return to their rightful place at the front.

The 1996 instalment of the permanent renaissance was not going well. Ever since the early discoveries of the F310's disturbing tendency to change its handling characteristics in mid-corner and the fragility of its expensive titanium gearbox casing, a programme of continuous modifications had been under way at Shalford and Maranello. First came a humiliating reversion to the previous year's gearbox and its associated aerodynamic components, while the titanium case was first strengthened and eventually replaced by a design in heavier but more robust steel. There was clearly still trouble with the car's clutch, and at some point the troublesome Japanese Daiko product was abandoned in favour of a mechanism by Fichel & Sachs. Barnard had spoken at the launch ceremony about the design being a unity, that to alter one component would mean changing everything because the whole thing was conceptually interlinked – yet in Canada such designer-speak had been rendered meaningless when the car appeared with a raised nose, copied from Benetton and Williams, representing a significant reconsideration of its aero-dynamics. Nevertheless, Montreal had been a disaster.

'A Calvary for Schumacher,' the *Gazzetta dello Sport* proclaimed when electrical problems on the grid forced the team leader to switch to his spare car, starting from the back and later retiring with a broken driveshaft; Irvine's suspension had already collapsed on the first lap. At the French Grand Prix it was Irvine's turn to start from the back row, the result of a protest by Williams against the legality of the Ferrari's air deflectors. True, Schumacher was on pole. But his car had not even completed the parade lap when smoke was seen to be issuing from the Ferrari's engine, and the car was out of the race before the grid had formed up. Irvine lasted only five more laps before his gearbox failed. 'Recriminations are useless,' Schumacher said, showing both loyalty and pragmatism. 'I couldn't have imagined so many problems all at once. But there's no point in getting discouraged. We must continue to work.'

On the Friday at Silverstone, Gianni Agnelli and Luca di Montezemolo had paid a morale-boosting visit to the team.

Wisely, they left before the race itself, although they could not escape the new round of recriminations and accusations back home. Schumacher, whose brilliance alone had been responsible for the new car's single victory to date, was not yet ready to admit in public the extent of his disillusion, but his face in the paddock afterwards suggested that he would be looking for honest answers to a few hard questions. 'We've done full race distances in testing without trouble,' he said. 'We came here to Silverstone and we ran on Friday and Saturday without problems. It's not easy to understand, after three races like this. But I'll keep my motivation, I'll keep trying to motivate the team and I still believe the rest of the season can be good for us.' An even larger knot of inquisitors surrounded Jean Todt, the beleaguered Ferrari team manager. 'I feel sorry for every member of our team,' he said, 'because they are all good people. I feel sorry also for our fans.'

All this was being observed by Phil Hill, the great American driver who won the world championship with Ferrari in 1961 — the team's fourth champion in the first twelve years of the competition — but left Maranello a year later after a season of bitter political infighting. 'I don't think what's happening now is a result of any of that sort of thing,' he said. 'I think it's just a terrible spell of bad luck, and they'll dig in and drag themselves out of it.' Nevertheless some commentators were already saying that if Ferrari had got themselves into this state despite spending $25 million a season on the best driver in the world, then it might be time to call it a day and disband the team. Rumours about Philip Morris' continuing involvement in Formula One, which had concentrated on the possibility of the company removing their sponsorship from McLaren, suddenly switched to their possible abandonment of the Italian outfit.

At Silverstone, a dull race was followed by a miserable epilogue when a technical protest was lodged by Benetton against the winning Williams, threatening Villeneuve with disqualification. After three hours of deliberation the Silverstone stewards rejected the allegation that the front-wing endplate of the Williams was of an illegal design. According to Benetton, it contravened the regulation which stipulates that its leading edge should be rounded, in order to avoid causing damage if it came into contact with another car's tyre. 'We brought it to the Williams team's attention in the morning, hoping that something could be done in an amicable manner,' Ross Brawn, Benetton's technical director, said, 'but they chose not to respond.' From the Williams camp came the eventual reply that the endplate had been designed according to the letter and the spirit of the regulations, and that it had been used on their cars since the first race of the season, on the cars in which Villeneuve and Damon Hill had won seven of the season's ten events.

Now these are clever chaps. Nothing escapes their attention. From halfway down the pit lane they can spot a millimetre's difference either way in a hidden grommet. So did it really take the best brains at Benetton four months and ten races to spot something like that in plain sight? There were dark mutterings in the paddock that Benetton had been alerted to the supposed infringement – put up to it, in other words – by the engineers at Ferrari, in revenge for what they had suffered at the French Grand Prix two weeks earlier as the result of Patrick Head's protest against their cars.

The world of Formula One probably contains more first-class brains than any other three sports put together, but all the intellectual activity in the world could not compensate for a colourless race or render the subsequent business anything other than a squalid mess. The fruitless protest, which wasted a lot of people's time, was the final play in a day that, one way and another, summarized most of grand prix racing's contemporary defects.

Forget the protest for a minute and think about the racing itself. After the first corner you could have been forgiven for thinking that overtaking had been banned. Gerhard Berger was typically forthright when he was asked afterwards to sum up the race. 'To overtake with a Formula One car these days is nearly impossible,' he said. 'There's too much risk involved.'

I I

It was ten minutes past noon on the Wednesday after the Belgian Grand Prix when the phone rang on the desk of Michael Breen, the London lawyer who was acting as Damon Hill's manager.

'Good morning, Michael,' the voice of Frank Williams said.

'Good afternoon, Frank,' Breen corrected.

The conversation did not get a chance to recover from that unpromising start. Within a minute Breen had discovered that Williams Grand Prix Engineering were terminating negotiations over a renewal of Hill's contract. In effect, Williams intended to dispense with the services of Breen's client at the end of the season. Later it emerged that a deal had been concluded with Heinz-Harald Frentzen, the German Sauber driver.

'We only began negotiations with Frank Williams in mid-August,' Breen said at a hastily convened Sunday morning press conference at a hotel in Chelsea Harbour. 'Obviously, there were several points put on the table. But on Wednesday Frank called to withdraw from discussing Damon's contract any further, giving no reason for his decision.' Then Breen suggested that Frank Williams had never truly intended to sign a deal with Hill, who had stayed at home in Ireland with his family rather than attend the press conference. 'Damon was keen to drive for Williams. He's been there six years, why would he not want to continue? Personally, I feel we could easily have done a deal if there was a deal to be done.' He added that at the end of last season, when Hill signed a one-year contract with Williams, the team boss had told him: 'Let's see what happens. If you win the championship, you know we have already lost enough world champions and I will be berated by my sponsors, so I would never do it again.'

The timing of the announcement, Breen said, was 'not ideal', with the championship battle building to a climax. 'I find it rather strange that at all material times we were given the impression they were keen to do a deal then, suddenly and without explanation, negotiations were terminated abruptly. People don't normally waste each other's time if they're not interested in reaching an agreement. Damon was shocked as he was expecting to reach an agreement. He is disappointed and, of course, sad.'

Money, Breen asserted, had not been a factor, although he had been trying to persuade Williams to agree to a contract raising Hill's annual retainer from £5 million to something closer to £8 million, still only half the amount Ferrari were paying Schumacher.

Once the news got out a great deal of anger was directed at Williams. It started with Hill, who clearly felt he had been humiliated at a point in his life when confidence and mental equilibrium were particularly vital. Nor did it please the people at ITV who had concluded a £70 million deal to lift the Formula One television rights from the BBC at the start of next season, and to whom Hill's continuing rivalry with

Michael Schumacher represented a key strand of the narrative of the grand prix soap opera.

But these special-interest feelings were drowned in the clamour from the ordinary fans who had grown to admire Hill's dogged performance for the Williams team over the past four seasons, from his quiet beginnings as Alain Prost's number two to his emergence from the shadow of Ayrton Senna's death, taking the responsibility for leading the team back to victory. Their outrage was heightened by the swift conclusion that the decision would seriously endanger Hill's chance of winning the drivers' title. Having watched his solid mid-season lead eroded by the efforts of his own team-mate, there was an immediate suspicion that if Hill were not going to be driving for Williams in 1997 the team would inevitably concentrate their efforts behind the French-Canadian in order to get the champion's No. 1 on the nose of their lead car next season.

In some quarters, sympathy for Hill's plight was muted by the memory that, four years earlier, he had landed the Williams seat in similar circumstances and at a time when many observers thought he had done little to deserve it. When Nigel Mansell walked out of the team at the end of 1992 after learning that the arrival of Alain Prost would deny him the deal he wanted as the newly crowned world champion, Hill was the unexpected beneficiary. He made the best of his good fortune and over the years had grown in stature, gradually adapting his approach without compromising his straightforward and modest nature.

Were he to win the championship, it would be less a tribute to his natural talent and his efforts over a single sixteen-race season than a reward for six years of dedication to the team's cause – two years as a tester, four as a racer. A victory for Villeneuve, on the other hand, would be mildly tainted by the knowledge that the precocious newcomer took the crown in his first Formula One season driving a car that was the best in the field largely because Hill's and the engineers' efforts had made it so.

But Formula One is an unsentimental business, and none of its leading players is less likely to be swayed by emotional considerations than Frank Williams. After parting with three world champions – Piquet, Mansell and Prost – on less than gracious terms, he was building a reputation as a latter-day Enzo Ferrari, apparently happy to follow in the footsteps of a man who made it his business to destabilize one great driver after another, as soon as their egos threatened to overshadow the achievements of his precious cars.

There may indeed be something of that dark urge in Frank Williams, coupled with a competitive instinct developed to the point where no chance of improving the team could be neglected, irrespective of its effect on personal relationships. When Williams entered his first grand prix in 1969, running a Brabham for his friend Piers Courage, he was a fully-fledged product of the free-wheeling, hard-partying Sixties. But there was already a core of steel, to be tempered further the following season when Courage, the heir to a brewery fortune, crashed his Williams-entered De Tomaso in the Dutch Grand Prix at Zandvoort and burnt to death in the ensuing inferno.

In 1973 the first Williams Formula One car appeared, named the Iso-Marlboro, after its sponsors. Two sixth-place finishes, in the hands of the Dutch driver Gijs van Lennep and Howden Ganley of New Zealand, earned the team its first two championship points. A year later that total was doubled, but Williams' financial fortunes were so low that his home phone was cut off. At the end of the season one sponsor withdrew and the other went bust. This was a time when, in the words of Williams' young wife, Virginia, 'business entertaining was done at home, for the simple reason that it was cheaper'. But nothing deterred Williams, who scraped and scuffled and did whatever was necessary to maintain his presence in a sport he loved and which he was determined to conquer. For 1975 the cars adopted the Williams name, but the great leap forward did not occur until 1978, when the team acquired sponsorship from Saudi Arabia, a fast and ambitious Australian driver called Alan Jones and, from the drawing board of the young Patrick Head, a small, nimble and very quick car, designated the FW06. A year later Jones won the British Grand Prix for the team and maintained the astonishingly rapid rate of improvement by leading them to the double of the drivers' and constructors' championship a year later. Thereafter a bad season would be a rare exception to the rule that the Williams team had become contenders.

Jones had a blunt-minded approach to racing. 'The sport is work and money,' he once said, a view reflected in his uncompromising driving style. Williams and Head adored his attitude, against which they tended to measure all his successors, often to the disadvantage of those in possession of what the designer, in a clear reference to Damon Hill, once memorably described as 'fragile egos'.

And then, on 8 March 1986, driving away from a test session at the Paul Ricard circuit near Marseilles, Frank Williams drove his rented Ford Sierra off the road, landed upside down in a ditch and suffered injuries that made him, at the age of forty-three, a quadriplegic. That he survived at all seems to have been the work of his wife, who cajoled and bullied the Marseilles hospital doctors into action during the subsequent days, and Prof. Sid Watkins, the professor of neurosurgery who became the Formula One medical chief in 1978, and who supervised the operation on Williams at the London Hospital.

The consequences of the accident altered Frank Williams' life in every way. Ron Dennis defined the change it was to make to the way he ran his racing team: 'Now he's even more dangerous,' Dennis said, 'because all he can do is think.'

Some people took a while to realize that. The biggest mistake was made by Honda, who moved their engines from Williams to McLaren at the end of 1987 because they couldn't imagine that the team could continue to operate in the same way with a boss who had lost the use of his arms and legs and who, when he wasn't being trundled around in a wheelchair, had to hang limply from a metal standing-frame. Williams had one bad season after that, but in 1989 they secured Renault engines and were on the way back.

Leaving Patrick Head to supervise the design and production of the cars, Williams concentrated on acquiring sponsors and picking drivers. And, as the manager of any team sport knows, the secret of selection is not just knowing when to pick players but when to drop them. By the time he came to drop Hill, practice had certainly improved Williams' timing. Doing the deed before the team had wrapped up their eighth constructors' title with a one-two finish in Hungary in mid-August would have imperilled the collective effort.

Making the call after Hill had won the drivers' championship would have created an even larger wave of wrath than the one that broke over Williams in the weeks between Spa and Monza.

The Frentzen deal had been rumoured since before the end of the 1995 season. The story went that Williams, frustrated by Hill's poor showings in the two Japanese races at Aida and Suzuka as Schumacher cruised to his second championship and anxious about the prospect of Schumacher in a Ferrari over the next couple of seasons, was said to have concluded a secret agreement with Frentzen there and then – only to see a rejuvenated Hill, his mind reset, sweep to victory in Adelaide before beginning his 1996 season with four wins in the first five races. But when a story to that effect was splashed over the cover of *Autosport* magazine ten days after Silverstone, there were swift denials from Williams and an enraged reaction from Hill himself towards Andrew Benson, the journalist whose high-level contact had provided the tip-off. 'You've made yourself look very stupid, Andrew,' Hill had told Benson while inviting him to leave the Williams motor home at Hockenheim on the day of publication. But Benson's source was to be proved correct – and he later furnished the additional information that the deal had been done in November 1995, nine months before it was announced. And it was Hill who was left looking stupid, he and Breen having failed to play their hand properly, or at least to have guessed the intentions of their opponent in the negotiations.

Why would Williams prefer Frentzen to Hill? The positive reasons included Frentzen's long-standing reputation for being quicker than his Formula One equipment had ever allowed him to reveal, the legend of his superiority over Schumacher when they were both with the Mercedes sports car team, and the fact that the presence of a German driver might be thought to help Williams in their efforts to attract BMW as a replacement for Renault if the French manufacturer carried out the announced withdrawal from supplying the team's engines at the end of 1997.

Those who imagined Williams had only just made up his mind looked for confirmatory evidence at the results of the last three races, following the disappointment of Silverstone. At Hockenheim, Hill had won from pole position with Villeneuve third, although the victory would have been Berger's had his Renault engine not blown up with three laps to go. Villeneuve won again in Hungary, the third victory of his maiden season, his stubbornness keeping Hill safely back in second place after the Englishman had made a poor start. At Spa, despite problems with the Ferrari's steering, Schumacher put everyone else into perspective with a brilliant win on the circuit where he had registered his first victory while Hill finished a humiliated fifth, three places behind Villeneuve. The Canadian had astonished veteran observers by taking pole position on a track he had never visited before. He was particularly impressive through the tricky left-right-left plunge and climb at the corner called Eau Rouge, a feature that remained more or less intact from the old Spa circuit and which continued to present the drivers with their greatest single challenge of skill and, principally, courage in the entire season.

Hill was slower than Villeneuve through Eau Rouge, where the driver must keep his eyes closed and his right foot nailed to the floorboards. It put another question mark against his ultimate talent, something of which Frank Williams had never been entirely convinced. Hill's seven wins to date in 1996 could not be denied in statistical terms but they would not have been enough to modify the boss's cold, hard and accurate opinion – the only one that counted.

The truth behind Williams' logic had been there to see, with embarrassing clarity, in a single incident halfway through the telecast of the Belgian Grand Prix. Hill, his nerves jangling as the race for the championship neared its climax, had already messed up the job of getting pole position, foiled when the rain came during the qualifying session and ceding the initiative to Villeneuve. Bad luck. Bad timing. But a truly great champion suffers from neither. The likes of Fangio and Senna had a poker player's sixth sense which told them when to draw and when to hold. In this generation Schumacher has it. By those standards Hill is mortal, like the rest of us.

In the race he made an indifferent start. He had been doing that all season, leading to the extraordinary sight of a potential world champion being treated like a learner driver. It was impossible to imagine Schumacher allowing himself to be dragged into public explanations of co-ordinating the movement of the clutch and throttle pedals and trying to describe why he needed three pedals while his team-mate could manage with only two. And then, for one reason or another, Hill's pit-stop routine went wrong, making him look foolish as he dodged in and out of the slip-road barriers like an advertisement for the Cones Hotline or one of those programmes of video howlers. Even when he found himself back in thirteenth place after that misadventure, there was a chance to show what he could do in hot blood, one of those little episodes of misfortune that Fangio, Moss, Clark, Senna and, on one occasion, even Prost exploited as opportunities to demonstrate their virtuosity, thrilling the spectators by slicing through the field and back up the leader board.

Maybe Hill was just unfortunate to have a helicopter-mounted television camera focused on him as he came up behind Martin Brundle on lap twenty-one and tried to overtake the fifth-placed Jordan into Les Combes, a right-hander which offers the circuit's best passing opportunity. At this point in the race Hill's Williams, the best car in the field, was running three seconds a lap faster than Brundle's Jordan, a margin that should have made overtaking a virtual formality. But the world could see what happened when Hill drew alongside, taking the correct overtaking line on the inside as they approached the corner. Suddenly he seemed to think better of it, braking early and dropping back, letting Brundle take his usual line through the corner. Schumacher – and Villeneuve, Alesi, Hakkinen and probably one or two others – would have outbraked the Jordan, leaving Brundle to sort out the consequences. There is no time for second thoughts in the business of driving a racing car. But Hill is a thoughtful man and it took him five more laps to get back up on Brundle's tail, ready for another go at the same corner. This time he brought it off, but as he went past a strange thing happened. He made the Williams lunge across the track at the Jordan, as if unconfident of his ability to bring off the manoeuvre cleanly, without a hint of intimidation to deter Brundle from counter-attacking – or as if, after his failure five laps earlier, he felt he had to redeem himself with a public show of aggression.

A whole theory could plausibly be erected on the basis of a single incident such as this, but there had been several other examples of Hill's flawed decision-making in the heat of battle. It seemed as if Frank Williams had seen enough to reach the logical conclusion that, although he may be a first-class test driver, Hill lacked a racer's edge and, at thirty-six years old, was unlikely to develop one.

Hill's financial demands were beside the point. They were not, in any case, excessive for the job in question should he win the championship. No, Williams knew that in the following season, facing Schumacher and a faster, more reliable Ferrari, his team would need every ounce of competitive advantage, and one way to achieve that would be to raise the level of internal competition by introducing a new threat to his remaining driver. Hill's dismay was immediate and obvious, even though he was a couple of hundred miles away playing with his kids in the garden. But at least his fate was clear. Maybe the man who needed to give most thought to the implications of Frank Williams' behaviour, and to the unfolding pattern into which it fitted, was Jacques Villeneuve.

'No, no,' Mary Spillane said. 'I'm just here as a fan, that's all.'

She was protesting too much. In her short cornflower blue linen dress, cardinal red cashmere cardigan, shiny gold pumps, thick black wraparound sunglasses and a quantity of jewellery, Mary Spillane certainly blended into the human zoo of the Monza paddock. But her presence, as a member of Damon Hill's inner circle, was one of the most interesting elements of the whole Italian Grand Prix meeting.

Mary Spillane is what is known as an image consultant. A forty-six-year-old American who followed a degree in politics by writing speeches for Ronald Reagan, she set up a company at the beginning of the Eighties called Colour Me Beautiful, advising business people and politicians on how to project themselves. She also became a widely quoted authority on the body language and general self-presentation of the Princess of Wales and the Duchess of York. Now her clients included Damon Hill, who was coming under closer and more intense scrutiny than ever as he prepared for the race in the shadow of his sacking from the Williams team a week earlier.

'Machiavelli would be at home here,' she observed accurately enough as we stood in the sun, watching the paddock people exchanging greetings and gossip on a particularly intense day for the rumour-mongers. 'It's so wonderful to see the energy of it all, the chaos, the politics and machinations.'

Monza is traditionally the prime venue for the wheeling and dealing over next season's drivers. Behind Mary Spillane, as she spoke, the Williams motor home was the focus of people watching for a significant exchange between Hill and Frank Williams, who had not spoken since Williams' phone call a week earlier. The Benetton hospitality centre hummed with rumours that Flavio Briatore was about to sack Alesi in order to be able to hire Hill for 1997 – allegedly at the request of Renault, who were unhappy that Williams would be throwing their probable world champion on the scrap heap. (The unhappiness was real enough: the Renault people had a genuine respect and fondness for Hill and were sorry that his No. 1 would not be on a car propelled by their engine.) Over at Sauber, Frentzen was preparing a modest little gathering to celebrate the announcement of his move to the best team in the paddock. Groups of people stood about in the sunshine, looking over each other's shoulders and talking out of the sides of their mouths. An anthropologist's dream, really.

Like those of a doctor or a psychiatrist, Mary Spillane's relationships with individual clients are confidential. She was not keen to talk about her work with Hill, refusing even to say how long she had been on the payroll (although she did say, when talking about the world of Formula One, that 'the whole of the last year has been a learning curve for me'). But she was part of the group of people who had been playing their parts in building and maintaining his psychological equilibrium, and whose presence as a team within a team had unquestionably irritated Frank Williams and Patrick Head.

A true creature of the modern world, her business is not with essence but with perception. 'In politics I work on some essence stuff,' she said, 'because I've two degrees in politics and that was my former life in America, so I throw that in because I love it and I can't avoid it. But when it comes to business I leave it to them to tell me what their strategy is, how it's coming across and how the key communicators of the company can address that.'

Since she would not discuss her work with Hill, I asked her to talk in general terms about what her clients want. 'I'm called in to give people an outside assessment of how they present themselves and what they might do to improve,' she said. 'First of all I critique their television performances, how they're written up, whether they're analysed as being strong, being in charge, being committed, doing the right thing. Or, if they're in deep shit, what they need to do to turn that around.'

What changes did she usually advise her clients to make? 'It's so variable that there's no one formula for it. It can be how they look, how they sound, it can be whether they speak in certain contexts or whether they leave other people to do it for them.' I suddenly remembered that she had been sitting alongside Michael Breen at the crucial press conference in the hotel in Chelsea Harbour a few days earlier, while Damon stayed in Ireland. Now I knew whose idea that had been. Not a good idea, in the view of an 'image consultant', to advertise your own vulnerability.

She is from Washington and Massachusetts, but married an Englishman. 'I came over here, thought that image consulting and executive coaching was something we did in America and that it really was time for it here.' How had she prepared for the job of image consultant? 'I did communications training, I did politics, I was at Harvard Business School. You throw all that together and you never stop learning, being perceptive and trying to give people a little bit of an edge they don't know about. Just being ahead of it, really.'

In Britain she had worked with all three main political parties at various levels. 'I've worked with them, and some fringe parties, for the last six or seven years. But now that the election's hotting up, I have candidates, MPs and party organizations that have asked me for help.'

I told her that someone in the paddock had said she worked for Tony Blair. 'No, no, no. I'm not working with him. No. Uh-huh.'

Teaching politicians methods of looking more confident while they tell us that black is white is one thing. But don't we want sportspeople to be nothing more or less than themselves? Isn't that the point of it? 'Absolutely.' So does she help them to be more themselves, or less? 'More themselves, but in a way that works through visual media and the press. Some people say, "Tell me what to do, tell me what to say." That's done day in and day out with a lot of public figures, sports figures, business leaders, whatever. But then there is an individual character – like, say, a Damon Hill – who just won't be packaged or programmed like that, who needs to make sure that what he says is perceived effectively but is still what he believes in and feels strongly about. Often the individual is misunderstood because the message is unclear, or the way they behave when they're delivering the message contradicts what they're trying to say. People have become so sophisticated at analysing how someone walks into a room, how they sit down and handle a press conference, whether they look on top of things or beleaguered. The general public is incredibly perceptive. Not just you guys.'

She was wrong there. The public's perception is not the product of its own highly debatable sophistication but is almost entirely shaped by 'you guys' – journalists who need to put a spin on reality in order to dramatize their stories and who have a range of skills designed to magnify minor flaws until they can no longer take the strain and an otherwise sound structure is shattered.

Tennis players and golfers are among Mary Spillane's other clients from the world of sport. There are similarities with racing drivers, she said: 'These are individual sports, in which much of their success comes from sponsorship. And sponsorship means recognizing that you're a product that has marketing pluses and minuses, so it's not just a question of having the skills and ability to bat a ball around or to play a great round of golf. There's a lot more to it than that if you want to have a longer career and have options when you're past your prime.'

Does her work actually help her clients play their game more effectively? To hit a better second serve, to putt straighter or to drive faster? 'Well, when they feel less beleaguered and more understood for who they are and what they want to get across, that cheers them up. And if they're cheered up rather than brought down by speculation about their shortcomings, then they're able to perform better. I just try to give them confidence in areas that they haven't been schooled in, because so many of them are catapulted into the limelight without the proper training and preparation. An analogy could be made with John Major who, catapulted into the limelight, wasn't prepared for the act and had a rough time getting there. It's the same thing here.' (Not really, I thought to myself later when I listened back to the tape, because Damon Hill spent all his childhood watching this kind of scene and developing a profound distrust of it. What he is having to learn now is how to accept the very thing that he once so firmly rejected.) 'So anyone in business, anyone in sport, needs to start early to build those skills,' she continued. 'Then they fly faster.'

What she was describing sounded very much like a branch of sports psychology. 'I can't just package people . . . It's got to come from within if it's going to be sustainable, whether it be how they look, how they sound, how they behave, changing the way they speak or whatever. So you have to understand what makes that person tick. We're pseudo-psychologists, I suppose, on top of it all.'

Are their clothes and their hair important? 'Yeah, yeah, yeah. Not with someone as good-looking as Damon, but with many other people it's essential. In business and politics, looking authoritative is something you achieve one way. Looking user-friendly you achieve another way. How do you make yourself look less stuffy, out of puff and out of ideas? In the Tory government, pinstriped suits on a Saturday afternoon reinforce that message. You might do something a little bit different. Think about what normal people look like on a Saturday afternoon. A little bit of that might make people think that you really cared about them and might be able to change their lives for the better. So there are some subtle things that can be done, but we don't think about a lot of this non-verbal stuff that is actually very powerful in the way that our society communicates – mainly by TV.'

The Damon Hill who gathered Mary Spillane and the rest of the Team Hill around him was the familiar one who turned twitchy under pressure, his eyes darkening and his mouth twisting as, in an environment where the ability to dissimulate is almost as valuable as a driving licence, he fought a battle with his natural desire to tell the truth at all times. Off duty, Hill seemed the most natural and companionable of men, his straightforwardness a remarkable response to the peculiar circumstances of his upbringing. In the Monza paddock on the day before the race I watched him having a long conversation with a couple of journalists. Animated, often laughing, he looked more at ease than anyone in the place. Afterwards I asked one of the journalists what they'd been talking about. *Trainspotting*, he said. Exactly as you and I would talk about the movie we'd just seen.

But the other side of the coin was revealed when I heard about interviews that had been scheduled in the event of the title being wrapped up in Italy and were now being abruptly cancelled. And someone told me that Damon had asked Frank time and again about Frentzen throughout the season and been told no, it's OK, nothing to worry about. Nor, significantly, had Renault known anything about the Frentzen deal before the story broke. They were upset – although their ability to exert influence had probably been reduced by the announcement several weeks earlier of their intention to quit at the end of 1997.

The circumstances behind the rupture of the relationship between Hill and Williams became only marginally more clear to the outside world when the world championship leader gave his usual Thursday press conference at Monza, with just one item on the agenda: why had he been given the sack, and what did it feel like? Hard information was not forthcoming from a sensitive man feeling the pain of rejection. Inevitably, Hill was more intent on maintaining his dignity than on opening his heart. But between the pauses and behind the evasions, some reasonable assumptions could be made.

'I've just been to see the team,' he said, a few minutes after arriving in the paddock, 'and they've all given me a good welcome and expressed their support.' But the key support had been withdrawn just over a week earlier, when Frank Williams telephoned Michael Breen. According to Breen, Williams had refused to explain his decision beyond stating categorically that money was not a factor. Now Hill intimated that, in telephone calls, Williams had given him the real reason. But he refused to say what it was. 'I did ask Frank, but I'm not prepared to disclose what he told me,' he said. 'It's a matter for you to discuss with him. I can't help you, I'm afraid.'

Unfortunately Williams, after issuing two opaque statements, was not making himself available. And so, inevitably, it was assumed that Hill could not bring himself to convey the burden of Williams' message because it reflected badly on his own competence.

As Hill faced the press, he was flanked by Breen and various other members of his entourage. Their efforts on Hill's behalf were now believed to have irritated Williams, who prefers to deal directly with his drivers and who expects them to speak up for themselves. He had also been annoyed by stories about a £10 million offer to Hill from Ron Dennis, which appeared to have been leaked in an effort to get Frank to the negotiating table and to raise Hill's price. Similar problems were behind the departure of Nigel Mansell from the team in 1992. Frank Williams is not a man with whom complaints about the team's performance and the strategic release of private information aimed at improving a driver's negotiating position go down well.

Hill made no effort to conceal his disappointment. 'I wouldn't say I could be anything other than disappointed to hear news like that,' he said. 'It doesn't really matter how it was communicated. Frank obviously wasn't comfortable about breaking the news to me himself. And I was disappointed by the way Frank conducted the negotiations. From our side, Michael Breen conducted them in a diplomatic and effective manner, in the same way that led to my contract for this season, which was an excellent contract for both parties.'

His deeds so far in 1996, he felt, had been good enough to ensure him the award of a new contract. 'I've led the championship all season, which I thought would be an ace in negotiating terms. But you can't count on anything. I believe that during the winter I turned myself around and made myself into a leading driver, if I wasn't one before. I concentrated on dedicating myself to winning races and winning the championship. I've won seven races this season, which is more than I've won in any season before. I'm still leading the championship, with three races to go, and my view has always been that my reward for winning races would be the opportunity to drive the best equipment. You may say that's naïve.' Williams, he claimed, had given him no indication of dissatisfaction. 'I had every reason to believe that Frank was extremely happy with my driving all season. I had many reactions from him and Patrick this season which suggested that they were not only impressed but astonished and extremely pleased by the way I was driving.'

He had now been given assurances, he said, that he and Villeneuve would receive equal equipment as the fight for the championship reached its climax. 'I believe that to be the truth. I expect it will be a professional situation. I'll continue to work for the team to the very best of my driving abilities.' His relationship with his team-mate, he said, had always been a healthy one. But he responded sharply when told of the suggestion the previous week by Jock Clear, Villeneuve's race engineer, that his driver might be less inclined to share technical information as the battle came to a climax. 'We'll have to discuss that between ourselves if he's up to those little tricks,' Hill said, and it was clear that a statement which might have conveyed a slightly bogus machismo a year ago carried a real conviction now.

'I've been through a lot of pressurized situations in my career,' he said. 'In a way, what's just happened relieves the pressure. I went to Paul Ricard for testing last week, knowing about the decision, and I was pleased to find that I was driving even better. The things that have happened will make me more determined than ever. I've won twenty races in my career and I'd like to have won twenty-three by the time I leave Williams.'

Beyond the championship, he was already looking ahead. 'On reflection, maybe it's time I flew the nest. I started at Williams as a test driver and I feel I've grown over these past six years. Now I have the opportunity to explore other teams to whom I can bring my expertise. I consider myself to be one of the best in the business at producing a car that is competitive in all conditions. But it's not enough just to take on a development project. I want to win.' He declined to be more precise, but the obvious candidates for his services included Jordan-Peugeot and the new Stewart-Ford team, although he was willing to respond to an amusing piece of speculation that he could join Michael Schumacher at Ferrari, with Eddie Irvine moving back to Jordan. Such a move would probably be to the taste of Bernie Ecclestone, who had been making supportive telephone calls to Hill since the news of the sacking broke. If it had a positive side, the affair at least proved that not everything in Formula One was controlled by Ecclestone. Now he was keen to find a way of preserving the box-office value of the rivalry between the Englishman and the German.

'I've enjoyed my races with Michael over the past two or three years,' Hill said, before hitting a surprisingly elegiac note. 'Between us we've won more races than anyone else. That created a rivalry. But it can't always be between the same two protagonists. Things change.'

Set in a royal park in a town fifteen miles north-east of Milan, Monza is full of the echoes of history. Only one circuit still in use can rival it, the difference being that on the morning after the Monaco Grand Prix the streets of the principality are full of the bustle of normal life. The Autodromo di Monza just sits and broods.

It was built just after the First World War, designed as a temple of speed fit for Italian heroes, combining an artificial road circuit with a banked speed-bowl. Cars could run practically flat out, straining their engines in the way that Monaco, with its endless corners, strained gearboxes. It was a place to hear the howl of a highly tuned, unsilenced racing engine running at peak revs. What I missed in 1996 was the sound of the Ferrari twelve-cylinder engine wailing past the pits and disappearing towards the forests, its pitch a full octave higher than the V10s and V8s of the rest of the field.

Chicanes inserted for safety reasons at the end of the main straight and in the middle of the back leg have all but ruined Monza. Yes, it was dangerous. Giaccone, Materassi, Arcangeli, Borzacchini, the opera singer Giuseppe Campari and Count Czaykowski were killed there between the wars. In 1955, Alberto Ascari died in a mysterious testing accident at the curve which was later given his name. Wolfgang von Trips killed himself and several spectators in 1961 at the Parabolica curve, the place where Jochen Rindt perished nine years later when something broke on his Lotus during practice for the grand prix. (Rindt might have survived had he done up the crotch straps of his safety harness.) Drivers were dying at other circuits during these eras, but there was something in the sheer flat-out nature of Monza that spooked people.

On one of the practice days I walked up the track, past the pits and the great ochre futurist grandstand just beyond the start line, up the strip of grass inside the barriers all the way to the first chicane. This is where the drivers shuffle down to second gear for the twiddle instead of holding the throttle pedal to the floor while rocketing towards the Curva Grande, as their ancestors did. Never mind. I turned round and discovered that it was still possible, looking back down the straight towards the Parabolica, to enjoy the unique sight of a car catapulting into view, no bigger than a beetle, squashed even closer to the ground than usual by the effect of high-speed aerodynamics and growing larger as it hammered past the pits at peak revs.

As one car went past, I turned to follow its progress into the chicane, listening for the impossibly rapid downshifts permitted by the semi-automatic gearbox, watching as the driver pitched it into the right-left-right combination, noting how he almost clipped the tyre barriers which had been freshly installed to prevent the drivers cheating by driving through in a straight line over the low kerbs. When I turned back, a Benetton was coming straight at me.

Gerhard Berger had left the pits in the normal way and had accelerated out of the exit lane on to the main straight when something went wrong and the car took on a life of its own, smashing into the barrier and bouncing back on to the tarmac, where it spun along under its own momentum and finally came to a halt at the edge of the track, level with where I had just been standing behind the barrier.

In a moment like that, it is interesting to discover what your instinctive reaction is. You run, of course. But where to? Not just away; something tells you that you won't be fast enough. Your reaction is to run inwards, away from the track, at ninety degrees to the car's direction of travel. Useless, of course. Had the car flipped itself over and jumped the barrier, its trajectory would have changed and it could have landed anywhere, most probably on me. The best choice would have been to remember the old racing driver's advice to anyone confronted by an accident: head right for the centre of it, on the assumption that by the time you arrive it won't be there any more.

While the tow-truck removed Berger's bent car, and after listening to a lecture from a policeman who thought I'd been too close to the barrier when the accident occurred, I resumed my walk up the track. Just by the chicane is the place where the cars used to veer off the road circuit and begin the loop of the banking. After scrambling through a hole in the wire netting and dodging between a few saplings I found myself on the old wall of death, the Pista de Alta Velocità itself, its concrete surface now dilapidated but still intact despite decades of neglect, pleasantly dappled on this day by the sunlight through the tall trees. So steep towards the top that it can barely be climbed, the track still has a painted yellow line denoting the zone, low down, to be used by cars not running at racing speed. And every few hundred yards, out of the high rim, there protrudes a platform on which flag marshals once kept watch.

The banking was abandoned many years ago. It didn't suit a new generation of racing cars, the spidery lightweight machines pioneered by the men Enzo Ferrari used to call the *garagistes*: Colin Chapman and John Cooper. Cars created for the billiard-table surfaces of English aerodromes were shaken to pieces in the high bowl. Mind you, it was rough on all sorts of machinery – there have been few post-war single-seaters cruder in conception than the Eldorado Special, a car specially constructed by the Maserati factory to a commission from an ice-cream magnate in order to compete in the 1958 Trophy of Two Worlds, a sort of challenge match between the Europeans and a contingent of US Indianapolis cars, using only the banked bowl. While the Americans were winning more or less hands down, the Maserati, painted a deceptively innocent white to match its sponsor's product, was trying to kill Stirling Moss. Doing 160 miles an hour on the banking, six or eight feet below the lip, he was worrying about the fact that the directional control of the car was feeling rather vague when the steering suddenly sheared entirely, sending him careering up and along the steel barrier that prevented the cars from hurtling over the rim, sparks flying from the contact and a wheel breaking off before the car spun itself to a halt in the ditch at the bottom.

Almost forty years later, on another hot afternoon, the bowl held only its memories, enfolded in the silence of decades.

On Friday night at Monza, Ron Dennis was asked if Hill figured in McLaren's plans for 1997. In other words, whether he would be prepared to replace Mika Hakkinen or David Coulthard with the Englishman. As usual, Dennis mulled the question over before delivering a reply of characteristic opacity. 'Our position on the drivers for next year is really quite clear,' he said. 'Our objective is to sit and discuss the options with Mercedes-Benz during the course of the next week. It could be that we do not make a decision at that stage. But whatever the outcome is, it will be based on the best available drivers. What I should do is correct the belief that we have had dialogue with Damon. It's not true, not in respect of him driving for the team. And certainly there hasn't been any money discussed at any stage. It is true to say that while on holiday we spent some time together, but that's purely because we enjoy each other's company. There was nothing said about him driving for the team.' Clear enough. By Formula One standards, at least.

Eddie Jordan was asked the same question and came up with an equivalent masterpiece in his own special vernacular of obfuscation. 'We'd be delighted to have Damon in the team, he'd be a major asset to us. He's a fantastically professional person who has won twenty grands prix. His record stands up for itself. He's driven for me in the past and he's about as fine a gentleman as you could meet, on and off the track. I think it would be a boost for Jordan if he were to come to us, but we have never had any dialogue. This is just my own opinion, it's a very personal opinion and, of course, we mustn't let personal opinions interfere with the commerce and the business of running a company. But I do hope that he gets a very good drive because it would be a great shame if, whatever happened for him, he didn't get the opportunity to continue in grand prix racing.'

The boys were playing games. And none with more enthusiasm than Schumacher, who was asked for his reaction to the news about Frentzen, his former team-mate in the Mercedes-Benz sports car team, his rival for national favour and the man from whom he lured Corinna Betsch, Frentzen's girlfriend, to become Frau Schumacher. 'It's interesting,' Schumacher said with a smile. 'We know each other from past times. I look forward to competing with him. Hopefully I can compete with him. That's the question mark, whether we're going to have a car good enough to give him difficulties.'

Then came a question of diabolical ingenuity, inviting Schumacher to make mischief: whom did he fear most, Frentzen in a Williams or Hill in a Williams? 'I don't think it's a good question.' No, it is a very good question . . . 'It [the answer] would be good for Heinz-Harald. I don't know how good it would be for Damon.' So that was the answer, then. But Schumacher had more to say. 'I think we should say something else which hasn't been said so often. We always talk about, yeah, Damon wins races and some people think, including myself, well, how good is he? Is it the car that wins the races or is it him? I think by changing to another team next year, which obviously he's going to do, we're going to see who Damon really is. It's going to be an opportunity for him to prove that he's better than some people might think. We might be going to see a surprise in that respect. Then we'll know where the ability is. How good is the car, how good is he?'

The message from the reigning world champion being that whatever Hill achieved this season, its true valuation would have to wait.

Hill put the car on pole at Monza, which was a terrific response to his trials of the preceding week. At the Saturday night press conference, talking about the special tyre barriers placed at the chicanes at the drivers' request, he seemed a different man: suddenly sure of himself, much more impressive when he was dealing objectively with a concrete problem rather than being forced to contemplate and analyse the abstractions of his own performance. Flanked by Villeneuve and Schumacher, who would start the race alongside and immediately behind him, he had a new authority.

It was, he said, a particularly satisfying pole position in the light of the events of the preceding fortnight. 'I haven't lost anything as a driver. I'm still as quick as I ever was. I performed like I've performed all season.' Would he and Villeneuve, both on the front row, team-mates fighting each other for the world championship, consider talking about a non-aggression pact at the first corner? 'Pretty pointless conversation, I would have thought.' Villeneuve, next to him, laughed. On the other side, Schumacher rubbed his hands gleefully and smiled. 'There's going to be a fight tomorrow to win the race,' Hill said.

Then he was invited to talk about the new tyre barriers, arranged to prevent drivers taking short cuts. 'I think we're all agreed that something needs to be done,' he said, 'because if you don't have anything then there's no way of legislating as to what is an unfair advantage when the car's going over the kerbs, because you can gain quite a lot of time. But there's no way of saying how much of a kerb is too much and how much is acceptable. It could lead to a lot of arguments. So we decided that the best thing was to put those tyres there. I'm not happy, it's not a perfect solution, but I think in the circumstances it's better than not having anything. Jacques went over the kerb this morning and a car that had gone over previously had pulled out a great lump of concrete. The whole run-off area is made of these T-shaped concrete blocks. You can't afford to have them pulled out during the race.' He reminded us of what had happened the previous year when Berger hit a camera that had fallen off a car. 'It doesn't bear thinking about what a concrete block would do. So the best thing is to try and keep everyone off the kerbs. But you don't want to hit the tyres either.'

Villeneuve observed: 'You have to hit the kerbs hard here if you want to get a good time.' He was trying to take his mind off what had happened that afternoon when he came up to overtake Diniz at 180 miles an hour, only to find the Brazilian turning straight into his path at the entrance to the Parabolica curve, having failed to look in his mirrors. 'I just happened to come upon one of those few idiot drivers who shouldn't be in Formula One,' he said, to the sound of laughter from the assembled journalists, thrilled by such unusual forthrightness. 'He came to see me but I was talking with the marshals so I didn't see him.' Diniz, who had been given a suspended sentence of a one-race ban for another offence earlier in practice, was later summoned to explain himself to the stewards and, amazingly, was absolved of all blame for an incident which most observers thought rated an instant suspension from that weekend's race, and perhaps a few more as well.

'Third place,' Schumacher said coolly. 'It's a good starting position. I'm not worried about it at all. We'll see what the race brings.'

Sunday morning, five to seven. A sickle moon loitered in the china-blue sky. The smoke of a thousand camp fires settled as a head-high mist across the old parkland. Helicopters clattered down behind the paddock. Fans already pressed against the paddock chicken-wire, clamouring for their arriving heroes. It didn't seem like a day for an ordeal, but by the end of it Damon Hill was in worse shape than ever.

After taking the lead from the start, the world championship leader committed a simple mistake which cost him the outside chance of wrapping up his first title and presented Schumacher with the opportunity of bringing the crowd to the point of delirium by giving Ferrari their first victory at Monza since 1988, ahead of Alesi's Benetton-Renault and Hakkinen's McLaren.

Hill made his now-customary poor getaway from pole

position, conceding the lead to a rocket-assisted Alesi as they went into the first chicane at the end of the main straight. But, smarting from the humiliations of the last week, Hill charged back to repass the Frenchman, feinting at him going into the first Lesmo corner and then diving inside at the second. When Alesi attempted to mount a counter-attack at the Ascari chicane a few moments later, Hill held him off with a display of disciplined aggression which made it look as if, at last, he had become a fully-fledged racing driver. Not, in other words, just a man who drives racing cars. 'That's how I like to race,' he said afterwards. 'I'd like to race like that more often but the truth of the matter is that it's very rare to get the opportunity in Formula One.' Not entirely true: the opportunity had been there at Hockenheim, where he failed to mount a convincing challenge to Berger despite the clear superiority of the Williams over the Benetton.

At Monza, though, he was away and gone, or so it seemed. His lead over Alesi had grown to two seconds when, at the start of the sixth lap, his car clipped the tyre barrier marking the inside of the Goodyear chicane – the very thing whose presence he had defended so eloquently less than twenty-four hours earlier. The impact on the front wheel flicked the Williams into a spin until it came to a halt in the middle of the road, its steering broken and its engine stalled. A minute later the television cameras picked up the figure of Hill leaning over the steel barrier at the side of the track, hitting his helmet with his gloved hands in a fury of frustration. As he walked back down the side of the straight, all he could think of was the likelihood that Villeneuve would recover from his own bad start and win the race, thereby cutting the championship lead from thirteen points to three. But when he got back to the pits it was to be told that his team-mate had already experienced his own misfortune, hitting the tyre barrier at the second chicane on the second lap. Three pit stops failed to repair the damage to his car's steering and he was to finish no higher than seventh, one place out of the points.

Hill was open about his own misjudgement. 'I threw it away,' he said. 'I was pleased with the way the race was going initially and I was enjoying myself. I've only got myself to blame.' He came out of the race with a measure of new credit among those who heard Alesi's subsequent description of their battle during the first lap, when the Benetton had gone from sixth on the grid to the lead in the few seconds before the cars reached the chicane. The vigour of Hill's reply surprised and impressed his opponent. 'When Damon came by he was fighting like it was not the first lap but the last,' Alesi said. 'From someone who was fighting for the world championship, that surprised me. He was taking big risks.'

An hour and a half later, Hill's fortunes were of little interest to the tens of thousands of flag-waving fans who stormed the fences and thronged the track to welcome Schumacher to the victory rostrum. The last time a Ferrari won at Monza, in the hands of Gerhard Berger, old Enzo Ferrari had been dead barely a month and the victory took on the elements of a valediction. Schumacher's win, by contrast, was a celebration of rebirth. The heavily reworked F310 was still far from being the best car in the field, or even the second best, but Schumacher's genius could sometimes override its defects. At Monza he drove a superb strategic race, overcoming his own poor getaway to profit, early on, from the temporary disappearance of Mika Hakkinen, who went into the pits to fit a new nose after hitting a tyre barrier on the third lap, and from the permanent removal of Hill.

Holding station in second place, less than a second behind Alesi, Schumacher waited for the Benetton to make its pit stop. 'I had quite a lot of fuel on board,' he said, 'and I knew I could wait until later to stop. Jean's car had a good top speed and I couldn't overtake him, so the safe strategy was to overtake him in the pit stops.' Another measure of Schumacher's genius: how many past Ferrari drivers would have had the self-control to demonstrate patience and prudence in front of a frenzied Monza crowd? Sure enough, Alesi came in on lap thirty-one to take fuel and tyres in a nine-second stop. Two laps later Schumacher followed him, and so slick were his entry and exit that although the stop itself was only a fifth of a second faster, he came out of the pit lane with a lead of four seconds over the Benetton. After that he drew away, increasing his lead by an average of more than half a second a lap, the romantics among us relishing the sound of his Ferrari changing up to top gear in its new seven-speed gearbox every time he passed the timing box, the only alarm coming when he momentarily lost concentration with thirteen laps to go and brushed against the first pile of tyres at the very chicane where Hill had come to grief. The outgoing champion's luck held.

Alesi, unable to respond, was thinking wistfully during the closing laps of his own barren years with Ferrari and, in particular, of his awful experience at Monza in 1994 when what looked like a certain victory was removed by a gearbox failure during a pit stop. He might also have been nursing vain hopes that Schumacher's car, which barely lasted the course while winning at Spa, would break – as had the second Ferrari of Eddie Irvine, which retired from third place just before half-distance.

As for Heinz-Harald Frentzen, the man scheduled to join Williams next season lasted only five minutes longer than the driver who had been sacked to make way for him. Hill had barely begun his walk home when Frentzen spun his Sauber into the sand and out of an undistinguished eighth place.

13

It is half past seven on the night before the grand prix at Estoril. The season is almost over, autumn has come and night has already fallen on the paddock. The poseurs were back in their hotels hours ago; by now they have probably changed and are sitting down to dinner. But all the way along the pit lane, lights blaze in the garages as the mechanics perform the final rituals of fettling the machinery in preparation for tomorrow's race.

In the Ferrari pit a familiar figure leans against the skeleton of the No. 1 car, which is jacked up high with most of its externals – wheels, wings, engine cover – removed. Alone of all the twenty drivers in tomorrow's race, Michael Schumacher is still around, changed out of his driving suit into jeans and a white polo-neck sweater but still intent on monitoring the final details of preparation. There are no team managers or designers in sight, just three mechanics and the world champion, who watches keenly and talks quietly to them as they work in, around and under the car.

This, you think, is a bit of a throwback to how it used to be in the days before cars were set up by computer. The days when drivers and mechanics worked and lived together, when a Surtees or a Brabham was not above wielding a spanner when necessary. The engineers no longer appreciate a driver who thinks he knows how to design a car better than they do, but the mechanics still warm to one who shows his understanding and appreciation of their work, who will stay late into the night watching them trying to produce a car that will go a quarter of a second faster, and who will then go out the next morning and turn that quarter of a second into half a second through his own commitment and virtuosity. No wonder Schumacher is a class above the rest. He's the one who stays late.

His qualities were already making the big difference at Ferrari, the difference between a struggling, directionless team and one which might not yet be in sight of its objective but was at least working with a confidence that it would come into view only just around the next bend. After raw talent, focus is the attribute most prized among top sportspeople: the ability to concentrate on the task at hand. Schumacher has it, along with the linked ability – even more important in this case – to prove that it is a transferable asset, by infecting every other member of the squad with the same degree of commitment and optimism.

So at half past seven that night in the Estoril paddock, with the lights on in the pits, Schumacher is still doing his work when his race engineer, Ignazio Lunetta, brings in a friend and introduces him to the world champion. Then Jean Todt comes in and joins the group in a quiet, relaxed conversation.

All this time Schumacher is leaning on his race car or resting a hand on some part of the bodywork. I don't think I've ever seen a driver looking more a part of his machine, more naturally proprietorial, as if he had a special relationship with it. Not anthropomorphic, not sentimental, but a feeling for what he and it could do together.

Once upon a time, the scene in the Ferrari pit during a race was like the last act of a comic opera – all red wine and tantrums, oily rags and Italian imprecations. The mechanics were all shapes, sizes and ages, but all somehow distinctively Italian. Not any longer. Beneath the shiny red cars, the grey-painted garage floor is untainted by spilled liquids. The uniformed technicians, staring at the squiggles on their computer screens, speak to each other calmly. And, quite a lot of the time, they speak in English. For Ferrari, the team to which the Italian people entrust their dreams, the last one to maintain the tradition of painting its cars in the designated national racing colour, is now the most multinational of the lot: French, Dutch, Swiss, Japanese, German, Irish. Most surprising of all, the chief mechanic is from Warwickshire.

Nigel Stepney has been a familiar figure in Formula One for eighteen of his thirty-seven years. He worked with Clay Regazzoni at Shadow, with Elio De Angelis and Ayrton Senna at Lotus, and with Nelson Piquet at Benetton. But when he joined Ferrari and moved to Italy, he became famous.

The consequences of his move became evident right away. After all, two of his predecessors, Giulio Borsari and Ermanno Cuoghi, published their autobiographies. The handsome Borsari, who 'came over' from Maserati, Ferrari's great Modenese rivals, was a familiar figure throughout the Sixties. Cuoghi was Niki Lauda's mechanic in the championship campaigns of the mid-Seventies. Yet when Nigel Stepney moved to Emilia-Romagna and found a house in the hills above Maranello, he discovered that the phenomenon of the celebrity mechanic could be a mixed blessing. 'Every bar you go into in Maranello has a picture of the Old Man on the wall,' he said, leaning against a bench in the Ferrari truck at Estoril. 'It's part of life there. The restaurants and hotels, they live on Ferrari. The biggest problem is that whenever I go out someone always wants to talk about Ferrari. Everybody knows who you are and what you're doing. But now I've got a group of friends, five or six families, who I can go out with and it'll be three or four hours before someone brings the subject up. It's not the first topic of conversation and that's important for me, to change the air.'

Stepney left school with qualifications and began his career with an apprenticeship at Broadspeed, a tuning firm once famous for turning out Mini-Cooper racers. 'I wasn't much good at school, except for metalworking. I hadn't a clue about motor racing but Broadspeed was only four miles from home. I'd never even seen a race. So I went in at the deep end, just turned seventeen. I started from scratch, doing the shitty jobs. After I'd finished at Broadspeed I had the opportunity to start in Formula One with the Shadow team in Northampton. I was there for a year and a half, and that was my apprenticeship in Formula One. Regazzoni and Stuck were the drivers, then Lammers and De Angelis in the second year. But the company was struggling and De Angelis was going to go to Lotus. He asked if I wanted to go with him, so I got in my car and went and had a look at Norfolk. I started there as the number one mechanic on his car. Mario Andretti was there, too, that year. Again I was thrown in among the animals, as it were, but I was prepared to learn, as I am now. They'd won the championship with Andretti, they'd been through a bad spell and they were trying to rebuild. Colin Chapman died, there were some hard times, but when Senna arrived in 1985 we knew we'd been progressing and eventually we had good times. In those days you could work hard and then play hard.'

De Angelis had been the first driver with whom he developed a close relationship, but the Italian's death in a testing accident the year after he left Lotus made Stepney wary of getting too close to the pilots. 'He was a nice guy. When he left Lotus for Brabham he asked me to go with him again. But it's not good to follow a driver around. I did it once but I wouldn't do it again. If he left the team or got injured or something, you'd think, hang on, what do I do now? But then I lost a friend anyway because he got killed a year later. A fantastic guy. Very *simpatico*. Very gifted. We used to sit and listen to him play the piano. When I went to the funeral one of his brothers gave me a bit of shit: "If you'd gone with him . . ." This, that and the other. Crazy talk.'

Still, Senna's presence was enough of an inducement to keep him at Lotus. 'That was a good experience. He appreciated people, appreciated the effort. And we appreciated working with him because he put in the effort. If you work with a driver who puts the car on pole and wins races, it all helps. We used to go out together at night, go round to his house. But the thing is not to get too close. Then, if a driver is killed, it's a bad, bad feeling. You have to draw a line. It's difficult. The drivers rely on you so much – even Senna. And they have to trust you.'

When Stepney went into Formula One with Shadow, he was paid £100 a week. The rewards had improved but the hours hadn't changed much. 'At the beginning of the season you work more because nobody really knows the car. Sometimes at a race weekend you can work for four days with four hours' sleep. And as you work longer hours things start to slow down, because you've got to keep your concentration. With a car that'll do 340 or 350 kilometres an hour, you've got to get it right. But at this time of year, on a normal weekend towards the end of the season, you work fewer hours, unless the driver's had an accident. But even if the driver destroys a car, we can change the chassis in six hours.'

It was John Barnard, the chassis designer, who took Stepney to Ferrari at the beginning of 1993. 'I'd worked with John at Benetton. We had a good relationship through some difficult times and we kept in touch. He's a pretty hard person to get on with because he likes everything perfect, which isn't always possible. But having stuck by him through those days, when the opportunity came to go to Ferrari I dropped everything. I wanted to have a go.' At the time, the team was in a bad way. 'There was a lot of despondency. People were working, but not with the motivation that was required. The management kept changing.' For a few months, culturally stranded and horrified by the team's legendary infighting, Stepney wanted to return home. 'It was a big shock, in every area. But I thought, no, you made the decision, you've got to go through with it. It was hard. Rebuilding a team takes time. Creating a structure was the first priority. Without that, you can't operate. You don't know what anybody's doing and if somebody wants to go round you, they can.'

It's one thing to turn up at the factory of a company with the traditions and ingrained habits of Ferrari telling everybody that you're the new chief mechanic, but it's another thing to prove your right to the title. 'It was difficult, not knowing the structure – or, if there was no structure, who did what – because with the size of it, the amount of resources and the number of people . . . it took me a few months just to get used to what we could do in the place, compared to where I'd been before. We never had those resources at Benetton or Lotus. At Ferrari we could have everything we wanted. And because it's there, you've got to use it. The resources weren't really being used to the fullest.'

There were those in the team who resented the newcomer. 'I knew a lot of them from the days when everything was more relaxed, when the mechanics used to have water fights, the English versus the Italians. But I still had to prove myself. You can't just walk in. There's always somebody wanting you to fail. I didn't intend to fail.' Gradually the remodelled team took shape. 'Now we're a lot more organized. We can work from one month to the next, from one year to the next, without having to rush everything. It's a gradual development. If you look at Williams, that's what they've done, they've been very stable. A few engineers may leave but it doesn't change the structure or the performance. It's taking us time to get to that level, but now we're looking forward.'

The big step came with the arrival of Schumacher to drive Barnard's new V10-engined car alongside Eddie Irvine. 'It's always good for the driver to come around and speak to the mechanics. They're always talking to the engineers but they don't speak so much to the mechanics. With the drivers we have at the moment, German and Irish, the language is a little bit difficult. They communicate, have a joke and a laugh, but probably a little less – no, a lot less – than you'd normally get with an English team.' In fact, neither pilot could speak a word of Italian. 'The drivers talk to the engineers in English because it's the only way they can communicate. And the debriefing meetings are in English.' The mechanics, most of whom are from Modena, still speak a local dialect among themselves, which can make life difficult for the outsider. 'The words are completely different. The mechanics speak the dialect more than standard Italian. But if they know you don't understand the dialect they'll speak Italian to you. Most of the people are from around the Modena area.'

His own role had changed with the evolution of the new structures, particularly in relation to Barnard's Ferrari Design and Development office in Surrey. 'Now I'm more of a co-ordinator between the test team and FDD. At the very beginning I spoke with FDD a lot because they wanted a contact. There was nobody they could speak to at the basic level of the building and maintenance of the cars. John wanted a direct relationship, he didn't want to have to go through twenty people. If you do that, you lose something.'

There were still those in Italy who resented Ferrari's 'rainbow coalition' of multinationalism, but Stepney felt the results were beginning to justify Todt's decision to look far beyond the team's domestic recruiting base. 'In England, as in America, you have so much depth of experience to draw on. If you want to build a team you can go around and pick people with experience in any area. And there are plenty of people to choose from. In Italy it's different. Not bad, just different. The idea is not to change things – you can't change Ferrari, Ferrari is Ferrari – but perhaps we can try and help them in their methods to improve the situation. Not to make it like an English team, you can't do that. But we want a depth of personnel with experience, which we haven't got in all departments. That takes time to build up.'

The sheer size of a company that produces its own engines as well as its chassis presented problems of its own. 'It's the first time I've been involved in a team like that. Ferrari is the only one left now. Years ago there were lots of them. There are good things about it and bad things. When you're working with Cosworth or Renault, it's a different relationship – you'd receive an engine and put it in the car. OK, they'd allow you a degree of input on the installation. But here, because you're involved so closely, there's more integration.'

But also the potential for greater conflicts, in the grand Ferrari tradition? 'Sometimes. When you have the same engine as another team you can measure your performance, like Williams and Benetton with the Renault. You can see if you have to do some work on the chassis. With us, we don't have that benefit. We can't do as much testing of the engine as two teams testing two cars each. That's a big disadvantage.'

The decent performance of the new V10 engine and Schumacher's readiness to give value for his £16 million a year had already paid off with the wins at Hockenheim, Spa and, before the team's home crowd, Monza. 'That took a lot of pressure off,' Stepney said. 'It's given us a breathing space. Now the team can work quietly. We still have problems, for sure, but we keep them internal. A couple of years ago everyone would have known about them. It's a much easier environment to work in.'

The last vestige of the old atmosphere of chaotic improvisation had gone for ever. 'There's no magic to this,' he said.

'It's hard work. We know we can do it. We know we have the best driver. We haven't got the best car at the moment, but it's coming.' And he was glad he had stuck it out. 'I love the lifestyle now,' he said, remarking that his new rented house was no more than an hour away from the nearest skiing, and not much further from the sea. His English had already acquired Italian cadences and formulations.

There would, he said, be only one way to celebrate the fiftieth anniversary of the appearance of the first car to bear Enzo Ferrari's name. 'I want to win the championship,' he said, 'and I can't think of a better team to win it with than Ferrari. In Italy, whenever there's a sporting event the people are so emotional, whether it's motor racing or football. They're really involved. The English are cold, in many respects, with things like that.' Is he interested in the company's history? 'I'm interested in making it. One day, when I have the time, I'll sit down and read about it.'

'I prefer to have critics and win races,' Damon Hill said at Estoril. But by contrast with Schumacher, Hill's demeanour in Estoril could not be described as serene. Giving an impromptu television interview in the paddock, something he was accustomed to doing as regularly as putting on his helmet, his body was still and his face composed in an expression of calm seriousness, but his hands, clasped together in front of him, told a different story. The fingers were knotted and writhing. I remembered a famous photograph of Princess Diana taken at some big function or other during her marriage, superficially radiant in a black evening dress, all diamonds, velvet and a halo of blonde hair. But her fingers, behind her back, were twisted into a contorted shape that made you wince with pain just to look at them, saying a lot more about what was really going on than the smile on her face.

Hill wasn't talking about his plans for 1997. 'I've got a lot of things to look at and I'll let you know in due time,' he said. But higher up on the agenda came the question of whether he had considered the possibility of shunting Villeneuve off the track, in a recreation of the climactic battles of Prost and Senna. 'My situation is quite simple,' Hill said. 'I have to finish ahead of Jacques to end the whole thing, but I can still win the championship if I'm behind him. I do not want to resort to unfair tactics. We both want to win, but there's no problem anywhere. He's been tough all season. In Melbourne he made it plain that he was not prepared to be pushed around, and nothing's changed. If I'm in the lead I'll defend it vigorously.'

It was pointed out that Martin Brundle, in a newspaper article, had advised him to knock Villeneuve off the track. 'I clearly feel I can win the championship on merit, on my own driving performance,' Hill responded. 'There are all sorts of views on how drivers should conduct themselves out on the circuit and some drivers have different views from my own. But I don't have any ambition to be involved in that sort of tactic.'

Ted Macauley of the *Mirror* wanted more, or at least the same thing phrased in a more headline-friendly way. 'You're an honourable man,' he said. 'Would you rather not win the championship than drive dirty to secure it for sure by knocking Jacques off?'

Hill tried to point out that he had already answered the question, but Macauley persisted. 'After all,' he pointed out, 'it's been done to you.' He was referring to Adelaide in 1994 and the conclusive collision with Schumacher.

'That's your opinion,' Hill replied airily, indicating that he didn't want to be dragged back into an old and irrelevant debate. 'It's always a matter of opinion what's fair and not fair in sport. I drive in the way I feel fitting at any given time, and I'm still at liberty to drive in a way that may not actually be the way people expect me to drive. So I have everything at my disposal. I don't always have to give way.'

Stan Piecha, Macauley's opposite number at the *Sun*, did his bit for the morning's back pages. 'I think what Ted was getting at,' he ventured, 'was that you wouldn't deliberately ram Jacques to win the title.'

Hill looked a bit mischievous. 'Wouldn't I?' Now he was playing along, trying to find his own advantage in the game that had so often been played out in someone else's favour.

'I thought you just said you wouldn't,' Piecha responded.

'What I'm saying,' Hill continued, 'is that anything's possible. I currently lead the championship, I'm determined to win the championship and I reiterate, so that you're absolutely clear on it, that I do not want to resort to unfair tactics. Personally I'm against them. I've seen championships settled in ways before which I think are unsatisfactory and I don't want that to happen this time. I believe I can win the race cleanly. I believe I can start on pole, lead the entire race and not have to see another soul. Whether that's what will happen or not I don't know.'

Was it possible to go about his business in a team run by Frank Williams without being affected by a degree of bitterness? 'I'm here to get on with my job, which is driving.

Frank is here to see his cars perform to their best and, on a professional level, we're getting on with our jobs, both of us. I wasn't happy about Frank's decision but that's over, that's past. We'll just get on with the race weekend. He wants to see his cars win, I want to win, so we're both hoping for the same thing.'

I asked him about the Monza débâcle, and whether the uncharacteristic display of hot-blooded aggression that took him past Alesi on the first lap might have been the very factor that cost him the race, when he misjudged the chicane a few laps later. At that stage of the season, with things as they were, was it difficult to balance aggression and prudence? 'Well, listen,' he said with some asperity, 'I made a mistake at Monza. The things that go through your mind when you're in the lead of a race are those things which determine your mode of driving. I made an aggressive start to the race and thereafter I was determined to drive more cautiously. But sometimes, in the attempt to drive more cautiously, you can make mistakes. I'm not the first or last driver to make a mistake under those circumstances. It was unfortunate. But there have been fourteen races so far and I've won seven of them. I would love to have a perfect CV, but show me a driver who has.'

It was a superabundance of caution, then, rather than an excess of uncontrolled aggression that had led him into the crucial error. Well, it had happened before. Ayrton Senna was at the top of his form at Monaco in 1988, driving with supernatural brilliance and running away with the race when he lost concentration near the end and hit the barriers at the entrance to the tunnel, putting himself out and handing victory to his team-mate and bitterest rival, Alain Prost.

Instead of returning to his pit to talk to the team, Senna went home to his apartment, took the phone off the hook, ignored the doorbell and spent the night in tears, knowing that he had betrayed his own talent.

Hill's reaction had been quite different, conditioned by the outcome in terms of championship points. 'Monza proved two things. One is that God is truly on the side of Ferrari, and also that he wants me to win the championship. Because to actually knock myself out of the race and then end up not losing any points was a miracle. So I went away from Monza quite relieved rather than dejected.'

That relief had persisted, according to him. 'I feel quite relaxed, actually,' he said. 'I don't feel anxious. My nerves are not jangling, as some people would have you believe. I've been relaxing and preparing for this race. On the Monday after Monza I was up a mountain in Austria. It was good to get out of the gym, which can get a bit monotonous. You can feel like a laboratory rat sometimes. Then I spent some more time at home, training.'

Wasn't the build-up of pressure getting to him? 'I don't think so. I'm looking forward to this weekend. I like Estoril. I test here a lot. I know the place like the back of my hand and I believe I'll be able to get the best set-up on my car. There'll be a certain amount which will be down to chance, not everything is under my control. But certainly everything that is under my control I will be doing my best to keep that way. Here we've got a long straight, one kilometre long, which gives a chance for the cars to overtake, and we've got this fantastic 180-degree corner, the last corner, where we'll be pulling 4G for something like six or seven seconds. It's very physical, but I'm absolutely confident of my fitness and that I'll be able to push all the way through the race. To do a quick lap you have to have the right blend of aggression and finesse. But, apart from that long straight, the overtaking opportunities here are not that good and tyre wear is quite high, so it's a good place for taking a tactical approach.'

If it were just down to performance and driving, he said, he'd be very confident. 'With the car I have and feeling the way I do at the moment, I believe I can go out on Sunday and win the race. But there have been enough times this season when we've had proof that grand prix racing can throw up the unexpected.'

It was already clear that even the influence of Bernie Ecclestone had not been powerful enough to get Hill a seat in either the Ferrari or the Benetton teams next year, replacing Irvine in the former team or Alesi in the latter. Ferrari liked the way Irvine was prepared to play the role of the loyal back-up man, while Benetton would not countenance the cost of paying off Alesi's contract and replacing him with a driver who might be better at technical development but was not as quick. Hill's only chance of a competitive drive seemed to rest with the Jordan-Peugeot team, where he might partner Ralf Schumacher, the world champion's twenty-one-year-old brother, who was introduced to the press with a small ceremony in Estoril. For Eddie Jordan, Hill's proven competence as a test driver would make him the ideal complement to the German novice, who was said to lack none of his elder brother's self-confidence. For Jackie Stewart, that same quality would be invaluable in the process of developing not only his team's first Formula One car but its first car of any kind. The option of joining the Scot's team was not favoured by Ecclestone since it could hardly satisfy the requirement of putting him up among the front-runners, thereby pleasing the new people at ITV.

It was a game of bluff and counter-bluff, played in two dimensions: the race for the championship and the skirmishes leading up to 1997. Don't say you will do it, don't say you won't. Across the Williams pit, Villeneuve was being asked similar questions and was carefully playing down reports that he had criticized Hill for squeezing him out at the start of the Italian Grand Prix two weeks ago, while not actually denying his disapproval of the manoeuvre. 'It's just a different mentality,' he observed. 'When I make a start, I go straight until I'm up to speed. Then I look to see where everyone else is. It seems the mentality in Formula One is more to try and go to left and right as much as possible so that if someone makes a better start than you, you block him. You just have to adapt to that. I'm not saying it's wrong.' Did that mean he might adopt similar tactics tomorrow? 'I don't like doing stuff like that. But you never know. When you are in a critical position you sometimes do stuff you wouldn't normally do. We'll see.'

How was he handling it? 'Just by being myself and not thinking from morning to night that we'll have to beat him. We'll do what we can. If we can beat him, great. If we can't, we'll just have to swallow it.'

For Villeneuve there were no permutations to clutter the strategic thinking. 'I need four points more than Damon this weekend just to have a chance of taking it to Suzuka,' he said. 'It's going to be a tough battle and I hope we can fight right up to the last lap of the last race.'

Schumacher, hoping to watch them fight it out in his rear-view mirrors, was asked which of the two he would like to see taking the championship. ' "Like",' he said with a grin, 'is the wrong word.' Next season, he was implying, he would get his title back.

We learnt a bit more about Hill's state of mind during an exchange at a press conference with Mark Fogarty, an Australian freelance journalist, who asked him if Jordan and Stewart were his only options for 1997, or if he was in negotiation with other teams.

'I want you to appreciate that discussions are going on, they're confidential and I'm not going to discuss what is happening here and now,' Hill replied. 'In the future we'll know more. I'm talking only about this race weekend. You can ask me anything you like, go ahead. But I'm telling you that I can't give you an answer about who I'm discussing driving for next year or what goes on in those discussions.'

'I wasn't asking you for intimate details,' Fogarty continued. 'I was just asking whether it's two teams only or if you have more.'

'I'm not telling you,' Hill responded.

'If you were to go to Jordan, driving with Michael Schumacher's brother, wouldn't that be an uneasy situation, hypothetically of course?'

'Hypothetically, I'd prefer to drive for Williams. In a hypothetical world that would be the best place for me to stay.'

'Hypothetically, you don't have that option.'

'No, in actual fact I don't have that option. That's the reality. We could bat this hypothetical thing around for a long time, if you want, but I'm not going to divulge what's going on. I'm talking to a number of people and that's all I'm going to say.'

'How do you reckon you stack up against Heinz-Harald Frentzen?' Fogarty persisted. 'In equal cars, could you beat him?'

'No question. Why don't we put me in an equal car and we'll find out? But that's just a hypothetical situation . . .'

'Do you think it's unlikely that you will be in an equal car next year?'

'I know I'm not going to be in a Williams next year, and that's where he's going to be. So we'll probably never get an answer to that one.'

'Whichever way you look at it, whatever happens, you're going to have to take a step backwards next year, aren't you?'

'Um, let me see.' Hill reflected. 'I've enjoyed driving for Williams. I've been driving the most competitive car in Formula One. I started with them, if you disclude Brabham, and right from the start I had the opportunity of winning. I've won twenty grands prix and my winning ratio is one of the highest in the sport. In my first season with Williams I was under team orders to finish second to Alain Prost, which I duly did. Whether I should have done that or not is debatable, but I did what I thought was right at the time and I went on to win more grands prix than any of the team-mates I've had since. One of my team-mates, unfortunately, was killed, and we'll never know. But I certainly have made the best, I believe, of the opportunity I've been given with Williams. And things never stay the same. Williams may not remain the top team in Formula One. They weren't always at the top but they've made themselves into a very successful race team and, in all probability, will always be there or thereabouts. Things change in Formula One and that goes for drivers, too. But that's not to say that there's not the opportunity for a challenge, the opportunity to display what a driver can do, what other attributes can be employed to demonstrate your worth as a grand prix driver.' He paused and smiled. 'I lost you there, didn't I?'

The question still was: could Damon Hill actually overtake people, or couldn't he? Did someone whose credentials as a racing driver were in doubt actually deserve to add his name to the list of world champions? Some people said the problem was that he hadn't been brought up racing karts in the way Mansell, Senna and Schumacher had. Karts got you used to racing wheel to wheel. You learnt to dive in at the slightest hint of an opportunity.

'I've done eight years in go-karts,' Rubens Barrichello said, 'and I think 50 per cent of what I know comes from that. You'll certainly learn how to be aggressive there, but that doesn't mean you'll be aggressive in Formula One.' Barrichello's lacklustre performances in his fourth season of Formula One, after arriving as a potential new star in 1993, were no great recommendation for whatever type of training he may have received.

David Coulthard was another advocate. 'I think that in karting I was doing four races a weekend between the ages of eleven and sixteen,' he said. 'That's 150 races a year, so it's a good way to learn how to race, how to make mistakes. You spin off and it doesn't hurt. It's a fantastic way to learn your craft.'

'I didn't race karts,' Hill said. 'I raced bikes. If you fall off, it hurts. You don't get quite the same freedom.' So what did he think of karts? 'There's no question that it's the right place to start. I didn't do any karting until I'd done Formula 3000. I went back and did some indoor karting, and some of the best races I've ever had have been in karts. Nose to tail, lots of overtaking, but of course you can take risks in a kart because you're unlikely to get hurt.'

The fact remained that the championship was being led by two men who had not come up through the kart school and they shared the front row again at Estoril, with Hill on pole once more, the twentieth of his career. 'I'm very proud of that,' he said. 'It's a meaningful statistic in Formula One. It's important to be in pole position and at Estoril it's particularly important because overtaking is difficult and the track is cleaner on the left-hand side. Now I have to do the job I've been doing all year, which is to get a good start and make it through in the lead. If I can get into the lead I'll be comfortable. If I'm not, and I'm sitting behind Jacques, I'm still in good shape and there'll be plenty of pit stops coming up, I imagine. I feel more relaxed than I've felt in a long time and I feel I'm freer to enjoy my driving now because I've come to terms with the fact that . . .' The sentence went unfinished.

For all his assurances, Hill blew it so badly at Estoril that he seemed to be about to throw the whole season away. He led for fifty laps, with Villeneuve in close attendance, but slick work by the Canadian and his crew enabled him to take the lead during the third round of pit stops. He pulled away from Hill, but with sixteen laps to go the Englishman was warned of a clutch malfunction by his engineers and slowed down to preserve his second place ahead of Schumacher and

Alesi. Although his long quest for the world championship would now go down to the wire, at least the official odds kept improving. By finishing second to Villeneuve, Hill ensured that he needed only a single point from the final race of the season, at Suzuka, wherever Villeneuve finished. One point, of course, was the margin by which Hill had lost the championship to Schumacher at Suzuka two years earlier.

Villeneuve kept the championship alive with a drive of impressive power and purpose, cutting Hill's lead from thirteen points to nine: just within range. He would need not only to win the Japanese Grand Prix but to see Hill finish lower than sixth. But if Villeneuve won and Hill took the single point available for sixth place, they would be level on eighty-eight points. In that case Hill would take the title by virtue of having won seven races in the season to Villeneuve's five.

The supremacy of the two Williams-Renault cars was as clear from start to finish at Estoril as it had been since Hill began the season with three wins in a row, a sequence broken only by Villeneuve's début victory. Hill was generous in defeat. 'Jacques was flying today,' he said. 'He drove a great race. To come from fourth after the start to win the race is no mean feat around here. There was no way I could stay with him. And then I got a warning about the clutch problems and I had to back off.' Nevertheless the frustrations were growing. 'Before the race I couldn't help but think that I was within an hour and forty-five minutes of perhaps becoming world champion. Now I'll have to wait until Suzuka to find out if it's going to happen. But I've waited all season. Longer than that, actually, so I can bear to wait the last three weeks. I'm looking forward to Suzuka. It should be very exciting.'

All the tension inside him came out in his behaviour at the start of the race. He got away well from pole position, on the left of the track, while Villeneuve spun his wheels. But Alesi, as he had done at Monza a fortnight ago, took off even better and came down the right-hand side, drawing almost alongside Hill as they passed the pits. Suddenly Hill swung to the right, off the racing line, forcing Alesi towards the pit wall. On the face of it, this was a piece of calculated blocking of the kind Senna introduced to Formula One, which many believed Schumacher used to deprive Hill of the title in Adelaide two years ago. Bloodcurdling stuff.

'I never even saw Alesi,' Hill said afterwards, with a somewhat disingenuous air. 'I was looking where I was going, keeping my eyes on the road ahead. You've got your hands full at the start, I can tell you.'

Alesi, seething behind the Benetton garage, had a very different view. 'Everybody is fighting for a place,' he said. 'In Damon's case it's to win the world championship. In my case it's to finish in third place in the championship. And I don't think it's correct to use the pressure of winning a race or whatever to block someone, especially at the start, the most dangerous moment in a grand prix.'

Hill had given a variety of light-hearted responses when confronted before the race with the suggestion that all he had to do to win the title was nudge Villeneuve off the track. A lack of aptitude for intimidation is greatly to his credit as a human being, but now it seemed that he was fed up with the idea that he was a soft touch and lacked the steel of a true champion. What he was still not any good at was the overt display of aggression that came with occasionally wince-making naturalness to Senna.

Villeneuve, on the other hand, had produced what many came to think of as the finest single moment of racing seen during the entire year when he overtook Schumacher around the outside of the long curve before the main straight. He had told his engineers before the race that he thought he could pull it off, using his experience of the long constant-radius bends on the American oval circuits. As Schumacher himself followed Giovanni Lavaggi's Minardi round the curve, preparing for a pass on the straight, he was astonished to see the front wheel of the Williams draw level with his own, hold its line on the exit to the corner and then pull across behind and round the Minardi as they hurtled past the pits, calmly holding off Schumacher's counter-attack into the first bend. It was a manoeuvre seen only once or twice in grand prix racing of the modern era, which was perhaps an indication of nothing more than the conservatism that had afflicted the sport since Jackie Stewart began his safety campaign in the late Sixties. One thing it proved was that you didn't need to have spent your teenage years in go-karts in order to pull off a pass requiring raw courage and fine judgement. It was the product of a competitive instinct honed in another arena. The world champion let it be known that he was impressed.

Villeneuve's character had taken on a clearer outline as the season progressed. Even in Melbourne it had been obvious that he wasn't going to use his freshman year as an opportunity to take the learning curve gently. As the reigning Indycar champion, he didn't feel it would be too presumptuous to start winning races straight away. His competitive instinct was evident from the moment he took pole position for his first grand prix and then tried to ignore the radio instructions to back off and relinquish the lead to Hill.

His untied bootlaces and untucked plaid shirts marked him out from the rest of the drivers, all of whom – even Hill, the one-time Sex Pistols fan – more or less followed the smart-casual mode of Formula One drivers: a tradition handed down from the Latin aces of the Fifties with their brown suede jerkins, pastel polo shirts, stone chinos and soft leather loafers. Look at pictures of Berger and Alesi and you can't miss the linear progression from, say, Eugenio Castelotti and Luigi Musso. Even when Villeneuve and Hill wore identical off-track team kit of discreetly logotyped button-down denim shirts, white T-shirts and chinos, they looked as if they'd attended schools in different parts of town.

On the weekends when Villeneuve's girlfriend, Sandrine Gros d'Aillon, took time off from her communications studies in Montreal and turned up at a race, she emphasized the difference. Unconventionally beautiful, she wasn't someone you could imagine in Seventies-revival hot pants and a fixed dolly-bird smile, holding up one of the Marlboro name-boards next to a car on the grid, any more than you could imagine Georgie Hill doing that kind of thing. But Sandrine, like Jacques, was from another generation. One weekend her hair would be dark brown with a yellow stripe, the next it would be white-blonde. Maybe she came from a rich family, but at the track she wore the sort of denims that she might have worn to class. It was easy to imagine a role-reversal: she could have been the lead singer with a band like the Cranberries or Garbage; he could have been her boyfriend. This was not a thought that would have formed itself around many other relationships involving grand prix drivers.

But, as his driving suggested, there was nothing soft or sentimental about Jacques Villeneuve. He was a hard little nut who used his partnership with Craig Pollock to ensure that his time at the top would, in commercial terms, reap the maximum reward. His Timberlands may have been untied but they were always spotless; his untucked plaid shirts were certainly not from a second-hand shop. Beneath the non-conformist image, here was a man as ready as anyone to wear the baseball cap bearing the tyre company's name on the podium and to ensure that each post-race soundbite contained a namecheck for the tobacco company which was, in effect, paying his retainer. His informal press conferences were remarkable affairs in which he switched from English to French to Italian and back again according to his questioner's native tongue, giving value with answers that were full, if seldom genuinely enlightening.

He was clearly aware of his own value. By the time he arrived on the grid for his first grand prix, his image had already been legally protected. This prevented computer-game manufacturers, for instance, from sampling his face and using his likeness in a Formula One race-simulation package. Later in the season he and Pollock took steps to deter Timothy Collings, the *Daily Telegraph*'s grand prix correspondent, from fulfilling a commission to write Villeneuve's biography. Not only was Collings denied access to Villeneuve and his family but also to the members of the Williams team, and seemingly all the driver's past and present associates were requested not to respond to the author's requests for interviews or background information.

Villeneuve had nothing personal against Collings. It was just that his own book would be coming out in time for the Christmas market and he didn't want the competition from another volume to cost him sales. Actually, his decision would have been more intellectually respectable if he had harboured some sort of genuine dislike of Collings, for it hardly needs pointing out that if all stories – sporting or otherwise – were recorded only in the participants' versions, in order to maximize their incomes, we would never get a fix on the truth about anything.

That, however, is the way of sport today, when the guiding principle is the brevity of an athlete's career and when the managers and agents are intent on pushing for every last penny, not merely for their client's benefit but in order to increase the sum of their own 10, 15 or 20 per cent cut. But it was another example of the cool, worldly style with which Villeneuve and Pollock had approached their first season in Formula One, respectful when it mattered but making it clear that they refused to be overimpressed.

Leaving Estoril, his attitude was downbeat. He would handle it, he said, 'by being myself'. He wasn't going to spend every day thinking from morning to night about how he was going to beat Damon Hill. 'We'll do what we can. If we can beat him, great. If we can't, we'll just have to swallow it.' It suited his purposes to underplay the mood, but as he prepared to face the final round of a long and gruelling season, the rookie had done enough to convince some observers that he was in better shape than the odds-on favourite.

14

At Monza she had worn a crisp white jacket on race day, her hair up and her *maquillage* perfect, looking every inch a world champion's wife. But it wasn't to be, not that particular Sunday. In Estoril two weeks later she was in denims and a white T-shirt, her hair loose, as if belatedly acknowledging the perils of hubris. Georgie Hill's strength of character, I thought, is matched by her enduring lack of pretension.

These were the days that would define the rest of Damon Hill's life. One single point in Japan would give him the world championship, whatever happened to the only other man who could win it, his team-mate. But there would be times when that little point would seem impossibly distant.

The title would allow him to banish for ever the tribulations of the last three years. Then he, and everybody else, could forget the criticisms heaped on his head after his failure to beat Schumacher to the championship in 1994 and 1995, when he was believed to be enjoying the advantage of the best car in the field but could not, in the end, make it tell. One point at Suzuka would put him irrevocably alongside the twenty-four men who had won the title since it was first awarded in 1950. And, if Damon Hill should win it, the twenty-fifth champion would be worthy of his crown, in his own way.

'A championship is not given to you like a present,' he had been saying. 'You have to go out and fight for it.' There are, nevertheless, many different ways of winning it. Some champions are unassailable, and the best yardstick of all-time greatness is winning the title more than once. Twice is never a fluke. Because of that, the status of Fangio, Ascari, Brabham, Clark, Graham Hill, Stewart, Fittipaldi, Lauda, Piquet, Prost, Senna and Schumacher is beyond dispute. Of the one-time winners, few would quibble with the achievements of Farina, Surtees, Hulme, Rindt, Scheckter, Andretti, Jones or Mansell. Which leaves four whose claims are more fragile: Mike Hawthorn, Phil Hill, James Hunt and Keke Rosberg. Hawthorn, the first British world champion, took the title in 1958, which should have been Moss's year. He won a single grand prix that season, to Moss's four (even the man who came third in the championship, Tony Brooks, won three), and took the title by one point. Then he retired, only to lose his life in a road crash a few weeks later. Phil Hill's title, again won by a single point, may be said to have come as a result of the death of Wolfgang von Trips, his team-mate, in the penultimate race of the season. Hunt's talent flared brightly but dimmed as quickly as it rose, which cast doubt on its integrity. Rosberg, like Hawthorn, won only a single race in his championship season and seemed to lose his motivation not long afterwards.

With twenty wins in four seasons going into the 1996 Japanese Grand Prix, Damon Hill had nothing to fear from statistical comparisons, a point he had begun to use in his own defence against insinuations of unworthiness. But the real significance of his accession to the title would be as a reward for the devotion which had helped the Williams team maintain their pre-eminence, so enabling them to entice the talents of Prost, Senna, Villeneuve and Frentzen into the other cockpit. Were Villeneuve to take the title in his first season, it would have been on the back of Hill's hard graft. Which is not to say that Villeneuve would not have deserved it, since there is no such thing as an undeserving Formula One world champion; just that he might have deserved it rather less than Hill.

Villeneuve had lost some sympathy at the pole position press conference, when he chatted to Schumacher behind Hill's back while the Englishman was answering questions, repeating a discourtesy the two of them had committed in the same circumstances at Monza. Hill's eyes flickered with disapproval. 'They're talking again,' he told the media in a mock-schoolmasterish tone before turning to his colleagues. 'Pay attention, boys. You might learn something.' You could see the generation gap open up. Villeneuve knew that his chance of winning the championship was slim, and anything legitimate that gave him an edge must be used. Schumacher, who could defend his title, was interested in causing confusion, although my guess was that of the two Williams drivers he would have preferred Hill to come out on top, since he had proved his ability to beat the Englishman many times and knew that the majority of fans would realize that only the Ferrari had disabled his challenge for a third consecutive title. In a sense, Villeneuve was already his target. If the Canadian won the title at his first attempt it would make him more relaxed the following season, and therefore potentially an even more formidable opponent when the Ferrari reached a pitch of development that would allow Schumacher to fight him on equal terms. If he lost, the adrenalin produced by redoubled motivation might make him jittery and more prone to mistakes. Still, Schumacher joined in Villeneuve's little game; out of habit, maybe, or just to keep his hand in.

One thing we knew about Hill by this time was that he had no need of the title of world champion in order to call himself a man. Whatever doubts may plausibly be raised about his gifts as a racing driver, there were none concerning his human attributes. But there was a better reason than that for wishing him a happy conclusion to the season in Suzuka, and it was to do with the nature of his true opponent.

At this level, each driver has his own motivation. Schumacher races against his opponents: he needs to be on the top step of the podium, looking down on those below him. Senna raced against himself, beating others chiefly in order to be alone at the front, finding a resolution in some sort of mystical communion with a higher being that was, in fact, a part of himself. Moss raced against the limitations of his machinery and his own inability to resist a high-odds challenge. Hill, whatever he might be saying, was racing against the memory of his late father. That might sound novelettish, but it was the truth. It was not a question of wanting to beat his father or diminish his memory, but, unlike Villeneuve, he had risen without being able to shake off his father's distinctive shadow. It was the reason why he was ill at ease in the public eye for so long and suspicious of success. 'A lot of the discomfort I feel is with myself as much as with anyone else,' he had told me at the beginning of the season, 'so I have to come back and have another go.' Realistically, one afternoon in Suzuka now represented his last chance to cast off the burden. For Villeneuve, no doubt, there would be other seasons. The odds favoured Hill, but once the race began they would be no more relevant than his wife's lucky outfit.

It had taken Tom Walkinshaw no more than an afternoon to convince Damon Hill that Arrows was the place to go if he wanted to use the 1997 season not just to cash in on his championship but also to have a chance of showing the world what a mistake Frank Williams and Patrick Head had made when they discarded him. And the result of Hill's decision was that, for the first time in his life, he wrong-footed absolutely everyone, including all those people in and around Formula One who thought they were a lot cleverer than him. The news that Hill would be driving for TWR in 1997, announced at a press conference between Estoril and Suzuka, came as a complete surprise to even the most assiduous and imaginative of Formula One's rumour-gatherers. Most people had believed he would wait to complete a deal until the championship was settled and his value established. After McLaren, Benetton and Ferrari had been eliminated, Jordan and Stewart seemed the only contenders.

A deal with Eddie Jordan would have given him a decent mid-table ride, but after six years in Formula One the team seemed to have stopped making progress. I had a conditional bet with someone that if he went to Jordan he would qualify no higher than sixth on the grid all season. His achievements there might well have been no greater than those of Rubens Barrichello and Martin Brundle, which would have auto-matically devalued his championship by suggesting that they, too, could have won twenty-odd races had they been lucky enough to find themselves in the cockpit of a Williams-

Renault. At least Jackie Stewart's team offered the prospect of starting from scratch in an environment in which no datum line had been established, meaning that any success at all, even qualifying for a race, would be seen as a positive result. It was, however, a terrific risk. The car might be a complete dud and the Ford engine might perform no better in a Stewart chassis than it had in the Sauber.

None of us had thought of TWR as an option. But the more closely his decision was scrutinized, the shrewder and more imaginative it seemed. Particularly to someone who, like Hill, had made the trip to Leafield that summer. Tom Walkinshaw and the revamped Arrows held out the prospect of allowing Hill both to participate in the evolution of what amounted to a new team and, perhaps, of being up there scrapping with the best. And Walkinshaw was prepared to commit himself to a contract whose terms would not change whether Hill won the title or not.

A few telephone calls and one trip around the new head-quarters had been enough to persuade Hill that TWR was a serious proposition. When Walkinshaw was able to follow up the remarkable coup of unveiling his new number one driver by announcing engine and tyre deals with Yamaha and Bridgestone, everyone else began to take the idea seriously. Walkinshaw had sometimes overreached himself in the commercial world, notably when he tried to create a chain of motor dealers in partnership with the Silverstone circuit (which is owned by the British Racing Drivers' Club, whose members became very irate and scotched the deal), but the blots on his competition record were not visible to the naked eye. When he took on a racing project, he was not in the habit of failing.

'True,' Hill told me later. 'But Formula One's the big one. And you know the old joke: how do you make a small fortune in Formula One? Start with a big one. But Tom's a big player anyway, outside Formula One. He's not a guy who mucks around. Nobody thought it was sensible to run an estate car in the British touring car championship. They aren't doing too badly now.'

The adventure of a new team, the sense of breaking new ground with people who meant business, was what, finally, had appealed to him most. 'Everything's going to be new. New tyres, new engine, new chassis, new team ... there's going to be a lot of finding out going on. That means there's going to be a lot of opportunity to go forward. There are going to be setbacks, but there's a lot of potential for improvement, and that's another thing which I enjoy.'

He remembered how the negotiations had started. 'I'd been having discussions with the teams you know about. And then I had a phone call from Tom. My reaction was exactly the same as everyone else's later on. I said to Georgie, "I don't believe it. Arrows have rung me up. Oh God." ' He mimed a sort of embarrassed wince. 'At first I totally dismissed it. Out of the question completely. And then I had a few more conversations with various people – I just enquired a bit more around the place and I thought, well, it's such a long shot but I'm not going to be satisfied until I've explored every possibility at this stage, so that when I do make my choice I'll know that I haven't missed anything out. Tom rang me up a few more times, he came to see me and I kind of listened, but not closely enough. Then I got another call from Tom when I was testing in Estoril saying, "Will you come and talk to me? Come to the factory, have a look, see what you think." I thought, nothing ventured, nothing gained. So I dropped what I was doing – this was right after the Estoril race, I'd done one day's testing and I was happy with what I'd done. I thought, right, I've got to go and do this because I've got to make a decision. So I jumped on a plane, went back and met Michael. Driving there from Oxford airport I was racking my brains thinking of everything Tom had done, thinking that he's a tough old cookie, Tom, he's been successful in virtually everything he's done. And when I got to the factory and I was shown round, I realized that this was a guy who'd made a decision that he was going to have a grand prix-winning team and a championship-winning team. He's not taking it step by step. He's made that decision and all the ingredients have been brought together. After we sat down and went through all the factors and questions and points I was worried about, looking at things that, on the face of it, would be real weak links, he seemed to have thought of everything and he was prepared to make the commitment. From what I knew about everyone else's offers, I thought this one seemed to have all the ingredients I was looking for. So it was quite an easy decision to make, at that point. When I sat in the press conference and said I was very excited, someone said, "Do you really mean that?" They thought I was being facetious. I wasn't. That was the point. There's such a lot of potential – we're not going to go out and win the first race and we're not going to be leading the championship. That's not going to happen. But I think we could be up there fighting at the front occasionally, and that would be extremely satisfying.'

*

Five million of us got up before dawn on Sunday 13 October to see the showdown and the end of this story. I made a cup of coffee and switched on the television. Across the street, lights were on in other houses. A whole community was watching, and wishing Damon Hill well. We could all have stayed in bed another two hours and watched the rerun, but it wouldn't have been the same. Time-shifting doesn't suit sport, not when the experience is available in real time. The tension is the thing. The truth of the moment. Watching a dramatic incident in the knowledge that its consequences have already been settled is not the same as knowing that you are participating, however remotely, in something whose outcome remains open. You want to feel that uncertainty, the sensation of fate in the balance and that odd, nonsensical feeling that your presence could somehow make a difference – that if you didn't join in, the ending might go wrong.

He knew how we felt, sitting in front of the television at five o'clock on a Sunday morning, waiting for the cars to smoke off the grid on the other side of the world. 'I understood exactly because I'd done it for Nigel in 1992,' he said a few weeks later, thinking back to the time, twenty-one grand prix wins and several million pounds ago, when he and his Georgie and their sons were living in the terraced house in Wandsworth. He was the Williams test driver that year, doing the development work on the car that took Mansell to the title in Japan, in the final race of the season. 'We had a party and stayed up to watch,' he said.

What Hill himself experienced as he waited for the red lights to go out in Suzuka, with his own championship chances at stake, he could barely begin to describe. 'Can you imagine the tension on that grid just before the race started?

Knowing that there were all these people sitting at home on the other side of the world? I knew what they felt like. Now I know what it feels like to sit in the car as well.'

At the end of a season in which he endured the most public of sackings and underwent a prolonged examination of his mental fortitude, he secured the title by leading the Japanese Grand Prix from start to finish. It was his eighth win in the season's sixteen races, giving him a nineteen-point margin over Villeneuve, and putting an end to four years in which his fortunes had fluctuated from triumph to disaster, with not much in between.

He went into the final round knowing that it would be his last race for a team whose principals had proved, in the most explicit manner possible, that they no longer believed in him. Both Williams drivers started from the front row of the grid, with Hill again on pole, but the outcome was effectively settled in the opening seconds when Hill, the one who was supposed to be destroyed by nerves and suspect technique, got away cleanly while Villeneuve, Mr Cool, spun his wheels on the start line and had dropped to sixth place by the time they reached the first corner.

To win the title, Hill drove his finest race, given the special circumstances, producing a performance that banished many of the remaining doubts. The defining moment came on the first lap, after he had got away in the lead. Gerhard Berger was up behind him in a Benetton which was clearly returning to form at the end of a bitterly disappointing season. Berger pushed Hill all round the lap and was right up behind him as they approached the first right-angled bend of the tight, narrow chicane, exactly the point at which Senna and Prost had calamitously come together in 1989. Like Prost, Berger took the inside line into the right-hander while Hill placed the Williams a foot or two wider than usual on the entry, just enough to make the Benetton driver imagine he had seen an overtaking opportunity. He hadn't. As the Williams turned in, aiming for the normal apex on the kerbing, Berger was forced into an instant reconsideration. He braked hard but could not avoid crunching his left front wing against Hill's right rear tyre. His car slowed, bucking harshly over the kerb. Clearly he had been expecting Hill to move over, prompted by an unwillingness to risk a hand-to-hand fight in the knowledge that a top-six finish would be enough. 'Unfortunately,' Berger said afterwards, 'the manoeuvre didn't come off.'

Hill's description was far more graphic, and demonstrated a new kind of confidence. He had heard Berger's engine, he said, the first time that had happened to him since his motorbike-racing days. 'Then I saw him in the mirror. There wasn't much I could do, once he'd decided to go for it. I carried on doing what I was doing and left him to make his own arrangements. The next time I looked, he was a lot further back.'

Villeneuve had clawed his way back to fourth when, towards the end of the race, his right-hand rear wheel and tyre came off at the first corner – a near relative of the accident that had ruined his team-mate's Silverstone race. The wheel bounced across the safety area and over the first layer of debris fencing at more than a hundred miles an hour, but was caught and prevented from going into the crowd by a second layer: a reminder, in case anyone had forgotten since 1 May 1994, of the dangers inherent in motor racing and a tribute to the efficiency of the current safety precautions.

When Hill heard over the car radio that Villeneuve was out and that the title was his, he had been momentarily disconcerted, unsure of how he was supposed to react. Should he ease off and stroke the Williams home, or give it the whip all the way to the finish? 'I went into a bit of a spin in my head for a few laps,' he said. 'I realized I didn't actually have to carry on driving any more. It was strange. The job was all done, but there were still fifteen laps to go. So I thought, what the hell? I've come this far, and it was worth pushing on to the end.'

As for Berger, he dived into the pits at the end of the first lap, changed his front wing, returned to the race and fought his way back up the field, only to attempt the same trick on Eddie Irvine a dozen laps from the end, punting the Irishman's Ferrari out of fourth place at the chicane. The Austrian earned harsh words from Irvine and a suspended one-race ban by the stewards, and a few people remarked that perhaps a hellish and somewhat humiliating season had finally got to him. Yet if that had been Damon Hill instead of Gerhard Berger, crashing into people right, left and centre, what would the Monday morning papers have said?

After taking the chequered flag, Hill announced that he would dedicate his twenty-first race victory to the Williams-Renault team. 'But if you don't mind,' he added, 'I'll take the championship myself.' He had given the car a final ear-bursting blip of the throttle when he returned to the pits before emerging from the cockpit to embrace Georgie. 'I can hardly wait to get back to my children, but it's especially Georgie I would like to thank for this championship,' he said. 'She has been a tremendous strength to me throughout the season and all the time I've been racing in Formula One.'

He had become the eighth British driver to win the title. 'This is a terrific feeling for me,' he said. 'It's a tremendous relief to have finally won it after all the anxieties and the sleepless nights.'

When he climbed the stairs and stepped on to the podium, he gave a smile that few outside his immediate circle had seen before. No more anxiety, it said; no more recriminations. It was all joy and relief, and it seemed to open a window into the soul of the real Damon Hill. 'That's our boy,' cried Murray Walker in the same instant, summing up the general reaction as dawn crept into front rooms around Britain. Our boy indeed. Our first sight of Damon Hill had been as somebody's son, which condemned him to a special and unenviable sort of treatment. Somehow he became everybody's son, to be praised and scolded and patronized as if he were our own. Even the unsentimental Frank Williams sometimes referred to him as 'our Damon', meaning to imply a degree of fondness but also conveying the hint that Hill was not to be taken quite as seriously as some of his predecessors and rivals. It wasn't fair, and it didn't help. Our scepticism was something else he had to fight against, along with the legacy of being his father's boy – an inescapable reality which may have opened doors in the early stages but, since inherited genius was not part of the legacy, turned out to be no use at all when it came to the real business of driving a racing car. Now he had proved that, in the context of an elaborate and very public battle, a man can fight his own private war between self-belief and self-doubt, and win.

What Damon Hill did in Japan, in taking the title by winning the race from the front, blew away all the humiliations heaped on his head since his vulnerabilities started to appear under pressure the previous year. It justified the mission that had begun after the disasters in Japan, when he decided to reorder his priorities and adjust his mentality in order to cope with whatever the season might throw at him. Now he could live with himself.

'It would be awful to have to bear any other kind of feeling into old age,' he had said before the start of the season. It would have been particularly awful for the son of Graham Hill to have lived the rest of his life knowing that he had been unable to match his father's achievements, despite favourable odds. In the public mind he would have become an eternal 'nearly' man. That is not, in Britain, necessarily a dishonourable title for a sportsman – as Henry Cooper, who put Cassius Clay on the canvas but couldn't keep him there, or Jimmy Greaves, who was dropped from the World Cup final team, could probably attest – but it would no longer be the prospect greeting Damon Hill in his shaving mirror on any morning for the rest of his life.

The final statistics showed that he had taken the title by eight race wins to Villeneuve's four. Those who browse casually through the record books in generations to come may see these figures and infer that he cantered to the championship. But none of the twenty-four champions who came before him had worked harder or longer for the title. Only Moss needed the same resilience in the face of adversity, and he never managed to reach the happy ending. Hill's was a championship measured not in points or race wins, or even across a single season, for it took many years to achieve.

But when he said that winning the title would mean 'a confirmation of the work I have done', he specifically meant the work that had begun, in effect, six years earlier, when he signed up as the Williams team's test driver. The path to his title was littered with deceptions and obstacles. The biggest of them all was in his own head, and the measure of his triumph was that he could confront his own vulnerability and conquer it.

Sour old Niki Lauda said he didn't think Hill was good enough to be called world champion. 'He undoubtedly gave the weakest performance because, with the best car, it took him such a long time to become world champion,' Lauda told the *Frankfurter Allgemeine*. 'He had the advantage of an ideal situation like no one else this season.' Villeneuve said he and Damon had both made mistakes, but that the title was decided over the whole season and Hill had done a better job. Prost pointed out that the car had given him 'a huge advantage' (something the Frenchman's own career made him particularly well placed to judge) but that his number of wins and his contribution to the team justified his victory. Coulthard, who could have been in Hill's car had things turned out differently, summed it up with notable fairness: 'Because it's Damon, people will point to the mistakes he's made rather than the races he's won convincingly. Credit to him, he did it.' Schumacher, too: 'He has waited a long time for this title and he deserves it. For sure it was a tough few years, but congratulations to him. He has had a great season, eight victories, and it's not just by luck. He really fought for it.'

But Frank Williams' words were the most intriguing. 'I believe what Damon has done is truly admirable,' he said. 'It is a great example for everybody wanting to learn the lessons of life – just keep going if you believe in yourself and you believe in something. It is a great demonstration of how life, generally, should operate. I must say he's been very masterful in the car this year, about how he conducts himself in the pits during practice, how he thinks through his race, plans strategy, everything. He is changed from last year. He is more mature and he's done it through a self-development programme. And, I emphasize, it was very successful. He controlled the championship. He was given some good equipment and he made 101 per cent use of it. He's also a rare breed as a gentleman. I've hardly ever seen him angry and I've never seen him come out with any invective at all. Damon has climbed a mountain for four years and he thoroughly deserves to be at the top.'

What we thought we learnt from that little speech was a hint of regret at having taken the decision to replace Hill before the beginning of the season. But that may have been deceptive. The fulsome praise, clearly sincere, may have been simply the most polite way of saying farewell to a driver who, even in his hour of triumph, never truly convinced Frank Williams that he was the man for the big job.

But he was part of history now, his name up there with the greats. Alongside his father. Whatever happened to him in the future could not change that; what he had achieved could never fade or tarnish. Even when he is old and grey, people will still come up to him, wanting to stand next to the man who won the title back in 1996.

What sort of a release had he experienced in the moment of triumph? 'I'd describe it as like being let out of a room that you've been locked up in, or maybe more like coming out of the end of a long tunnel, because I'd been so blinkered all year.' So cut off from the world, in fact, that when the fans who had made it to the final race began to sing in celebration, he didn't recognize the song. 'It went, "It's coming home, it's coming home . . ." I didn't know what it was. I'd never heard it. Then someone told me it had been number one for something like six months. I don't know about anything that happened in 1996 except for what I was doing. Now, suddenly, I can look around. I don't have that compulsion to focus on just one thing. That blockage has gone, that championship thing. Now things can flow.'

Before the season started he'd told me at length about how he was preparing for it. Had it all come off exactly as he'd planned? 'Pretty much, except for the slight twist over re-signing with Williams, which wasn't in the plan. I took the view that I had to come out strong at the beginning, because clearly Jacques would be learning the ropes but would get better towards the end when he found his feet, so I knew I had to capitalize on that at the end. When I had a lead of twenty-five points, people were saying, "If it goes on at this rate . . ." but it never does, you know. If you look back through championships, very rarely does a lead just expand and expand. I was fully expecting it to get tight at the end, which it did. In the same way that in a race I would make sure that I got to the finish, I took the view that towards the tail-end of the championship it was crucial not to do anything silly. Like I did at Monza.'

He had prepared himself physically and mentally with extreme care, as a direct result of what had happened before. Had he been trying to cover every eventuality? 'Well, I knew that in 1995 things had gone wrong for reasons other than purely driving a car. I wanted to have dealt with as many of the other aspects of driving a grand prix car as I could, to allow me more time to concentrate on the actual driving and for things to run smoothly. I think it went well.'

In Argentina, after his third win in a row, I asked Patrick Head about Hill's new serenity and where it had come from. Head, typically candid, said we'd see how serene he was when Ferrari and Benetton got their act together. In other words, he was saying we'd see if Damon was a choker or not. I asked Hill if there had been a point at which his confidence wobbled. If so, what did he do about it? A long pause. Then: 'No, I can't think of a time, in all honesty. I always knew that, excluding some extraordinary circumstances or extra-bad luck, I'd be able to deal with whatever came up, on or off the track, in order to win the championship and maintain my advantage. After Monza, for example, walking back to the pits I just thought, well, it's down to three points. I was preparing myself for fighting for the last two races with a three-point advantage. If it came down to a head-to-head, I'd be able to fight tooth and nail and I knew I'd be able to come out on top. But by the time I returned to the pits it was back to thirteen points, so I knew it was a slightly different agenda. I always felt I was able to deal with whatever circumstances came up, having had the experiences I'd had, particularly over the last three seasons. If that meant balls-out, no holds barred, taking all risks necessary, then I could do that, if the situation required it, and I was prepared for it. But if that meant hedging, to guarantee maintaining a points advantage, then I'd also learnt the discipline to do that, rather than exposing myself to too much chance.'

Had he learnt to deal with his tendency to show his feelings more than some of his rivals? Did it put him at a disadvantage? 'I think . . .' A really long pause. 'No. I wouldn't have anything any other way. I think I've learnt a lot about the way to deal with the sport, off the track. When I came into it I was focused entirely on what happened on the circuit and I disregarded whatever happened elsewhere. I considered it irrelevant, to be honest. But I think 1995 taught me that it's not irrelevant. It's very relevant. I'm now more comfortable in Formula One and, whatever happens, I can be myself and not be too concerned about politics and the rest of it. I can just enjoy my job, enjoy driving.'

I said I suspected that, like a lot of people subjected to incessant media coverage, he had difficulty recognizing himself in a lot of what he read. 'Um.' Had bringing in Mary Spillane been an attempt to find a way of presenting himself as an image that he could recognize, to construct a Damon Hill that could be presented to the world and wouldn't result in him getting hurt? 'Yes. There was a bit made of my use of Mary as an *image consultant*.' He emphasized the phrase, as if it had been made up by an enemy, although that is the way she describes herself. 'Well, that's one of her roles. But she doesn't image-package me. That's not what I've employed her for. She's very experienced in the world of politics and in helping people present themselves in interviews. I got in touch with her to get some advice, really, on why I'd got such a bad image at the end of last year, because I clearly felt upset that the image that was being portrayed of me was incorrect. I believed that it had got way out of line with reality. It was just a bandwagon thing. The press get on to a line and follow that, it gets expanded on, it gets repeated and eventually it becomes exaggerated out of all proportion.

And I didn't understand what was going on. I really did not understand how this had happened and what the workings of the media were. It was an attempt to bring things back towards what I thought was more representative of myself, so I could feel that when I walked into the paddock people would know who I was and not confuse me with some sort of misrepresentation. She helped very much in that, and really all she did was tell me to be myself. That's the bottom line. Be yourself and don't let it get to you. Lighten up. I think there's a lot of paranoia about people like Mary Spillane, but in truth she's actually helping everyone. She's helping me to get myself across, which means she's also helping you guys get to know me better and it allows me to drive better because every time I come out of the car and go to the motor home I'm not strung up by people asking questions which come from such strange angles that I don't even know how to begin to answer them. This year was really quite easy. It was made a lot easier than 1995 and, for other reasons, 1994 . . . In many ways, 1996 was actually my easiest season in Formula One. I drove better and I enjoyed myself more. I'm not saying that because I won the championship. At the beginning of the season I sat on the plane with you and said that's what I'm going to do, and I did. I can understand if you were sceptical at the time because everyone comes out every year and says, "Oh, I've changed. Don't confuse me with the old person." But really all I did this year was be more myself, and I think I benefited from that.'

Did the sudden and hurtful break from Williams feel as if it had put his chance of the championship in jeopardy? 'Of course I worried about it. The thought crossed my mind that if I wasn't going to be driving for the team next year and the other guy who stands a chance of winning the championship is my team-mate, and he's going to be there next year, was I going to be treated fairly? But if there's one thing I've learnt about Williams it's that they're sticklers for providing equal equipment to both drivers. And I was constantly reassured. They sent a spare car out to Japan, although it wasn't my turn for the spare car.'

No, he had misunderstood. I hadn't meant disruption within the team, I had meant the disruption to his own peace of mind. 'In the back of my mind I had allowed for the possibility of an upset during the season which could throw me off course. When it happened, I kind of figured, "Well, that's what I've been preparing myself for. This is it." It would have been easy to be distracted by that, but I was determined not to let it affect me because then I would have been a double loser, and I wasn't going to allow that to happen. It was an added workload, having to scratch around at that particular time of the season when I was fighting for the championship, to sort out my future as well. But I think things have turned out rather well.'

For four years he had been endlessly analysed by a lot of amateur psychologists. That, I suggested, must have been weird. 'I read what they write and I sometimes think, "My God, is there any truth in what this man is saying?" It's so bizarre, some of it, that it's worrying. That's when you start thinking, "If there's some truth in that, I'm really screwed." '

So what had he learnt about himself in the last year? 'I've learnt that all the things I worry about, all the things I get doubts about, in actual fact I usually manage to deal with those things and overcome them. So I don't really see why I shouldn't be able to do anything I want to. To answer your question, what I've learnt is to have confidence in myself. It's all very well standing on the sidelines, as I did when I used to go along to Brands Hatch and watch people racing, but standing on the sidelines and believing you can do it is very different from actually being there and being faced with the reality. I've been through it and, as I say . . .'

In order to succeed, had he needed to convince himself that he really was the best? 'I refuse to believe that anyone can do anything better than me. But at the same time I know that I probably give out too much of the desire to be better and not enough of the confidence that I am, actually, very good; better than the other guy. But it's there, believe me, otherwise I wouldn't be a racing driver, I wouldn't be competitive. And unfortunately being competitive can sometimes make life intolerable.'

The death of Hill's father when he was young had caused money problems. He had, until then, grown up in a degree of privileged comfort, so it must have affected him. Now, through his own efforts, he had regained that standard of living. Had that been part of the motivation all along, the desire to recover something that he felt was his by right? 'Yes.' Firmly. Another pause. 'I don't know how much of it was motivated by that. I think I was competitive before my father died. But . . . I don't want to drag this into a father-bloody-dying analytical thing again, you know . . . But I'm motivated to provide a standard of living that I was used to, and I want my children to enjoy what I enjoyed when I was younger. I had a fantastic upbringing. I had everything I could possibly want. I'd like my children to have that.'

Did it have something to do with his own loss of a sense

of security? 'No, because for me it was OK. I was quite able to take care of myself. They could take everything they wanted away. I mean, I'd lost my father and that was the only thing that concerned me. But I felt sorry for him. Everything he'd achieved in his life, all that success, was stripped away after he died. That was like ... almost an insult, in a way. But that's just life. It was very rough on my mother.'

So there must be a tremendous satisfaction in knowing that he had managed, in a sense, to make good that loss? 'Yes, but I've learnt that you can't go back and change things. You can persist in trying to recover something that you've lost, but you never actually get it back again. That's not possible. It might look the same on the outside, but really it's a different situation.'

The first Formula One world champion, Nino Farina, ticked the box marked 'No Publicity'. After wrapping up the 1950 title ahead of his team-mates Fangio and Fagioli with a win in the last race at Monza, he refused all interviews and went home. Damon Hill also went home after Suzuka, newly crowned as the twenty-fifth champion, but not until he had smiled for the final few hundred photographs and answered the last of a thousand questions.

Hill got up on the morning after his arrival at Heathrow and put on his driving suit to pose with his Williams-Renault on the traffic island beneath Marble Arch, which dreamers have sometimes envisaged as the focal point of a future London Grand Prix to rival Monte Carlo (a blast down Park Lane, round Hyde Park Corner, along Knightsbridge, right turn at Harvey Nichols into the park, past the barracks, across the Serpentine – great natural esses – and back along the Bayswater Road). The arch's triumphal nature explained its attraction to Hill's sponsors but had he failed to clinch the title he might have been summoned to the same spot to revive its ancient function as the site of the Tyburn gallows.

Office workers and tourists watched in the sunshine as he waved a Union Jack and hugged Georgie for the photographers in front of the trophies presented for each of his eight race victories during the year. This may not have been quite the size of the reception accorded to Fangio in 1951, when the entire city of Buenos Aires came to a halt to welcome him home and a limousine swept him straight to the Casa Rosada and the embrace of President and Mrs Perón; or to Alain Prost in Paris in 1993, when police closed the Champs-Elysées to allow him to blast his Williams up to the Arc de Triomphe and back. But it suited Hill's unassuming nature, as he proved when he couldn't get the cork out of a magnum of champagne, in front of a hundred cameras waiting for the pop and the spray. 'There's usually someone to do this for me,' he remarked.

15

I don't believe anybody goes to a motor race to see some-one killed or injured, but it would be ridiculous to deny that a sense of attendant danger is a factor in the sport's appeal. We want to see people doing something we are not equipped, by talent or temperament, to do ourselves; the fact that they do it in an environment of competition sharpens the flavour and adds another dimension.

When Senna died, the world was aghast. But the horror, whether genuine or otherwise, was not caused simply by the death of a racing driver. The proof of that had come a day earlier, when Roland Ratzenberger perished on the same track in an accident which took place without any great subsequent outcry. The fuss over Senna arose because he was a superstar, because he was handsome and intelligent, because he had been world champion three times and, last of all, because there was an aura of mystery surrounding the possible cause of the accident. Mostly, though, the headlines were written so large simply because Senna was known to the general public and his televised demise could be turned into what the media call a good story.

Curiously, by comparison with the old days when the risks were considerably greater, the drivers are nowadays paid far more money to stay alive. The sponsors need their longevity because so much has been invested in an individual driver as a symbol of the corporate image. The potency of such symbols can only be built slowly, by the gradual accretion of success and the emergence of the elements of personality. Similarly, the fans now have an investment in their heroes as characters in the celebrity soap opera, created by the symbiotic relationship between television and the tabloid newspapers.

The nature of motor racing has changed greatly and will perhaps change even faster in the coming years, under pressure from television and the need to compete for attention with virtual-reality games. The question is: how can the sport increase its levels of safety while maintaining the tension derived from the knowledge that its contestants are taking part in a profoundly perilous activity?

Here are some words written in 1958 by a man whose death at the end of 1996 reminded many people of how and why they had fallen in love with motor racing: 'In common with other organizers, the Automobile Club von Deutschland decided to reduce the German Grand Prix from its former powerful position down to a "milk-and-water" type of event by reducing the distance from twenty-two laps of the Nür-burgring to fifteen laps, a mere 342 kilometres . . .' The man who wrote that, almost forty years ago, thought that a race lasting two hours and twenty minutes over a fourteen-mile circuit featuring 175 corners lined with trees and ditches, contested by men in fibreglass helmets, string-backed gloves and cotton polo shirts driving fragile cars without seat-belts, roll-over bars or fire extinguishers, could reasonably be described as 'a "milk-and-water" type of event'.

The writer's name was Denis Jenkinson, and he was the

doyen of British motor racing writers when he died at the age of seventy-five. Jenkinson's most celebrated achievement had been to act as Stirling Moss's navigator during a famous victory in the 1955 Mille Miglia, when they averaged 97 miles an hour for more than ten hours over public roads from Brescia to Rome and back in an open two-seater Mercedes-Benz while Jenkinson shouted out instructions written on a long roll of paper above the bellow of the Merc's unsilenced straight-eight engine. But for me, as for many others, Jenkinson's contribution went far deeper than that. Over a period of years his writing implanted a set of beliefs that, for better or worse, defined what constituted a motor race and what it took to be a proper racing driver.

As the continental correspondent of the magazine *Motor Sport*, he spent the summer driving from one race to another, from the great temples of Monza, Monaco, Rheims, Spa and the Nürburgring to lesser meetings at Syracuse, Bordeaux, Bari and Naples. In those days there was little print or television coverage of grand prix racing and Jenkinson's lengthy, close-set reports, published weeks after the event, represented the authorized version.

Superficially, I suppose he was a bit of an anorak. There are many photographs of his tiny, bearded figure bending over Maseratis and Vanwalls, logging chassis numbers or spotting tiny modifications. He would be the first to notice when BRM moved their oil cooler from the left to the right of the engine, and he could tell his readers the exact angle at which Colin Chapman canted the engine of the Lotus 16 (and why Chapman had decided to do it). Jenkinson loved and understood good engineering and he thought the men who designed the cars were just about as important as the glory boys who drove them. But he was also, in his flinty way, a romantic. The technical exegesis always came after the report of the race itself, and he never hid his admiration for the courage and skill of the best pilots. He was interested in finding out what made a racing driver different from you or me, and he was intelligent enough to realize that the proportion of those qualities might vary between individuals of comparable achievements.

Along with enthusiasms came prejudices. For example, he despised the campaign of Jackie Stewart and others to reduce the risk to the drivers by introducing safety precautions, particularly to the tracks themselves. He liked road circuits with natural features: the manhole covers and kerbs of Monaco, the ditches of the Nürburgring, the tramlines of Porto. He wanted Stewart to prove himself against the same tests that Rosemeyer or Fangio had faced, which was an unrealistic expectation in a changing world. Yet he was never nostalgic or sentimental. In his eyes, Ayrton Senna was the equal of any of the idols of his youth.

How differently death was treated in Jenkinson's heyday. In that same German Grand Prix of 1958, Peter Collins was lying a close second to Tony Brooks' Vanwall when his Ferrari ran wide and hit an earth bank at the right-hand bend called Pflanzgarten. The car somersaulted, throwing him out and fracturing his skull against a tree. He died in hospital a few hours later. Collins was twenty-seven years old, handsome, well liked and newly married to a beautiful American actress. Two years earlier he had come close to being crowned the first British world champion; he deprived himself of the title by his chivalrous decision to give up his Ferrari to Fangio, his team leader, whose own car had broken during the final race of the season. Had he sat tight, Collins could have become world champion. His fatal accident took place only a few weeks after he had won the British Grand Prix at Silverstone. Along with his team-mate, Mike Hawthorn, and Moss, he was a favourite for the 1958 championship. Yet here are the sentences with which, in his *Motor Sport* piece, Jenkinson described Collins' death, on the third page of a report headlined 'Vanwalls Strike Back':

On lap eleven disaster struck the Ferrari team, for rounding the double right-hand curve after Pflanzgarten Collins was in his usual opposite-lock slide when he overcooked it and went off the road in full view of his team-mate, and while striving to catch the flying Brooks. Collins was taken to hospital with severe head injuries from which he later died and Hawthorn was left to carry on the struggle, but by the end of that lap his clutch began to show signs of failing and as the Ferrari went up the return road behind the pits it suddenly slowed and though Hawthorn continued on lap twelve he did not reappear. This little scrap that ended so tragically had been motor racing at its best.

Elsewhere in the issue, in his Continental Notes, Jenkinson grouped Collins' death with those in previous weeks of the Scottish sports car driver Archie Scott Brown and Luigi Musso, another of Collins' team-mates. They died, he concluded, doing something they enjoyed:

They were motor racing and 'having a go'. Or, as is often jokingly said, they were dicing with death. Death threw a double six and they had to pay up. Let us not bewail the fact; let us all pause in silent admiration of three fine men and remember the great pleasure they gave us all whether we knew them merely as names in motor racing, or as personal friends . . . They died fighting, and there can surely be no better death.

Jenkinson pointed out that it was hard to generalize about the causes of fatal accidents, and therefore to legislate against them. Seat-belts? Some deaths had been caused by harnesses imprisoning drivers in a burning car, while others had been averted untethered drivers had been thrown clear. A tree had contributed to Collins' death, but it was a tree that had prevented Jenkinson and Moss hurtling down a mountain in the 1956 Mille Miglia, thus saving their lives. 'If we can prevent accidents beginning,' he wrote, 'all well and good, but if we are going to take down all trees and fill in all ditches then the logical conclusion is to end up with Sorbo-padded walls round all the circuits.' Which is almost exactly what Formula One is likely to have when the FIA's safety commission comes up with its findings into the use of energy-absorbing materials in safety barriers and its recommendations have been tested and turned into reality.

If his attitudes seem barbaric by contemporary standards, it must be remembered that Jenkinson was writing in the context of a culture only lately immersed in a bloody war. Many of the people in motor racing had been involved in the fighting and had seen death at close quarters on a regular basis. The tariff on human life was assessed according to quite a different scale of values.

So, in financial terms, was success. If we cannot make any meaningful comparison between the track performances of men from different eras, here is one way of comparing their value. We can learn something about the evolving status of grand prix drivers by relating their annual earnings to the cost, at the time, of a new Rolls-Royce (an object which, since it has maintained its value and position in the market-place across the decades, represents as reliable a reference point as any). And what we learn is surprising, if not a bit shocking.

Stirling Moss earned £32,750 in 1961, his last full season, when he was unquestionably the world's greatest driver – enough to buy six Rolls-Royces. Not a fortune, but a substantial sum. In the mid-Seventies a world champion – James Hunt, say – could make a quarter of a million pounds a year, which would have bought him seven Rolls-Royces. In 1996, four years after Ayrton Senna had been paid $1 million a race by McLaren, Michael Schumacher and his manager, Willi Weber, persuaded Ferrari to make that £1 million, to which could be added enough in endorsements and personal sponsorship deals from Nike, Dekra and others to take his total earnings for the year beyond £25 million, enabling him to buy, should he wish, no fewer than 170 Rolls-Royces. In real terms, then, Schumacher earns twenty-eight times as much as Moss did at his peak.

Among the drivers of his time, Moss possessed an unusually acute awareness of his commercial worth, but his success and reputation were used to sell only items directly related to motoring: petrol and oil, spark plugs, brake linings and tyres. By contrast Schumacher acts, to all intents and purposes, as the front man for a multinational tobacco corporation. He is a marketing and promotional tool for a business which, faced with static or shrinking markets in the West, knows that it has only three available strategies if it wishes to avoid contraction. First, in its traditional markets it can survive only by increasing market share, which means establishing its brand in the minds of as many potential consumers as possible. The scope for this is limited by restrictions on tobacco advertising, particularly in the broadcast media. But the growing popularity of Formula One racing assures any company of remarkably free access to high-quality television time and the challenge for Marlboro, Mild Seven, West and Rothmans has been to utilize that time as efficiently as possible. Their cars need to be at the front, attracting the gaze of the cameras for as long as possible. The paintwork needs to react well with the 625-line transmission system, which means that the red on the coachwork of a Marlboro-sponsored grand prix car is not the same as the red on a packet of Marlboro cigarettes; instead it is a red developed in the Philip Morris laboratory to ensure maximum visibility and impact on television. Similarly, the Marlboro chevron and the Rothmans stripes are emphasized wherever possible, so that in those countries which do not allow explicit tobacco advertising on the cars, such as France and Germany, the removal of the actual names from the bodywork has very little effect, since the brand is identified by the shape and colour of the overall design alone.

The second avenue offering growth for tobacco companies is in new territories. Africa is one. A tactic there is to raise the level of nicotine in cigarettes in order to make them more addictive. As a promotional tool, however, Formula One is not yet much use in the devastated economies of Liberia or Mali. But the East is another matter, and that is where the third strategy can be employed to the benefit of Formula One. Led by the long-term enthusiasm of the Japanese, countries are starting to queue up not just to buy television rights to the grands prix but to be allowed to stage races of their own. And the laws on tobacco advertising are generally much more relaxed than in Europe, which means that a grand prix in Malaysia, South Korea or even China will see the cars carrying their full sponsorship regalia – and there will be nothing much that Western broadcasters, committed to taking the telecast of the races, can do about it. For these reasons the centre of gravity of Formula One racing seems about to make a sharp shift towards the Pacific Rim, which may eventually precipitate the biggest change in the balance of Formula One power since the British constructors emerged from their airfields to take on the Continentals.

So what is it we really like about Formula One? Is it the drivers or their cars? I once went to a race with the artist Ralph Steadman, who had been commissioned to produce a series of drawings evoking the atmosphere of the grand prix paddock. Steadman, as much a social commentator as a draughtsman, ended up making a lot of drawings of the fans leaning over the cars to peer at the innards, their eyes popping and mouths agape. He'd got the idea one evening when we left the circuit and went to one of those restaurants with fish tanks, where you choose your own supper. We'd been gawped at all evening by a shoal of big grey fish, examining us with exactly the same mesmerized, weirdly incurious stare that Steadman had noticed in the paddock.

It made me think about why we spend so much time staring at the cars, most of which look almost exactly alike. Perhaps it's a piece of inherited behaviour surviving from the days when they all looked different. It isn't as if today's cars are beautiful in the way they used to be; not, anyway, in the sense that Concorde or a Parker 51 fountain pen is beautiful, which has everything to do with purity of line, aesthetic balance and a common sense of form. The appeal of today's Formula One cars is entirely bound up in the knowledge of what they can do and in whose hands they will be doing it. But if you didn't already know, there would be nothing about their respective appearances to tell you that a McLaren should be faster than a Minardi.

Even the designers are getting self-conscious about it. 'I suppose they are getting a bit samey,' Patrick Head said after the season was over. 'It's the regulations. They used to be this thick' – he made a gap of a quarter of an inch between his thumb and forefinger – 'and now they're like this' – his palms moved three inches apart. 'The other thing is that we've all got the same measuring tools, in terms of wind-tunnels and so on, and we're finding that the same rules apply. The best way of mounting a front wing within the regulations is going to be the same in another team's wind-tunnel as it is in ours. If you didn't have the wind-tunnel you'd design whatever you thought might be best and then you'd probably see more differences. But when you've got the measuring tool giving you feedback when you test a number of different ways of doing it, then you tend to come up with the same answers.'

Apart from the little dorsal wings sprouting behind the drivers' heads on the 1995 McLaren and the 1996 Jordan, nobody was daring to try anything different. Even those wings were quickly outlawed because no one must be allowed to do anything that might either give them a considerable competitive advantage or involve the other teams in an expensive game of catching up. The days of the great conceptual leap – of John Cooper's decision to put the engine behind the car, of Colin Chapman's abolition of the tubular frame in favour of a one-piece fuselage – seem to have gone. Now the technical interest is in areas hidden from view, in the software controlling 'active' differentials and sophisticated clutch mechanisms, all of which are highly prone to rule-bending and of little immediate interest to the average fan peering at the cars from a safe distance behind the paddock's perimeter fencing.

You probably wouldn't expect the drivers to get worked up about the cars the way the rest of us do. But in all that long, bumpy year, when his emotions ran the gamut from A to Z and back again, I never heard Damon Hill sound more animated than when he was talking about the way the cars are built. It came up in the course of a fairly desultory conversation, when he'd already spent half an hour repeating the usual lines. But suddenly something inside him lit up and I could see what it is he really loves about what he does. It isn't the champagne on the podium, the five-star hotel suites, the private planes, the holidays, the potential access to endless supplies of beautiful women, or even the sheer mass of the acclaim. It is the cars.

'I'm interested,' he said. 'It's fascinating, the art of building cars. They're so beautifully made, some of them, and now with the computers, strangely enough, they're even more beautiful because the computer hones it down to the bare essential. The shape is exactly within the tolerances for the stresses it needs to bear, so you don't have any excess material there. That pure minimalist design is lovely.'

Tuesday evening, 15 October 1996. Terminal Four at Heathrow. And here is what it's really all about. Two or three hundred people are clustered around the exit from the arrivals hall as the British Airways flight from Tokyo touches down a few minutes before its scheduled arrival at half past six. An experience like this has a rare quality of innocence: nobody has sold you a ticket, nobody is trying to hustle you a T-shirt. The real business is over and done with, so what we have here is a transaction of admiration, affection, enthusiasm and pleasure.

I've turned up simply because I want to give Hill a cheer. And as he, his wife and his manager struggle through the applauding crowd, a ten-year-old boy wriggles his way to the front. A couple of minutes later he's back in triumph, waving his pen and a piece of paper with a squiggle on it. 'I think I'm going to faint,' he says.

The next morning I go to wake him up, to get him to school. His eyes open slowly. Before they've even focused, he says, 'Did I dream I met Damon Hill last night?' He reaches out for the autograph, lying on his bedside table. I think to myself, we'll get this one framed, too. It can go up alongside Pelé's.

READ MORE IN PENGUIN

A SELECTION OF FICTION AND NON-FICTION

The Evening of Adam Alice Thomas Ellis

The uneasy, unpredictable tales in this volume blend sharp-eyed humour and observation with myth and imagination to depict the dark forces that lurk beneath life's calm exterior. 'In these brief, ambiguous tales wisps of meaning float across the road like patches of mist, and wraith-like endings hang in the air ... Even at its lightest, the author's whimsy is unnerving' – *Observer*

Notes of a Native Son James Baldwin

Richard Wright's *Native Son*, Hollywood's *Carmen Jones*, boyhood in Harlem, the death of his father, recovery and self-discovery as a black American in Paris – these are some of the themes of James Baldwin's early essays, which established him as among the greatest prose stylists of the century.

Nelson: A Personal History Christopher Hibbert

'Nelson is the authentic hero of English history and in Christopher Hibbert he has found a biographer to suit the complex personality which made him the most glorious and romantic figure of his time' – *Mail on Sunday*

Barbara Hepworth Sally Festing

On her death in 1975, Barbara Hepworth was acclaimed as 'the greatest woman artist in the history of art'. 'Compelling ... the brilliance, dignity and pain of this conflicted life shine through' – *Sunday Times*

The Penguin Guide to Jazz on CD
Richard Cook and Brian Morton

'An incisive account of available recordings which cuts across the artificial boundaries by which jazz has been divided ... each page has a revelation; everybody will find their own' – *The Times*